China and Southeast Asia's Ethnic Chinese

China and Southeast Asia's Ethnic Chinese

STATE AND DIASPORA IN CONTEMPORARY ASIA

Paul J. Bolt

Westport, Connecticut
London

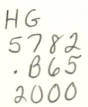

Library of Congress Cataloging-in-Publication Data

Bolt, Paul J., 1964–
    China and Southeast Asia's ethnic Chinese : state and diaspora in contemporary Asia / Paul J. Bolt.
        p. cm.
    Includes bibliographical references and index.
    ISBN 0–275–96647–X (alk. paper)
    1. Emigrant remittances—China. 2. Investments, Foreign—China. 3. Chinese—Asia, Southeastern. I. Title.
HG5782.B65 2000
305.895′1059—dc21   00–022347

British Library Cataloguing in Publication Data is available.

Library of Congress Catalog Card Number: 00–022347
ISBN: 0–275–96647–X

First published in 2000

Praeger Publishers, 88 Post Road West, Westport, CT 06881
An imprint of Greenwood Publishing Group, Inc.
www.praeger.com

Printed in the United States of America

The paper used in this book complies with the Permanent Paper Standard issued by the National Information Standards Organization (Z39.48–1984).

10 9 8 7 6 5 4 3 2 1

Copyright Acknowledgments

The author and publisher gratefully acknowledge permission to reprint the following material:

Excerpts from Paul J. Bolt, "Looking to the Diaspora: The Overseas Chinese and China's Economic Development, 1978–1994," *Diaspora* 5:3 (1996), pp. 467–96. Reprinted by permission of University of Toronto Press Incorporated. Copyright 1996.

Excerpts from Paul J. Bolt, "The New Economic Partnership Between China and Singapore," *Asian Affairs: An American Review* 23:2 (Summer 1996), 83–89. Reprinted with permission of The Helen Dwight Reid Educational Foundation. Published by Heldref Publications, 1319 1st. N.W., 8th St. N.W., Washington, D.C. 20036–1802. Copyright 1996.

For Betty Jo and our children, Matthew, Elizabeth, and David

Contents

Acknowledgments

Reflecting back upon the process of completing this work, it is clear to me that I owe a debt of gratitude to many people. My advisors at the University of Illinois deserve much credit for their roles in this project. George Yu is an example of a true and continuing mentor. Steve Douglas and Carol Leff were both insightful and helpful. Each one brought different perspectives and strengths to the project, which blended together in a harmonious manner.

Others played an important part in this work as well, in both discussing ideas and reading all or parts of the manuscript. I want to especially thank James Alexander, David Longenecker, Richard Leitch, and John Sloan. Haning Hughes gave invaluable assistance in research. Khachig Tölölyan had helpful suggestions on previous works related to the manuscript. Col. William E. Berry Jr., USAF, retired, graciously read through the entire manuscript and made many helpful comments. Col. Douglas J. Murray and the Political Science Department at the United States Air Force Academy provided invaluable support as well. My editor at Praeger, James Sabin, was extremely patient and understanding. My thanks go also to the United States Air Force Academy, the University of Illinois, the United States Department of Education, and the Taiwan Universities Consortium for funding for this project.

I also want to thank those who assisted me in my fieldwork. Those who allowed me to interview them in Singapore and China were most gracious. Special thanks goes to the members of the Institute for Southeast Asian Studies, Xiamen University. My deepest gratitude is extended to Huaiji and Xiao Li for their friendship and considerable sacrifices on my behalf.

Finally, I thank my family, without whose support this work would not have been possible. My wife's love, patience, and encouragement sustained me during the writing process. My three children also demonstrated great patience with their dad and helped me keep perspective on what is most important. My parents also deserve a great deal of thanks for their roles in my life.

Although many people contributed to this work, I am solely responsible for the errors that remain. This work in no way reflects the opinions, standards, or policy of the United States Air Force Academy or the United States government.

CHAPTER 1

China and Asia's Ethnic Chinese

CHINA'S ECONOMIC REFORMS AND ASIA'S ETHNIC CHINESE

In 1978, China embarked on a path of economic reforms that have fundamentally altered the country's economic and social landscape. These reforms have been remarkably successful in raising economic output and increasing wealth. For example, from 1980 to 1993, China's real gross national product (GNP) grew at an average annual rate of 9.4 percent. Rates of growth then slowly declined from 12.6 percent in 1994 to 7.8 percent in 1998.[1] The Chinese government reports that the number of people living below the poverty line dropped from 250 million in 1978 to 42 million in 1998.[2]

Two central components of China's reforms have been the household responsibility system in agriculture, leading to a doubling of agricultural output in the 1980s, and the open door policy. Under the open door policy the Chinese government has encouraged trade, foreign investment, scholarly exchanges, and increased contact with the rest of the world in a wide variety of arenas. Foreign investment has received special emphasis due to the jobs, technology, and export opportunities that it brings. China has been quite successful in attracting this investment. By April 1999, there were almost 330,000 overseas-funded firms in China with a total contractual investment of $580 billion and actual paid-in capital of $270 billion.[3] This made China the world's second-ranking host country for foreign investment after the United States. China has also made great strides in expanding its exports. In 1997, exports equaled nearly 20 percent of GDP, up from a negligible amount before the reforms were initiated.[4]

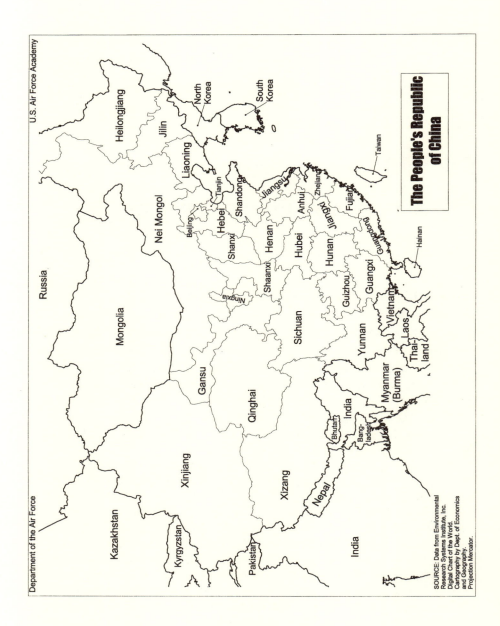

Department of the Air Force

U.S. Air Force Academy

The People's Republic of China

SOURCE: Data from Environmental
Research Systems Institute, Inc.
Digital Chart of the World.
Cartography by Dept. of Economics
and Geography.
Projection Mercator.

China's reforms have also brought difficult problems. Throughout the reform period the government has struggled to manage the consequences of unchecked growth, such as periodic inflationary surges and rising income inequalities between individuals and regions. For example, consumer price inflation in 1994 ran at 24.1 percent.[5] Although subsequently inflation was brought under control, in 1999 policymakers struggled with a deflationary spiral. The loss of state workers' jobs has brought discontent, and millions of migrant peasants roam the country in search of work. Furthermore, corruption is endemic, and at times Beijing seems to have little control over what happens in the provinces. However, what is most remarkable is China's long run of success in expanding its economy, a success that is especially noteworthy in comparison with the economic performance of Eastern Europe and the former Soviet Union.

The current study illustrates one of the distinguishing features of the Chinese economic reform: the active participation of Asia's ethnic Chinese. During the 1990s, the Western press began to pay more attention to the contributions of what it calls the "overseas Chinese" in explaining both China's success and the dynamic economic growth in Asia. For example, James McGregor of the *Wall Street Journal* described in 1992 how the "overseas Chinese" invested "at home," financing at least 75 percent of the foreign-invested enterprises in China and even more in areas such as the southeastern province of Fujian.[6] In 1993, Joel Klein in *Newsweek* noted three major factors in China's economic boom: China's transition model, the "entrepreneurial edge" of the Chinese, and "the power and pride of the Chinese diaspora." Klein went on to assert that diaspora businessmen "jump-started" China's boom and represent 80 percent of China's foreign capital.[7] Similarly, in 1996 the German weekly *Wirtschaftswoche* claimed that the overseas Chinese were taking control of Asia from Japan,[8] while in 1997 the Canadian magazine *Maclean's* asserted that "the world's 57 million overseas Chinese . . . rule the world's third most powerful economy."[9]

There are some inadequacies in these generalized popular accounts. One is the lack of distinction regarding the identity of the "overseas Chinese." Lumping all ethnic Chinese living outside mainland China into the category of "overseas Chinese" is simplistic and causes consternation in Southeast Asia, where this is a sensitive issue. In political terms there are clear distinctions among ethnic Chinese living in Hong Kong, Taiwan, and Southeast Asia. Similarly, referring to "overseas Chinese" as returning "home" is misleading. Most of Asia's "overseas Chinese" have citizenship in their countries of residence and have lived there for generations. Nor is it accurate to describe Asia's ethnic Chinese as members of a single economy whose output can be compared to that of nation-states. Nevertheless, the attention given to the "overseas Chinese" is important and deserving of closer scrutiny. Investments in China by ethnic Chinese throughout Asia have played a crucial role in propelling the Chinese economy. This has important implications for both China's development and the appropriateness of the Chinese model for other developing societies.

At the scholarly level, many Western writers on China's development have not paid adequate attention to the role that ethnic Chinese have played in China's development, focusing instead on government policies. When attention is given to the role of ethnic Chinese, usually it centers on those from Hong Kong and Taiwan rather than Southeast Asia. Furthermore, few writers have attempted to systematically describe the current political and economic implications of ethnic Chinese investments in China. Fortunately, this is beginning to change. For example, the Centre for the Study of the Chinese Southern Diaspora was recently established at the Australian National University to focus on issues regarding people of Chinese descent living in Southeast Asia and the Southwest Pacific.[10]

This work examines the role of Southeast Asia's ethnic Chinese in contributing to China's economic development since 1978 and the political ramifications of this role for both China and the region. Although investments from Hong Kong and Taiwan are larger than those from Southeast Asia, Southeast Asian ethnic Chinese are worth examining for several historical and political reasons. First, the popular and scholarly literature has given less attention to them than investors from Hong Kong and Taiwan. This has been due at least in part to their lower profile. A second and related point is that ethnic Chinese in Southeast Asia live in internationally recognized sovereign states. Thus, their interactions with China have a different character than the interactions of Chinese from Hong Kong and Taiwan and require separate analysis. Third, there is a need to account for shifting historical patterns of investment. Before 1949 most external investments and remittances that flowed into China came from Southeast Asia, raising questions about changing patterns of external engagement in China's economy. Nevertheless, it is sometimes necessary to place all ethnic Chinese outside the mainland in a single category, and thus this work examines the interactions of Chinese in Hong Kong and Taiwan with Southeast Asian Chinese and mainland China as well. For example, one cannot speak of ethnic Chinese networks and exclude the role of Hong Kong and Taiwan.

The relationship between Southeast Asia's ethnic Chinese and China is particularly interesting because it illustrates the ties between a diaspora community and a nation-state. Diasporas are by no means a new phenomenon in international politics, although with increased global migration and rising national consciousness they are perhaps more prominent. Gabriel Sheffer defines modern diasporas as "ethnic minority groups of migrant origins residing and acting in host countries but maintaining strong sentimental and material links with their countries of origin—their homeland."[11] As such, diasporas create a triadic relationship among "homeland," "host country," and "ethnic diaspora."

The concept of diaspora is inseparable from that of ethnicity. It is well recognized that ethnicity is a factor that can generate strife in both domestic and international politics. There are numerous examples of countries where ethnic conflict has brought bloodshed, such as the former Yugoslavia, Russia, Iraq, Rwanda, India, Indonesia, and Malaysia. Even wealthy societies such as Canada and Belgium have been threatened by ethnic divisions. However, ethnic identity may play a positive role too. For instance, Joel Kotkin describes "ethnicity as a defining factor in the evolution of the global economy."[12] In examining five global "tribes"—the Jews, British, Japanese, Chinese, and Indians—Kotkin explains their economic successes largely in terms of their ethnic identity, which has maintained unity among the groups through global changes, as well as provided a worldwide network of mutual trust that facilitated the expansion of business activity around the world.

It is useful to treat China's attempt to attract investments from economically successful Chinese located across Asia as a problem of relationships with a diaspora community. First, the People's Republic of China (PRC) government itself behaves in this context. Second, the relationship does potentially manifest the classic dilemmas of the triangular relationship among diaspora, home country, and host country. On the one hand, China wishes to attract overseas entrepreneurs by whatever means possible for its own development, and has seized on the diaspora link as an effective strategy. On the other hand, China does not wish to alarm Southeast Asian governments on an issue that has historically been sensitive. During the cold war, the loyalties of Southeast Asia's ethnic Chinese were often questioned, with suspicions reinforced by PRC support of insurgent groups in Thailand, Indonesia, and Malaysia. With increased investments and interactions between Southeast Asian Chinese and the PRC in the 1990s, such questions have occasionally resurfaced.

However, caution must be used in characterizing Southeast Asia's ethnic Chinese as a diaspora. The definition of diaspora uses terms such as "homeland" and "host" that seem to undercut the sense in which ethnic minorities can be seen as truly belonging to the countries in which they live. In short, the identity of the diaspora community—in its own eyes, the eyes of the "home country," and the eyes of the "host country"—is problematic in an era of state sovereignty, ethnic minority populations, and transnational business activity. In addition, the identity and relation to China of ethnic Chinese in Southeast Asia have changed over time and vary from person to person. While some ethnic Chinese may speak a Chinese language and adhere to Chinese customs, others have lost all cultural connections with China. Thus, labeling all ethnic Chinese as members of a diaspora implies a uniformity that does not exist.[13]

Some have suggested that networks, such as those that link members of a diaspora with each other and the "homeland," pose a threat to the utility of the nation-state. For instance, John Naisbitt claims that due to the demands of efficient production and distribution, "the world is moving from a collection of nation-states to a collection of networks."[14] One such network that Naisbitt has in mind is that of Asia's ethnic Chinese. Networks challenge state sovereignty by providing individuals with information, encouraging the formation of group identities, and facilitating entrepreneurial activity that crosses state boundaries. Some have argued, for instance, that Asian regionalization is network-based rather than institution-based.[15] While institutions are established by states, networks are established by individuals. In addition to the threat from networks, the sovereignty of states is being eroded at both the supranational and subnational levels by multinational organizations, nonstate actors, demands for regional autonomy, and natural economic territories that cross state boundaries.[16]

Nevertheless, this study suggests that states still play a major role in manipulating ethnic business networks and providing an environment conducive to the activities of such networks. For instance, the Chinese government played a central role in attracting investments from the ethnic Chinese business network. What is needed is a greater understanding of the context and specific issues in which states benefit from or are undermined by a transnational diaspora community. This study examines that context in the case of China and Asia's ethnic Chinese.

As previously suggested, there is a triangular relationship among China, the states of Southeast Asia, and Southeast Asia's ethnic Chinese. Each point of the triangle has both shared and competing interests with the other points, and influence flows both ways along all three legs of the triangle. In examining these relationships the study focuses on how the states of Southeast Asia and China attempt to use the diaspora for their own goals, as well as if and how the transnational activities of the diaspora threaten the autonomy of the various states that are involved.

Later chapters explore all three legs of this triangular relationship and its special features. However, most attention is given to the first leg, the interactions between China and Asia's ethnic Chinese. There are several facets to this relationship. The first is China's use of ethnic appeals to the diaspora, both at local and national levels, to leverage investment from Asia's ethnic Chinese. To a lesser extent the state also seeks charitable contributions. This is a process that has been going on for a century, but only since the early 1980s has it been significant in terms of the effects it has had on China's development. Also within this leg of the triangle is the response of Asia's ethnic Chinese to China's appeals. Is the blood tie more important, or is investment and trade with China largely a response to profit opportunities? In general, in spite of the resurgence of markets and neo-liberal economic logic, culture and ethnicity still play a limited role in economic calculations.

Also related to the first leg of the triangle, but extending outside it as well, is the question of whether ethnic ties that appear to cement the PRC economic relationship with Asia's ethnic Chinese have created a closed and exclusive economic trading area. Have China's efforts to attract ethnic Chinese created a context that discourages other potential investors, who cannot break into the system of ethnically conditioned connections? Or do ethnic Chinese serve as catalysts and partners for others with an interest in China's economy? In addition, can ethnic Chinese investors meet China's needs? Again, there is ambiguity on these points; the answers are complex, and probably point to the operation of both positive and negative effects of the close PRC ties to Asia's ethnic Chinese investors. This issue is particularly salient with falling Asian investment in China due to the region's economic crisis and China's desire to attract higher-end technology.

At the same time, this study demonstrates that the interactions between China and its diaspora also challenge the Chinese state. This occurs in a context of numerous problems confronting Beijing. China faces the same forces threatening sovereignty from above and below that other countries do. However, these challenges are compounded by the problems stemming from high but unequal economic growth, the struggle to gain macroeconomic controls, major ideological transition, the need for a new system of allocating power between the center and provinces, the predominance of personal rule in politics, and the Asian economic crisis.

In regard to the ethnic Chinese, Beijing's policies may weaken central authority. Ethnic Chinese have many advantages in investing in China, one of which is the close connections they can establish with local and provincial officials. This is both a result and cause of the rapid decentralization of power that is occurring in China, a decentralization that at times appears to threaten dangerous disintegrative consequences and certainly creates strong patterns of cross-boundary ties that reorient high investment regions away from the center. Thus economic interactions between Asia's ethnic Chinese and local officials threaten the authority of the center as local areas obtain greater revenues and feign compliance with Beijing's directives. At the same time, business activity may also create conditions for democratization in China, a prospect that is unwelcome to the current regime.

The second leg of the triangle connects Southeast Asia's ethnic Chinese with their Southeast Asian homes. There are two main issues here. The first is the identity and loyalty of Southeast Asia's ethnic Chinese. This identity and loyalty has long been questioned by the indigenous inhabitants of Southeast Asia. By increasing investments in China, Southeast Asia's ethnic Chinese have risked renewed attacks on their loyalty. Nevertheless, this is perhaps an inevitable contradiction in a world of sovereign states and transnational business. As transnational interactions become more common, the meaning of loyalty is changing, and Asia's ethnic Chinese are adopting multiple levels of identity.

The second issue relates to the ways in which Southeast Asian governments respond to ethnic Chinese investments in China. There are contradictory processes at work here. On the one hand, efforts have been made to improve the domestic environment in order to keep investments in Southeast Asia, coupled with occasional political pressure applied to Southeast Asia's ethnic Chinese to invest at home. This was more pronounced during the Asian economic crisis. At the same time, some Southeast Asian leaders are also encouraging investments in China, both for economic reasons and to integrate China into the wider region.

This leads to the third leg of the triangle, relations between China and the states of Southeast Asia. China wishes to attract ethnic Chinese entrepreneurs by whatever means possible for its own development. However, China does not wish to alarm Southeast Asian governments over a topic that has historically been sensitive. In the past Southeast Asian governments have feared that China would use the ethnic Chinese to promote its political purposes in the region, and these fears still linger. Thus, ethnic appeals on the part of China are particularly prone to cause problems. This illustrates how dealings with a transnational network can create competition and even friction between states.

In sum, interactions among China, Southeast Asia, and Asia's ethnic Chinese present both opportunities and challenges to China, as well as ethnic Chinese entrepreneurs and the states of Southeast Asia. The opportunities lie mainly in the area of economic development. The dangers are political and reflect the threats faced by both states and individuals as a result of the operation of transnational forces.

GREATER CHINA

The ambiguity regarding what we can expect from the widening linkages between a territorially based state, China, and ethnic Chinese throughout the world is clearly illustrated in discussions of "Greater China." This phenomenon is addressed by John Kao: "The very definition of 'China' is up for grabs. What we think of as Chinese now encompasses an array of political and economic systems that are bound together by a shared tradition, not geography. . . . Chinese-owned businesses in East Asia, the United States, Canada, and even farther afield are increasingly becoming part of what I call the *Chinese commonwealth*."[17] Xiamen vice mayor Zhang Zongxu's comments reflect this situation also: "Politics used to impose borders on business, but today, overseas Chinese from Taiwan, Hong Kong, and Southeast Asia are responsible for 90 percent of all foreign-invested enterprises in my city alone. What this is about is bigger than just politics, I think. What this is about is 21st century China."[18]

However, what "21st century China" means for Beijing and the Chinese nation-state is unclear. While some wonder if Beijing will control this entity, others believe that it spells the end of the nation-state as we now know it. Thus, Maria Hsia Chang states that the 21st century will be a "time of transition between nation-states and 'global tribes.' The first intimations of those future arrangements are current regional developments—such as Greater China I [China, Hong Kong, and Taiwan]. Such economically integrated regions might very well 'sideline' existing nation-states. As the strength of Greater China I increases, Beijing's control over what is now the PRC measurably diminishes."[19]

This entity of "Greater China" gained attention in the 1990s. The concept of Greater China is an outgrowth of geographic, technological, ethnic, and political factors. Thus discussions of Greater China can be traced to both the geographic proximity of various Chinese populations and breakthroughs in transportation and communications that make physical distance much less relevant. Regarding ethnicity, the term refers to a group that defines itself as Chinese. Politically, the concept has implications for both the current Chinese state and the concept of the nation-state in general. Thus, the concept of Greater China provides a focal point for issues that are relevant to this study, illustrating the ambiguity regarding territory and identity when a state interacts with a diaspora.

Perhaps the most striking feature of the term "Greater China" is its ambiguity. Although the term began appearing in Chinese in the late 1970s and in English in the mid- to late 1980s, it has no generally accepted definition.[20] This is perhaps appropriate, as the phenomenon which the term purports to label is evolving. Furthermore, the economic, political, and cultural differences that separate various Chinese communities in Asia and around the world make the very concept problematic.[21]

The most restrictive definitions of Greater China include only China's Guangdong and Fujian provinces, Hong Kong, and Taiwan (and perhaps Macao),[22] a definition that is no longer as applicable today with the geographic expansion of China's reforms. An expanded definition incorporates all of China, Hong Kong, and Taiwan.[23] A further enlarged definition lists not only China, Hong Kong, Taiwan, and Macao, but also ethnic Chinese living in Southeast Asia and even farther afield. For example, David Shambaugh says that Greater China is used "to describe the activities in, and interactions between, mainland China, Hong Kong, Macao, Taiwan and the offshore islands, and the Chinese overseas."[24] Harry Harding states, "In essence, it [Greater China] refers to the rapidly increasing interaction among Chinese societies around the world as the political and administrative barriers to their intercourse fall."[25]

In order to more closely examine Greater China, we will follow Harry Harding's lead and divide the concept into three spheres: economic, cultural, and political. In the economic realm, most works on Greater China focus on integration among China, Hong Kong, and Taiwan. Links among these three entities are long-standing. For example, a report from 1914 states that Hong Kong and Canton (Guangzhou) "could be viewed as a single entity because of their close working relationship."[26] However, the scope of the three-way trade and investment relationship today is unprecedented, especially in light of the many questions that preceded Hong Kong's reunification with China and the political differences that separate Taiwan and mainland China. Over half of direct foreign investment in China originates in or transits through Hong Kong, while China is Hong Kong's largest outside investor. Taiwan's cumulative investment in China jumped from an estimated $100 million in 1987 to an estimate of as high as $40 billion in 1999, while according to official Chinese figures, in 1996 and 1997 China's trade with Hong Kong and Taiwan totaled approximately 21 percent of its total trade.[27]

There are many names given to this triangular relationship. In addition to Greater China, it has been labeled the Greater South China Economic Region, Southern China Growth Triangle, Southern China Economic Zone, South China Economic Periphery, and the China Circle. These names, of course, are not neutral, and their proponents come to the terminological question with defined positions on the underlying political issues.

Several factors have been identified as generating the integrative links among China, Hong Kong, and Taiwan. Some are also relevant to the Southeast Asian Chinese as well. The main factor is complementary economic advantages. With high wages and rents at home, Taiwan and Hong Kong manufacturers have sought lower costs of production in China. China also has need of capital, technology, managerial talent, marketing, transportation, and finance which Hong Kong and Taiwan can provide. Second, more stringent environmental regulations in Taiwan and Hong Kong have played a role in leading businesses to invest in China. Third, cultural ties and a common language make business transactions easier. Fourth, the easing of government restrictions and even encouragement of economic interactions have fueled the trend, although currently Taiwan is attempting to slow investment in China as part of its "no haste, be patient" policy. Fifth, greater access to the Chinese domestic market has spurred investments in China by Hong Kong and Taiwan.

The economic relationship among China, Hong Kong, and Taiwan has largely been market-driven. However, before Hong Kong's return to China there were discussions among scholars as to how economic integration could be formalized. For example, in January 1992, experts from China, Taiwan, Hong Kong, and other places met to discuss "systems for economic cooperation among ethnic Chinese."[28] After Hong Kong's reunification with China in 1997, the issue of more formal links centered on Taiwan-mainland relations. Some progress has been made in this regard, such as the opening of mainland-Taiwan shipping links in 1997 for cargo ultimately destined for third countries. In 1998, a Taiwan Democratic Progressive Party legislator, Chang Chun-hung, proposed the formation of a "Chinese Financial Group" consisting of Taiwan, mainland China, Hong Kong, and Singapore in order to better deal with the Asian financial crisis. Nevertheless, overall progress in formal economic integration between the mainland and Taiwan has been slow.

The concept of Greater China also has a cultural component. Many ethnic Chinese around the world share certain cultural similarities that define their Chinese identity. However, with relaxations in political barriers and reform in China, cultural contacts among Chinese communities have greatly increased. Academic and intellectual exchanges are one such area where this is evident. For example, in October 1994, scholars from around the world participated in the inauguration of the International Confucian Association. At its founding, the association made Singapore's senior minister Lee Kuan Yew its honorary chairman, while former Chinese vice premier Gu Mu headed the organization. In the realm of popular culture, imports from Taiwan and Hong Kong play a prominent role on the mainland scene, especially in music and fashion.[29] Global Mandarin and Cantonese television broadcasting has become a reality as well.

On the other hand, Chinese culture is not uniform. Various subcultures exist in both China and the ethnic Chinese communities throughout Asia. These subcultures have their own dialects and traditions. However, China's rising world position does have a stimulating effect on the "great tradition" of Chinese culture and identity among the diaspora communities of Southeast Asia.

The political aspect of Greater China has meant reunification of China, Hong Kong, Macao, and Taiwan. Unification among the mainland, Hong Kong, and Macao has already been achieved under the "one country, two systems" formula. However, in the case of Hong Kong the maintenance of "two systems" is still under question, especially with the reversal of a Hong Kong Court of Final Appeal's decision on the right of abode for mainlanders in Hong Kong by China's National People's Congress in 1999. The case of Taiwan is more complex, with divergent agendas in Beijing and Taipei. Taipei hopes that a certain level of economic integration with China will give it influence in negotiating with Beijing, but also fears becoming economically beholden to the mainland. Furthermore, the whole issue is complicated by Taiwan's own domestic politics and pressures for independence, highlighted most recently by President Lee Teng-hui's characterization of mainland China—Taiwan ties as "special state-to-state" relations in July 1999.

Mainland China, on the other hand, believes that economic integration will speed reunification with Taiwan. This is clearly expressed by Ma Zongshi:

The ever-mounting economic integration among the four economies of Guangdong, Fujian, Hong Kong and Taiwan (wrongly called a "Greater China," the more accurate term is, perhaps, Southern China growth triangle), together with the current mainland fever in Taiwan, will sooner or later melt down the political barriers separating both sides of the Strait and drown the clamour for Taiwan independence. High economic complementarity, the converging market mechanism, narrowing income gap between some coastal areas and Taiwan, snow-balling trade and investment, booming tourism . . . diminishing skepticism as well as common roots—all point to eventual peaceful reunification, a win-win game, instead of one side swallowing up the other.[30]

Whether this vision will come to fruition is yet to be determined. It can also be argued that Greater China poses a danger to the mainland as Marxist ideology and legitimacy are undercut and "socialism with Chinese characteristics" becomes increasingly irrelevant.[31]

As was implied by Ma, Chinese scholars and officials do not publicly view the term "Greater China" with favor. For example, when former Chinese foreign minister Qian Qichen was asked about his opinion on a Greater China economic area, he stated that no such area has yet been formed. Although he did note that Chinese in Hong Kong, Taiwan, and Southeast Asia have economic strength, he claimed that conditions do not exist that could lead to a formalized Greater China economic area. He concluded by adding that the issues of Taiwan and Hong Kong are separate from those of other ethnic Chinese.[32]

China withholds official endorsement of a Greater China due partially to opposition to the term in Southeast Asia. Because of long-standing tensions regarding the role of the ethnic Chinese and the ambiguous nature of the term "Greater China," many Southeast Asians are uncomfortable with the phrase and what it might mean for Southeast Asia. For example, Jusuf Wanandi of the Centre for Strategic and International Studies in Jakarta has warned that the terms "Greater China" and "Overseas Chinese Network" raise sensitivities when they are used outside the context of China, Taiwan, and Hong Kong. He emphasizes the fact that the Chinese in Southeast Asia have roots in their own countries. Their economic successes, which should not be exaggerated, are unrelated to China.[33]

Nevertheless, an article in *China Youth Daily* in 1991 advocated the building of a "Greater China [*Da Zhonghua*] cultural and economic sphere" to include the mainland, Taiwan, Hong Kong, Singapore, and ethnic Chinese in Southeast Asia. According to the article, an important characteristic of the evolution of the international structure is the emergence of regional blocs such as the North American Free Trade Agreement (NAFTA) and the European Union (EU). In order to compete with such structures, China must take advantage of the opportunities offered by Taiwan, Hong Kong, and Southeast Asia. Southeast Asia, the "soft belly of Asia's economy," offers special opportunities because of its high population, demand for Chinese products, underdeveloped markets, natural resources, and the influence of Chinese culture in the region.[34]

The relationship of Greater China to the Chinese state is still unclear. Some believe that it presages a frightening increase in China's state power. Others see it as leading to the demise of the Chinese state.[35] The nation-state is tied to a geographically based form of organization. How this geographic entity known as China will mesh with the expanding linkages among geographically scattered Chinese is an important issue that will further unfold in coming years.

OVERVIEW AND TERMINOLOGY

This chapter has discussed diaspora and state in order to guide the examination of the relationship between China and Asia's ethnic Chinese. Chapter 2 begins with a demonstration that there are indeed close links between China and Asia's ethnic Chinese, proving the utility of the diaspora model. The chapter subsequently describes Asia's ethnic Chinese in terms of numbers, wealth, and business practices. It concludes with a discussion of how Asia's ethnic Chinese entrepreneurs are organized in a network-like fashion.

Subsequent chapters then examine the evolution of relations between China and Asia's ethnic Chinese over time. Chapter 3 offers a historical overview of overseas Chinese investments in and remittances to mainland China from the late nineteenth century until 1978, examining both the various Chinese governments' appeals to the overseas Chinese and the ensuing responses. The survey demonstrates how successive Chinese governments have attempted to tap the wealth and expertise of Southeast Asian Chinese for the past century. It thus supplies a basis for a historical comparison of the post-1978 period.

Chapter 4 examines Beijing's policies toward Asia's ethnic Chinese since 1978 and evaluates the response to PRC efforts to attract investments. The chapter demonstrates that the state does have an important role in providing incentives to Asia's ethnic Chinese investors, incentives that take place in the context of China's wider policy toward Asia's ethnic Chinese as well as China's historical relations with the Chinese abroad. The chapter explores the magnitude and sources of external investments in China by Asia's ethnic Chinese, the motivations of ethnic Chinese investors, as well as the remittances and donations that have been funneled into China. The chapter shows that in spite of the resurgence of markets and neo-liberal economics, culture and ethnicity still play a role in the way actual investment decisions are made.

Chapters 5 and 6 examine the consequences of ethnic Chinese investments in China. Chapter 5 analyzes the economic impact of investments, focusing on the extent of investments, ethnic Chinese as catalysts and partners for Western firms, and the technology and management skills provided by ethnic Chinese. The chapter also explores the political effects of ethnic Chinese investments, assessing whether investments are a democratizing force, destabilizing force, or both. It asserts that China's strategy of attracting investments has costs for the state. The center's authority is reduced by playing the ethnic card because cooperation between local officials and ethnic Chinese is not easily monitored by Beijing. Ethnic Chinese businesspersons and networks, local government officials, and the state are all key players. In addition, investments directly lead to regional imbalances and indirectly foster pluralizing forces that the state must deal with.

Chapter 6 focuses on the international implications of ethnic Chinese economic interactions with China. The first section examines fears, justified or exaggerated, in Southeast Asia regarding China and the region's ethnic Chinese. The chapter also looks at the difficulties ethnic Chinese face in Southeast Asia and analyzes how renewed interest in China among ethnic Chinese affects their prospects for assimilation into Southeast Asian societies. The chapter concludes with a discussion of relations between China and Southeast Asia, specifically noting how these relations are affected by China's policies toward the region's Chinese entrepreneurs.

Chapter 7 targets Singapore as a case study of Southeast Asian Chinese investment in China, exploring how economic interactions between China and Singapore skyrocketed in the 1990s. Singapore is the only state in Southeast Asia that is governed by ethnic Chinese. It is in some ways representative of Southeast Asia's ethnic Chinese in that the Singapore government must at times speak for them and defend their actions. On the other hand, Singaporeans are also different from other Southeast Asian Chinese in that the Singapore government takes the lead in investing in China.

Chapter 8 summarizes the findings of this study and explores their implications. In so doing it specifies how the study has contributed to our understanding of the role of states in today's world and how state-diaspora interactions affect both China and Asia's ethnic Chinese.

This work generally avoids use of the term "overseas Chinese" to refer to Asia's ethnic Chinese. Historically, the Chinese word used to describe Chinese people living outside China is *huaqiao, hua* meaning Chinese and *qiao*, meaning someone who lives abroad, or more specifically, sojourner.[36] The traditional English translation of *huaqiao* is "overseas Chinese." However, with the emergence of independent states in Southeast Asia and the accompanying nationalism, the term *huaqiao* came to be problematic because it carries implications of Chinese nationalism and Chinese citizenship. Therefore, in the late 1970s Beijing became more conscientious in distinguishing between *haiwai huaren*, ethnic Chinese living outside China, and *huaqiao*, those who held Chinese citizenship or were somehow closely associated with China.[37] Today the term *huaren*, or ethnic Chinese, is also widely used to describe Southeast Asia's Chinese.

Unfortunately, a literal English translation of both *huaqiao* and *haiwai huaren* is rendered "overseas Chinese." Many authors, however, have argued that it is no longer appropriate to label *haiwai huaren* as "overseas Chinese." For example, Stephen Fitzgerald, writing as early as 1972, noted that the term "overseas Chinese" is not satisfactory because of its unintended implications of sojourner. He suggested that for the Southeast Asian context, *huaren* (ethnic Chinese) or *huazi* (foreign citizen of Chinese descent), or even *Nanyang* (Southeast Asian) Chinese be used.[38] However, Fitzgerald himself continued to use the term "overseas Chinese." Two prominent ethnic Chinese scholars from Southeast Asia have taken different approaches to this issue. Leo Suryadinata, when writing of the ethnic Chinese in Southeast Asia, simply uses the term "ethnic Chinese."[39] Wang Gungwu, on the other hand, prefers the term "Chinese overseas" to refer to "everyone of Chinese descent living outside Greater China,"[40] in other words, outside the Chinese mainland, Taiwan, Hong Kong, or Macao.

This study will employ the term "Southeast Asian ethnic Chinese" to refer to those ethnic Chinese who are citizens of Southeast Asian states. This avoids more Sino-centric terms such as "overseas Chinese" or even "Chinese overseas" that may imply that Southeast Asia's ethnic Chinese somehow belong to China rather than Southeast Asia. However, when referring to ethnic Chinese in Southeast Asia before 1978, the term "overseas Chinese" will be maintained. When referring to both Southeast Asia's ethnic Chinese and the Chinese in Hong Kong, Macao, and Taiwan, the term "Asia's ethnic Chinese" will be used in order to indicate a degree of separation from mainland Chinese, in spite of the recent reincorporation of Hong Kong and Macao. This separation is reflected in Southeast Asian sovereignty, Taiwan's claim to Republic of China sovereignty, and Hong Kong's status as a special administrative region.

NOTES

1. Maria Hsia Chang, "Greater China and the Chinese 'Global Tribe,'" *Asian Survey* 35, no. 10 (October 1995): 956; John T. Dori and Richard D. Fisher Jr., *U.S. and Asia Statistical Handbook 1998–1999* (Washington, D.C.: Heritage Foundation,

1998), 51; and "Economic Growth for 1998 Confirmed as 7.8 Percent," *Inside China Today*, 26 February 1999, Internet edition.

2. Josephine Ma, "Families Fall Back Below the Poverty Line," *South China Morning Post*, 8 November 1999, Internet edition; and Embassy of the People's Republic of China, *Newsletter*, 7 July 1999.

3. Embassy of the People's Republic of China, *Newsletter*, 10 June 1999.

4. Calculated from Dori and Fisher, *U.S. and Asia*, 51.

5. Economist Intelligence Unit, *China/Mongolia*, 1st quarter 1995, 4.

6. James McGregor, "Overseas Chinese Quietly Invest at Home," *Wall Street Journal*, 16 June 1992, A10. The *Economist* also carries the going home theme in "China's Diaspora Turns Homeward," *Economist*, 27 November 1993, 33–34.

7. Joel Klein, "Why China Does It Better," *Newsweek*, 12 April 1993, 23.

8. Bernd Ziesemer, *World Press Review*, June 1996, 30.

9. Peter C. Newman, "Tapping into the Bamboo Network," *Maclean's*, 21 July 1997, 44.

10. Information on the Centre is provided at http://coombs.anu.edu.au/Diaspora. For a brief account of the history of overseas Chinese studies, see Wang Gungwu, "The Status of Overseas Chinese Studies," in *The Chinese Diaspora: Selected Essays*, vol. 1, ed. Wang Ling-chi and Wang Gungwu (Singapore: Times Academic Press, 1998), 1–13.

11. Gabriel Sheffer, "A New Field of Study: Modern Diasporas in International Politics," in *Modern Diasporas in International Politics*, ed. Gabriel Sheffer (London: Croom Helm, 1986), 3. For a discussion of the changing conceptions of the term "diaspora," see Khachig Tölölyan, "Rethinking Diasporas: Stateless Power in the Transnational Moment," *Diaspora* 5, no. 1 (Spring 1996): 3–36.

12. Joel Kotkin, *Tribes: How Race, Religion, and Identity Determine Success in the New Global Economy* (New York: Random House, 1993), 4.

13. For reflections on the concept of diaspora as it relates to the Chinese, see Adam McKeown, "Conceptualizing Chinese Diasporas, 1842 to 1949," *Journal of Asian Studies* 58, no. 2 (May 1999): 306–37.

14. John Naisbitt, *Megatrends Asia* (New York: Simon and Schuster, 1996), 49.

15. See Peter J. Katzenstein and Takashi Shiraishi, eds., *Network Power: Japan and Asia* (Ithaca: Cornell University Press, 1997).

16. For a discussion of the challenges that states face, see James N. Rosenau, *Along the Domestic-Foreign Frontier* (Cambridge: Cambridge University Press, 1997). For a discussion of natural economic territories, see Robert A. Scalapino, "The United States and Asia: Future Prospects," *Foreign Affairs* 70, no. 5 (Winter 1991/92): 20–21.

17. John Kao, "The Worldwide Web of Chinese Business," *Harvard Business Review* (March/April 1993): 24. Italics are in the original.

18. In Andrew B. Brick, "The Emergence of Greater China: The Diaspora Ascendant," *Heritage Lectures*, no. 411, 1992, 10.

19. Chang, "Greater China," 967.

20. For the origins of the term "Greater China," see Harry Harding, "The Concept of 'Greater China': Themes, Variations, and Reservations," *China Quarterly*, no. 136 (December 1993): 661–64.

21. See Harding, "Concept," 683–86; James T. Myers and Donald J. Puchala, " 'Greater China': Some American Reflections," *Asian Affairs: An American Review* 21, no. 1 (Spring 1994): 3–13; and Charng Kao, "A 'Greater China Economic Sphere': Reality and Prospects," *Issues and Studies* 28, no. 11 (November 1992): 49–64.

22. See, for example, Louis Kraar, "A New China Without Borders," *Fortune*, 5 October 1992, 124–25; and Myers and Puchala, "Greater China," 3–4.

23. See, for example, Harry Harding, "The U.S. and Greater China," *China Business Review*, May–June 1992, 18–22. Other authors that use this definition include Daojiong Zha, "A 'Greater China'? The Political Economy of Chinese National Reunification," *Journal of Contemporary China*, no. 5 (Spring 1994): 40–63; and Geng Cui, "The Emergence of the Chinese Economic Area (CEA)," *Multinational Business Review* 6, no. 1 (Spring 1998): 63–72.

24. David Shambaugh, "Introduction: The Emergence of 'Greater China,'" *China Quarterly*, no. 136 (December 1993): 654.

25. Harding, "Concept," 660.

26. Reported in George Hicks, ed., *Overseas Chinese Remittances from Southeast Asia 1910–1940* (Singapore: Select Books, 1993), 103.

27. Figures come from the China Council for the Promotion of International Trade, www.ccpit.org/engVersion/cp_inform/cp_cbg/cbg4_1.html; "China-Bound Investment from Taiwan Plunges Nearly 70 percent," *Inside China Today*, 1 July 1999, Internet edition; and State Statistical Bureau, People's Republic of China, *China Statistical Yearbook 1998* (Beijing: China Statistical Publishing House, 1998), 626. See also Robert F. Ash and Y. Y. Kueh, "Economic Integration Within Greater China: Trade and Investment Flows Between China, Hong Kong, and Taiwan," *China Quarterly*, no. 136 (December 1993): 711–45; and Yun-wing Sung, "Hong Kong and the Economic Integration of the China Circle," in *The China Circle*, ed. Barry Naughton (Washington, D.C.: Brookings, 1997), 41–80. China's trade figures with Hong Kong are disputed by many of China's trade partners, as China records trade with industrial countries as trade with Hong Kong if it passes through Hong Kong ports. Furthermore, a significant proportion of the "foreign" investment channeled through Hong Kong is mainland money disguised as foreign investment in order to receive preferential treatment.

28. T. Hashida, "The Greater China Economic Zone," *Nomura Asia Focus*, June 1992, 16.

29. See Thomas B. Gold, "Go with Your Feelings: Hong Kong and Taiwan Popular Culture in Greater China," *China Quarterly*, no. 136 (December 1993): 907–25.

30. Ma Zongshi, "China Dream in the Global 1990s and Beyond," *Contemporary International Relations* 3, no. 7 (July 1993): 11.

31. In this regard, see Myers and Puchala, "Greater China," 9–13.

32. Xie Yining, "Qian Qichen jieshou benbao zhuanfang changlun Zhong-Mei guanxi" ("Qian Qichen Receives a Visit from This Paper to Discuss Chinese-American Relations"), *Qiao bao* (New York), 17 November 1993, 2.

33. Jusuf Wanandi, "China's Asia Card," *Far Eastern Economic Review*, 25 November 1993, 32.

34. "Sulian zhengbian hou Zhongguode xianshi ying duiyu zhanlüe xuanze" ("China's Realistic Strategic Choice after the Coup in the Soviet Union"), *Zhongguo qingnian bao* (*China Youth Daily*), 9 September 1991. Reprinted in *Chung-kuo chih ch'un* (*China Spring*), 1992, no. 1:38–39.

35. For example, Friedman believes that China's current regime is doomed due to its Leninist past and the very identity of China is now being contested. See Edward Friedman, *New Nationalist Identities in Post-Leninist Transformations: The Implications for China* (Hong Kong: Hong Kong Institute of Asia-Pacific Studies, 1992). See also Edward Friedman, "Ethnic Identity and the De-Nationalization and Democratization of

Leninist States," in *The Rising Tide of Cultural Pluralism*, ed. Crawford Young (Madison: University of Wisconsin Press, 1993), 222–41.

36. For discussions of the use of the term *huaqiao*, see Wang Gungwu, *Community and Nation: Essays on Southeast Asia and the Chinese* (Singapore: Heinemann Educational Books, 1981), 118–27, 252–54; and Yuan-li Wu and Chun-hsi Wu, *Economic Development in Southeast Asia: The Chinese Dimension* (Stanford: Hoover Institution Press, 1980), 117–22.

37. For an explicit distinction between *huaqiao* and *huaren*, see Zhao Heman, "Huaqiao huaren jingji yu Zhongguo dui wai kaifeng" ("The Overseas/Ethnic Chinese Economy and China's Opening to the World"), *Bagui qiao shi* (*Overseas Chinese History of Bagui*), 1994, no. 1:8. However, for an argument that *huaqiao* still has broader meanings for China, see Ku Ch'ang-yung, "Cong zhengzhi jingji cengmian lun Zhonggongde Dongnan Ya huaqiao zhengce" ("Economic and Political Perspectives on Peking's Policy Regarding Overseas Chinese in Southeast Asia"), *Zhongguo dalu yanjiu* (*Mainland China Studies*) 37, no. 9 (September 1994): 16.

38. Stephen Fitzgerald, *China and the Overseas Chinese: A Study of Peking's Changing Policy, 1949–1970* (Cambridge: Cambridge University Press, 1972), x.

39. See Leo Suryadinata, "Ethnic Chinese in Southeast Asia: Overseas Chinese, Chinese Overseas, or Southeast Asians?" in *Ethnic Chinese as Southeast Asians*, ed. Leo Suryadinata (New York: St. Martin's Press, 1997), 1–24.

40. Wang Gungwu, "Greater China and the Chinese Overseas," *China Quarterly*, no. 136 (December 1993): 927.

CHAPTER 2

Asia's Ethnic Chinese:
Characteristics and Networks

THE ETHNIC BOND BETWEEN CHINA AND ASIA'S ETHNIC CHINESE

In the previous chapter, the connection between a diaspora and its "home" country was discussed. Indeed, much of this work is based on the premise that a bond exists between China and Asia's ethnic Chinese. Does the relationship between China and Asia's ethnic Chinese exhibit such a linkage based on ethnic ties?

Ethnicity is a difficult concept to define. Among those who study ethnicity, there is a debate between primordialists, who see ethnicity as historically given, and instrumentalists, who see ethnicity as being fluid, a cultural construct.[1] Horowitz suggests that ethnic identity can best be seen as a continuum, with voluntary membership at one end and membership at birth at the other end. Various ethnic groups are located at different points along the continuum in terms of the way in which individuals become part of the group. Nevertheless, for most people ethnicity is an identifier that they receive at birth. Accordingly, most groups conceive of ethnicity as common ancestry, with the ethnic group being conceived of as extended kinship networks.[2]

This is clearly the case with the majority of Chinese. Over time the Chinese have viewed race as culture, type, lineage, nation, species, seed, and class.[3] For example, Sun Yat-sen, in the *Three Principles of the People*, claimed, "For the most part, the Chinese people are of the Han or Chinese race with common blood, common language, common religion, and common customs—a single, pure race."[4] Of these supposed commonalities, Chinese identity is based most strongly on biology or race. Theories of descent have been central to ethnic identity in China, supported by beliefs held at the folk level and the official level. Thus "Chineseness" is seen as being biological, defined by common racial roots.[5] This may partially be driven by the fact that the long-term features which define Chinese culture are ambiguous.

The racial or ethnic ties between China and ethnic Chinese throughout the world are still emphasized by mainland Chinese scholars, the Chinese government, and some of Asia's ethnic Chinese. Xiang Dayou of the Guangxi Overseas Chinese Affairs Office claims: "The Chinese mainland is the foundation of Asia's ethnic Chinese (*haiwai huaren*). Offspring of China both inside and outside the country, descendants of Yan and Huang, have identical nationality, ties of blood, the same language, a common culture, emotional bonds."[6] Sun Xingcheng of China's State Council Overseas Chinese Affairs Office uses former premier Zhou Enlai's metaphor to compare relations between China and Asia's ethnic Chinese to the bond between a mother and her married daughter. Although the daughter now belongs to her husband (the foreign country), she still is filial and loving toward her mother.[7] Furthermore, as part of the international Human Genome project, the Chinese government planned a project to "isolate the quintessentially Chinese genes among the 100,000 terms of genetic code borne by human DNA." In commenting on this, the *Renmin ribao* claimed that the research will "supply a biological basis to discern the dissemination and distribution of the Chinese race."[8]

In Southeast Asia many Chinese have genealogies charting their descent from *Huangdi*, one of the earliest mythical emperors of China and supposed father of the Chinese race, and some attribute their success in Southeast Asia to ethnic and racial superiority.[9] References to ethnic solidarity also come from Singapore officials. In a speech given to the World Chinese Entrepreneurs Convention in 1991, Singapore's then minister for information and the arts George Yeo stated that the migration of Asians to the United States, Canada, Australia, and New Zealand will continue because the "white peoples" in those places "are in relative decline. They are hardly reproducing themselves. Asians are needed to top up the numbers and also to revitalize their economies."[10] He noted that Chinese communities outside China should be considered part of the periphery of Chinese civilization, and called for the establishment of a Pacific Foundation to teach Asian languages and cultures in California, British Columbia, and Australia. This is because "among Asian migrants, there is always a fear that the next generation will lose their Asianness. If they speak only English, half the battle is lost."[11] Yeo concluded by commenting that although whites would like their Asian populations to be assimilated, this is unlikely. If "Asian migrants were to become white in everything but skin colour, their dynamism will surely be affected." Therefore there should be mutual accommodation and learning in the encounter of cultures.[12]

The rather startling biological and racial emphases in this perspective on ties between the homeland and ethnic Chinese should not be taken at face value, however. References to "Chinese" or "Asian" identity operate at too broad a level of analysis, in light of the cultural differences among Chinese from different regions, as well as their political and ideological differences. Certainly "Chinese-ness" has not always been sufficient to unify Chinese in the past, and there are great differences between and within various Chinese in different countries in regard to language, culture, identity, and political loyalty.

For example, in the past 150 years tens of millions of Chinese have died at the hands of compatriots in China due to civil war and domestic unrest. Currently mainland China and Taiwan face off in a showdown that could lead to war, creating divisions among Southeast Asian Chinese who may support one side or the other. In the economic sphere, Chinese companies compete against each other in fierce struggles for profits and markets. From a cultural perspective, Chinese in Southeast Asia have undergone varying degrees of assimilation into the indigenous cultures. For instance, *totok* Chinese have lived in Indonesia for two or three generations, speak Chinese (Mandarin or a dialect), and observe Chinese customs. *Peranakan* Chinese have been in Indonesia for at least three generations, are usually of mixed descent, and most often do not speak Chinese. Thus, even if one were to accept the primordial view of Chinese ethnicity, it is not clear what implications that would have for unity among Chinese.

Of course, there are those who challenge the primordial view. For example, Edward Friedman, responding to mainland assumptions regarding a unified Han race, argues that Han racial nationality is a modern invention, not genetic reality. The advent of reforms has brought about the contestation of national identity in China, with different visions existing between the inward-looking north and outward-looking south.[13] The outcome of this struggle will determine the future of China.

CHARACTERISTICS OF SOUTHEAST ASIAN CHINESE

The Number of Southeast Asian Chinese

Establishing the number of ethnic Chinese in Southeast Asia is not an easy task. If ethnicity is at least partially a subjective indicator, then ethnicity depends upon a person's self-identification and the label that others ascribe to him. Thus, it can be difficult to define who is and who is not Chinese. Many Southeast Asian Chinese have mixed ancestry and have adopted local names and the same customs as their neighbors. Under such circumstances there is no simple, objective test for an outsider to determine who is Chinese. Further, counting the number of ethnic Chinese can be politically sensitive.

Thus, researchers must attempt to estimate the number of ethnic Chinese in Asia and the world. Figures for the number of ethnic Chinese outside mainland China, Hong Kong, and Taiwan range from 26 million to 33 million (see table 2.1). Roughly 80 percent of such ethnic Chinese live in Southeast Asia. Therefore, the number of Chinese in Southeast Asia ranges from 20.2 million to 25.7 million, approximately 5 percent of the total population of the region.

Table 2.1
**Estimates of the Number of Worldwide Ethnic Chinese Outside China,
Taiwan, and Hong Kong (in millions)**

Source	Ethnic Chinese Outside China	Huaqiao[a]
Yu Chung-Hsun	24	2
Wang Gungwu	25–30	2.5
Poston et al.	31[b]	—
ROC Overseas Chinese Affairs Commission	33	—

[a] Defined as Chinese nationals. This figure is in addition to the number in the first column.

[b] Poston's original number is 37 million, which includes Hong Kong residents. Subtracting Hong Kong's 6 million yields the 31 million figure.

Sources: Yu Chung–Hsun, "Japan's Role in Southeast and East Asia During the Post-Cold War Era: In Relation to the Expanding Economic Power of the Ethnic Chinese," *Proceedings of Research Institute for Asian Development International Symposium* 1992 (Research Institute for Asian Development, International University of Japan, 1993), table 1, 110; Wang Gungwu, "Greater China and the Chinese Overseas," *China Quarterly*, no. 136 (December 1993): 927; Wang Gungsu, *China and the Chinese Overseas* (Singapore: Times Academic Press, 1991), 223–25; Dudley L. Poston Jr., Michael Xinxiang Mao, and Mei-Yu Yu, "The Global Distribution of Overseas Chinese Around 1990," *Population and Development Review* 20, no. 3 (September 1944): 631; and "Number of Overseas Chinese Tops 33 Million," Taiwan Central News Agency WWW in English (19 April 1998), FBIS, 19 April 1998.

Table 2.2 tabulates estimates of the ethnic Chinese population of Southeast Asia by country.

Two other groups of ethnic Chinese need mention here. The first is the *qiaojuan*, family dependents or relatives of Asia's ethnic Chinese who live in China. Yu estimated the number of *qiaojuan* to be over 26 million in 1986. The second group is the *guiqiao*, or returned overseas Chinese. Yu estimated their number to be over 900,000.[14] However, these numbers too are difficult to determine precisely. *Qiaojuan* and *guiqiao* are important due to their contacts with Asia's ethnic Chinese. Many *qiaojuan* and *guiqiao* have received money from abroad which they use for living expenses or investment, and have been an important link in Beijing's efforts to attract capital from Asia's ethnic Chinese.

The places of origin of Asia's ethnic Chinese are not evenly distributed across China. Most descendants of Chinese migrants can trace their family roots to Fujian province, Guangdong, Guangxi, or Hainan Island (now a province as well). The five major classifications of Asian ethnic Chinese (based on dialect and place of origin) are Hokkien (from Fujian), Teochiu (from the Chaozhou-Shantou area of Guangdong), Cantonese (from Guangdong), Hakka (scattered throughout southern China), and Hainanese (from Hainan Island). Within these groups are various subdialect groups as well. For example, subgroups of the Can-

Table 2.2
Ethnic Chinese in Southeast Asia (in thousands and percent
of total population)

Countries	Poston et al. 1990		Suryadinata 1990		*Economist* 1996	
Brunei	44	17.8%	41	16%	N.A.	
Burma	1,500	3.7%	466	1.4%	N.A.	
Cambodia	300	3.7%	50	1.0%	N.A.	
Indonesia	7,315	4.1%	5,460	3.0%	8,000	4%
Laos	160	3.8%	10	0.4%	N.A.	
Malaysia	5,472	30.0%	5,261	29.6%	6,000	32%
Philippines	820	1.3%	850	1.3%	1,000	1%
Singapore	2,113	77.7%	2,253	77.7%	2,000	76%
Thailand	6,000	10.8%	4,813	8.6%	6,000	10%
Vietnam	2,000	3.0%	962	1.5%	1,000	1%
Totals	25,724		20,166		24,000	

Sources: Dudley L. Poston Jr., Michael Xinxiang Mao, and Mei-Yu Yu, "The Global Distribution of
Overseas Chinese Around 1990," *Population and Development Review* 20, no. 3 (September
1994): 636; Leo Suryadinata, "Ethnic Chinese in Southeast Asia: Overseas Chinese, Chinese
Overseas, or Southeast Asians?" in *Ethnic Chinese as Southeast Asians*, ed. Leo Suryadinata (New
York: St. Martin's Press, 1997), 21; and "The Limits of Family Values," *Economist*, 9 March 1996,
Business in Asia 10.

tonese include Siyap, Taishan, Sanwei, Tungkoon, Sun Tuk, and Chungshan,
each with its own unique variation of the Cantonese dialect.

The countries of Southeast Asia have varying concentrations of Chinese dia-
lect groups. For instance, Thailand, Cambodia, and Laos have a majority of Teochiu
Chinese. The largest group in Malaysia and Singapore (although not a majority)
is Hokkien, while half or more of Indonesian and Filipino Chinese are Hokkien.
In Vietnam the majority of Chinese are Cantonese. However, most Southeast
Asian countries have Chinese from all five dialect groups in varying proportions.
Dialect groups are important because traditionally Southeast Asia's Chinese
communities were organized according to dialect. Thus neighborhoods, associations, and even occupations were strongly influenced by dialect group. For example, the Teochiu traditionally have controlled the food trade in Southeast
Asia. Although dialect groupings are not as significant as they once were, they
still form an important resource for networking.[15]

The origins of Asia's ethnic Chinese in southern China are of importance to
the explanation of regional variations in China's overall development and to the
dynamics of development in southern China in particular. Predictably, the lo-

cales of southern China today trumpet their connections to Asia's ethnic Chinese and try to use them to their economic and political advantage. Nevertheless, it is also true that since 1978 there has been a new wave of Chinese migration, estimated at over a million people. Large numbers of these migrants have settled in Burma, Laos, Cambodia, and the Philippines, as well as countries farther from China such as the United States. This wave of migration has differed from previous waves in that migrants usually speak Mandarin and come from across China.[16]

The Wealth of Asia's Ethnic Chinese

The Chinese outside mainland China are known to have substantial financial assets. This does not mean that all Chinese are rich. Chinese throughout the region are found in various socioeconomic levels, a point that is often lost in discussions of Chinese wealth. Nevertheless, large Chinese companies have access to substantial sums of money. However, estimates of Chinese wealth are even more speculative than estimates of the number of Chinese. Because ethnic Chinese capital is so difficult to identify, one observer has labeled it "shadow capital."[17] Due to frequent violence against the ethnic Chinese and efforts by governments to access Chinese wealth, it makes good sense for companies and individuals to camouflage their assets. Adding to the difficulties of assessment, the effects of the Asian financial crisis on Chinese wealth are not fully known at this point, although one estimate calculated a near-halving in the asset value of the top five hundred overseas Chinese companies in 1998.[18]

The accumulation of Chinese wealth has been based mainly on business activities across Southeast Asia, where ethnic Chinese have been a vital part of the economy for many decades. A report issued by the Department of Foreign Affairs of the Taiwan Governor General's Office (an arm of the Japanese colonial government), originally published in 1943, defines official Japanese interest in the overseas Chinese in Southeast Asia in terms of their economic dominance in the region: "Although they are only immigrants, it is no exaggeration to say that without the Chinese the economies of these countries would not have developed."[19] For example, before 1942, the overseas Chinese reportedly owned 80 percent to 90 percent of the rice mills in Thailand. Before 1932, they controlled 70 percent to 80 percent of the retail trade in the Philippines, and in 1948 held over 20 percent of commercial assets there.[20]

Estimates of the wealth of the ethnic Chinese in the 1990s vary, based on the analyst and the measure used. One gauge that is commonly utilized is economic output, assuming that Asia's ethnic Chinese have a GNP similar to a nation-state. The World Bank estimated that in 1991 the Chinese diaspora (including Taiwan and Hong Kong) had a combined economic output of $397 billion, which the *Wall Street Journal* reckoned to have risen to around $500 billion by 1995,[21] larger than mainland China's gross domestic product (GDP). Murray Weidenbaum and Samuel Hughes surmised in 1996 that the combined economic output of Asia's ethnic Chinese was as high as $600 billion,[22] while Hong Kong professor Gordon Redding makes a much more modest 1993 estimate of $200 billion, smaller than the output of the mainland.[23]

Another measure of wealth that has been cited is assets. During the Second World Chinese Entrepreneurs Convention in 1993, convention literature asserted that overseas Chinese businesspersons owned a total of $200 billion to $300 billion in global assets.[24] However, a London report, citing the estimate of a Singapore banker, claimed the 1997 liquid capital of the "Offshore Chinese empire" was up to $2 trillion.[25] The *Economist* provides an identical estimate of liquid capital, further stating that as of late 1995 nine of ten of East Asia's billionaires are "overseas Chinese," while Chinese control two-thirds of the region's retail trade.[26]

The position of Chinese in the economies of Southeast Asia is similarly impressive. Iman Taujik, vice chairman of the Indonesian Chamber of Commerce and Industry, stated in 1998 that Chinese run 90 percent of Indonesia's largest conglomerates and control approximately 50 percent of the Indonesian economy.[27] It is commonly said that Chinese control 70 percent of Indonesia's wealth,[28] in spite of the fact that they only comprise 3 percent to 4 percent of the population. In fact, Liem Sioe Liong's Salim Group by itself accounted for about 5 percent of Indonesia's GNP in the early 1990s.[29] In Malaysia, it is estimated that 80 percent of small and medium-sized industries are Chinese-owned.[30] In the Philippines, Chinese-owned companies generate two-thirds of the sales of the 67 largest commercial outfits and dominate the smaller companies as well.[31] Another estimate gives the ethnic Chinese control of 58 percent of the Philippines' commerce.[32] In Thailand, Chinese are said to control 81 percent of the wealth.[33] Table 2.3 provides further estimates of Chinese wealth in Southeast Asia as measured by market capitalization and business output as percent of total local economy.[34]

Table 2.3
Comparative Wealth of Chinese in Southeast Asia

Countries	Chinese Business Output as Percentage of Total Local Economy	Percent of Listed Companies Owned by Chinese
Malaysia	60%	61%
Indonesia	50%	73%
Thailand	50%	81%
Philippines	40%	50%
Singapore	76%	81%

Sources: "The Limits of Family Values," *Economist*, 9 March 1996, Business in Asia 10; and John Naisbitt, *Megatrends Asia* (New York: Simon and Schuster, 1996), 19–20. Naisbitt's figures on listed companies come from Fijitsu Research.

These figures on ethnic Chinese wealth in Southeast Asia are not very precise, and there are various methodologies for attempting to calculate wealth. Some methodologies omit the value of important assets such as land that would reduce the percentage of ethnic Chinese wealth.[35] Wealth estimates are also controversial because of their political ramifications. Mainland analysts tend to play down the wealth of Southeast Asia's ethnic Chinese. For example, Zhao Heman of the Guangxi Social Science Institute warns against exaggerating estimates of ethnic Chinese capital because it makes life difficult for ethnic Chinese. Zhao notes that claims regarding the amount of ethnic Chinese capital cover a wide range and are difficult to substantiate. He goes on to assert that compared to Western firms, ethnic Chinese are not especially wealthy.[36] Indeed, of the one hundred largest nonfinancial transnational corporations listed by the UN, the only Asian companies hailed from Japan and Korea.[37]

It is also true that the Asian economic crisis has taken a major toll on ethnic Chinese businesses. Indonesia's Salim Group, for instance, was devastated by Indonesia's economic collapse and is struggling to pay off debt. Thailand's CP Group, a major investor in China, is saddled with debt and making efforts to consolidate its far-flung businesses. Furthermore, many of Asia's millionaires moved money out of Asia and into the West during the Asian economic crisis. Nevertheless, the fact remains that ethnic Chinese produce wealth in Southeast Asia that is greatly disproportionate to their percentage of the population. This has two ramifications. First, it provides investment capital, some of which entrepreneurs have invested in China. Second, the amount of wealth triggers resentment in Southeast Asia, resentment that sometimes turns to violence. This is especially true where Chinese are least assimilated, such as Indonesia, and less so where Chinese are more assimilated, such as Thailand. Resentment in turn provides incentives for ethnic Chinese to move their money overseas, but at the same time creates within Southeast Asia more scrutiny and sensitivity toward capital flows moving out of the region.

Chinese Business Structures

There has been a great deal of interest in the structure and business practices of ethnic Chinese-owned companies, an interest reminiscent of the fascination with Japanese firms in the 1980s. Most writers emphasize the success of Chinese companies, although there are several areas of disagreement. These disputed issues include the place of Chinese culture in accounting for entrepreneurial success, the role of professional management versus the intuition of an all-powerful head in Chinese firms, the existence of an ethnic character to large multinational companies that are controlled by Chinese, and the technological level of ethnic Chinese enterprises. There also tend to be differences in the evaluation of ethnic Chinese businesses, with some analysts seeing them as praiseworthy and others viewing them suspiciously. Furthermore, there are many different factors put forth as being key to the business success of the ethnic Chinese. These issues will be laid out here. Although no attempt will be made to settle the controversies, the main themes are relevant to ethnic Chinese commercial dealings in mainland China. Across the categories of explanation it will become apparent that a key thread that runs through the debate over these many issues is the question of how or if a distinctive "Chineseness" is reflected in the structure and operation of companies owned by ethnic Chinese.

The generalized picture of the ethnic Chinese company is a small to medium-sized family-owned firm that is controlled by the family patriarch, who rules in an authoritarian manner with the support and cooperation of other family members. This structure allows for quick decision making and flexibility. Employees and owners of the company alike work hard. Owners traditionally try to avoid debt and preserve a good reputation, spending considerable effort in building and maintaining *guanxi*, or connections, with other Chinese companies. Therefore, the firm has strong but informal links with Chinese-owned companies throughout Asia, making Chinese businesses seem clanlike and elevating trust as a crucial value in business dealings. In fact, a single informal capital market is said to exist throughout the Chinese diaspora. Although most businesses are quite successful, succession is a major problem due to the family-oriented nature of business. Companies therefore tend to both rise quickly and fall quickly within a few generations.[38]

One of the major debates among those attempting to explain Chinese business success centers on the role of Chinese culture. Gordon Redding, taking a Weberian perspective in searching for a spirit of Chinese capitalism, traces how culture and values influence the business practices of Asia's ethnic Chinese through an economic culture that is distinctively Chinese.[39] Redding thus insists on the continuing "Chinese" characteristics of Asia's ethnic Chinese. He states that "the Chinese who moved have remained in some deep and significant sense still Chinese; the majority of them have not psychologically left China, or at least not left some ideal and perhaps romanticized notion of Chinese civilization. This is the feature which unites them, and which provides them with one of their most distinctive strengths—a capacity to cooperate."[40]

Redding sees the family business as being central to ethnic Chinese economic activity for cultural and environmental reasons. Thus, he notes that Chinese companies, even large firms, retain the traits of family businesses. He regards this characteristic as enduring because it is rooted in Chinese history and culture and is well suited to its particular East Asian milieu. The second key defining feature of Chinese businesses is their networks. Networks are based on clan or regional identity, personal obligation (such as the relationship between classmates or friends), and the unifying force of Chinese culture and identity.

Redding links the organizational structure of Chinese businesses to a management style that can best be described as patrimonial and personalistic. This, too, is a reflection of and response to Chinese society. There are advantages to this type of organizational style in facilitating flexibility and initiating rapid changes of direction, but such a style also inhibits talent at lower levels of management, depends on continued family unity and talent, and inhibits size and therefore technological sophistication. It also inhibits influence by professionals from outside the family who may be experts in areas such as accounting or finance. This is an important point, as it affects China's goal of attracting foreign investment in part to learn management skills.

Rupert Hodder, on the other hand, rejects the view that culture can explain Southeast Asian Chinese business success.[41] Hodder argues that there is no single Chinese culture that can account for a Chinese approach to business. This is due in part to doubts over the question of who is Chinese, based on the heterogeneity of ethnic Chinese communities and the mixing of ethnicity that occurs throughout Southeast Asia. Hodder also asserts that those who defend cultural explanations merely assume the linkage between culture and the variables they wish to explain, instead of proving that such linkages exist. He points to phenomena such as networks and family businesses, supposed results of Chinese culture, but found in the Philippines in both Chinese and Filipino business communities. Instead, Hodder argues that the success of ethnic Chinese should be explained by examining the "constantly changing and multidimensional institutions, values, actions, and behavior, conducted by and comprising individuals who also possess many different aspects."[42]

Other explanations of Chinese business success attempt to meld descriptions of culture and environment. For example, Rajeswary Ampalavanar Brown discusses how family and networks provided vital advantages in the East Asian environment due to their role in reducing transaction costs, increasing productivity, and overcoming the barriers put up by sovereign states.[43] Victor Limlingan argues that the Chinese have succeeded because they have developed a business strategy based on their value and social systems that works well in the particular Association of Southeast Asian Nations (ASEAN) environment.[44] The overall debate on the role of culture mirrors the wider debate in the social sciences on the utility of various levels of explanatory variables and their interaction with the environment.

Another area of debate concerning ethnic Chinese businesses revolves around their structure. As ethnic Chinese firms often are centered around a family, introducing modern management techniques is a challenge. John Kao of the Harvard Business School notes that most Chinese companies are small. However, even large companies maintain simple organizational structures to keep centralized control in the hands of the patriarch and family members. These "imperial organizations" are passed on to sons after the fathers retire. Nonfamily members can never get too close to the top. The major strength of these companies is "knowledge arbitrage," wherein entrepreneurs use their understanding of differing labor costs, consumer trends, technological developments, and resources in various countries to make profits.[45] However, a weakness is found in the area of management. Although many children of Chinese entrepreneurs do get their master of business administration degrees, it is difficult to incorporate outside managers with real authority into a family-run business system that tends to carefully guard information.[46]

Linda Lim differs from Kao in her analysis of the uniqueness of ethnic Chinese businesses. On the basis of her study of the electronics industry, Lim argues that ethnic Chinese companies that engage in modern manufacturing for export do not operate any differently than other multinational corporations (MNCs).[47] Lim's thesis is that "Chinese business loses whatever 'ethnic' character it has when it enters modern, technologically-based industries oriented to the world market. Although some firms may have *origins* linked to traditional Chinese business, their *operations* are quite different from traditional Chinese business practices, and no different from those of other modern capitalist industrial enterprises operating on profit-maximising principles in the world market."[48] As evidence, Lim points to the disappearance of traditional Chinese business practices in the modern electronic sector in Singapore and Malaysia, where capital is raised through impersonal means, foreigners are included as partners, and mass hiring is conducted on open labor markets. Similarly, Cai Renlong, in an analysis of the Indonesian Lin Shaoliang's First Pacific Enterprise Group, emphasizes how the group has broken away from the family management tradition.[49]

In spite of Lim's and Cai's assertions, the general consensus among organizational experts is that there do seem to be characteristics of many multinational Chinese firms that set them apart from other multinationals. This is not surprising, in that even American, European, and Japanese multinationals have been found to be different from each other due to varying national structures within their home countries.[50] Although the organization of large ethnic Chinese multinational companies is complex, the purpose of this complexity is usually to maintain family control over a network of companies. Holdings are often pyramidal in shape, with private holdings at the top. Other groups can be viewed as treelike, with the trunk being a holding company with shares in group companies. These group companies in turn have their own subsidiaries. Companies in a group are linked through complex shareholding relationships that allow groups to raise funds internally and protect themselves against takeovers. Deals between the various companies are common, and the whole structure can be convoluted, frustrating outsiders and potential investors. Besides lending itself to secrecy, these structures also can allow the shifting of assets between public and private stocks.[51]

This style of organization of many Chinese firms does have a cost. Lack of highly professional management makes it difficult for ethnic Chinese firms to move into sectors where sophisticated management is required, such as heavy industry and some high-tech applications. When firms do move into high-tech and heavy industries, it is largely by acquiring technology and management skills through joint ventures, acquisitions, and mergers. This weakness in the area of technology limits the value of ethnic Chinese firms to China's developmental efforts.[52] A further difficulty for Southeast Asian Chinese firms in developing heavy industry and high technology is their lack of strong connections to a supportive state, in contrast to the benefits enjoyed by firms in Taiwan, South Korea, and Japan. Even in Singapore the government has favored multinationals and its own state-linked enterprises over its domestic Chinese business community.

Other issues face ethnic Chinese businesses as well. One is the tendency of large companies to become conglomerates, spreading into numerous fields with few connections between them. Management experts such as Michael Porter have argued that in today's global economy firms must instead focus on their core areas.[53] Due to the Asian financial crisis, firms have been doing just that in an effort to survive. Another organizational issue faced by firms is that of survival past the founding generation. A Chinese proverb states that wealth does not survive the third generation. In order for family firms to survive in the long term, means must be found to separate family from firm at some point in a company's existence.

Chinese Business Networks

In discussions of ethnic Chinese businesses, much is made of the concept of networks. Networks are conceived of as one of the pillars of ethnic Chinese business success. Some go so far as to see small businesses linked by networks as supplanting large, bureaucratic MNCs, while others predict networks will replace the nation-state.[54] At times the links between Chinese enterprises are described in ominous tones. For example, one analyst states: "Many of the Chinese entrepreneurs operate through secretive transnational economic networks of Byzantine complexity beyond the control of the individual states, but with close links to Singapore, Hong Kong, and Taiwan, and shadowy connections with the PRC."[55]

A network can be defined as "a web of free-standing participants cohering through shared values and interests," while networking consists of "making connections among peers."[56] Thus, networks in principle are nonhierarchical. In the case of ethnic Chinese business networks, the participants cooperate through shared values, interests, and culture, although great competition occurs as well. Networks provide support, information, credit, and a sense of belonging in a sometimes hostile environment.

Chinese business networks are both formal and informal. At the informal level, which is most important, entrepreneurs with ties based on birthplace, common history, friendship, third-party introduction, or previous business dealings cooperate in sharing information, extending credit, or partnering in profit-making ventures. At a formal level, various mechanisms have been established to foster relations among Chinese businesspersons. For example, the First World Chinese Entrepreneurs Convention was held in Singapore in 1991. Subsequent conventions were held every other year in Hong Kong (1993), Bangkok (1995), Vancouver (1997), and Melbourne (1999). In a keynote address at the second convention, Singapore's senior minister Lee Kuan Yew extolled the benefits of *guanxi* and told the assembled gathering not to be ashamed of cultivating networks.[57]

In addition, traditional associations based on clan, hometown district, or dialect have revived and hold frequent conferences. It is estimated that over one hundred world conventions of Chinese voluntary associations have been held, backed by prominent business leaders and politicians. For example, the Second World Fujian Convention, organized by the Federation of Hokkien Associations of Malaysia, was held in Langkawi, Malaysia, in September 1996. It was attended by 2,500 delegates from 16 countries; Prime Minister Dr. Mahathir Mohamad gave the opening address. In 1999, the Federation of World Hakkas held its fifteenth biennial convention in Kuala Lumpur, Malaysia. The Gan, Guo, Lin, and Shun Clan Associations have all held international conferences as well, and new societies, such as the Chinese Entrepreneurs Society of Canada, are cropping up. Many of these bodies have permanent secretariats and other institutional structures that facilitate worldwide network building and promote dialect-based identities.[58]

The Internet provides another tool for networking. The Singapore Chamber of Commerce has created a World Chinese Business Network website to provide information on ethnic Chinese companies and to create business opportunities for them.[59] The World Huaren Federation maintains a website designed to provide information on the Chinese diaspora and further its well being.[60]

The establishment and maintenance of networks has been important to ethnic Chinese business success in Asia. Before the development of modern banking systems, networks provided credit based on reputation and trust. Trust is a vital part of networks, allowing deals to be sealed without an extensive bureaucracy or numerous lawyers slowing the process. One example of the workings of the ethnic Chinese network occurred when Singapore needed to raise $460 million in 1988 to build Suntec City. Officials turned to wealthy Hong Kong businessmen for the financing, and the deal was put together within a week.[61] With the opening of China in 1978 and the end of the cold war a little more than a decade later, Chinese ethnic networks expanded as entrepreneurs sought new connections to do business across China and a booming Southeast Asia.

Ethnic Chinese business networks also contribute to the economic integration of Asia as a region. Because networks cross political borders, cross-border economic interactions are common in spite of the fact that Asia has few formal integrative institutions. Nor are ethnic Chinese networks limited to Asia. Chinese students abroad and ethnic Chinese emigrants expand networks around the globe. For example, one-third of the engineers in California's Silicon Valley are ethnic Chinese.[62] Many of them can be expected to maintain contacts in Asia and return there to begin businesses.

Research has demonstrated the importance of networks in day-to-day business activities. Kao has found that Chinese conduct a large number of their dealings within their own ethnic networks. According to his survey, 52 percent of ethnic Chinese respondents said that over half their domestic working relationships were with Chinese principals, while 39 percent of their international working relationships were with other Chinese. These percentages are disproportionately high compared to other multinational firms.[63] Another study found networks to be important to Asia's ethnic Chinese doing business in China, playing a major role in the success of diaspora businesses in China.[64] A third study has found that the success of Chinese middlemen in Asia "was due chiefly to Chinese ability to protect contracts under conditions of contract uncertainty via their networks of kinship and ethnic relations among the Chinese dealers."[65]

This latter study points to an important reason for the centrality of networks in Asia. Networks evolved in a historical context of economic uncertainty and continue to be important in an environment where one's connections are often more important than rule of law and trust is a valuable business asset. In formal economic terms, ethnic networks reduce transaction costs in environments with poor legal frameworks where contracts cannot legally be enforced. In such an environment, who one does business with matters. Ethnic networks can reduce contract uncertainty by identifying who is trustworthy.[66]

This leads to one explanation for why ethnic Chinese entrepreneurs have tended to dominate investment in China. Since China's opening to the outside world, investors have found that good *guanxi* is important to doing business. Lucian Pye defines *guanxi* as "friendship with implications of continued exchange of favors."[67] *Guanxi* is often necessary to do the everyday work of business, such as obtain permits, hire employees, and deal with local officials. Although the PRC government is attempting to develop a system of commercial law, *guanxi* is still important in getting things done in China. Ethnic Chinese investors are, on the whole, better at establishing and using *guanxi* than multinational corporations. This is due partially to a greater understanding of Chinese language and culture, and partially to the experience of working in a similar environment in their own home countries. Thus, ethnic Chinese encounter lower transaction costs in doing business in China.[68] Transaction costs are also lowered by the tendency of many ethnic Chinese firms to invest in small towns, where local officials are cooperative and Beijing does not interfere.

In spite of the importance of networks for ethnic Chinese entrepreneurs, their significance must not be overblown. First, networking among Chinese does not eliminate divisions. Political tensions still create barriers, and dialect group and cultural differences continue to be relevant. Even language can be a problem. Among many Chinese, English is the only common language. Further, networks are not exclusive to the Chinese. All around the world, in business, government, and other professions, knowing people is helpful for advancement. Nor do Chinese network exclusively with other Chinese. In Southeast Asia there are increasing numbers of business dealings between Chinese and indigenous business groups. Similarly, the role of the United States and Japan in East Asia is too strong for them to be excluded from any type of economic arrangements.

More significantly, networks have been vitally important in Asia due in part to underdeveloped legal systems. In such an environment, networks establish who is trustworthy and assist entrepreneurs in dealing with bureaucratic obstacles. However, networks can fail in these functions, leading to carelessness in

dealing with "connected" individuals and corruption in dealing with government officials. Thus, a clear case can be made that overreliance on network capitalism contributed to the Asian economic crisis. If states in Asia can strengthen
the rule of law, networks, while still important, will become less crucial, leveling
the playing field for those companies without extensive networks in the region.
This will benefit overall economic development.

This chapter has described the bond between China and Asia's ethnic Chinese. It has also introduced important characteristics of the ethnic Chinese, with
a special emphasis on ways in which Chinese businesses excel at networking.
The key point in this discussion is that the ethnic Chinese business community
has been uniquely qualified to invest in China. First, there are strong bonds of
culture and identity between China and Asia's ethnic Chinese that have made
ethnic Chinese investment especially welcome in China. This was critical in the
early days of reform, which closely followed the autarky of the Cultural Revolution, when any outsider was under heavy suspicion. Second, ethnic Chinese
have had sufficient assets to make a major economic impact on China, although
these assets have been reduced due to the Asian economic crisis. Third, ethnic
Chinese business structures and networks are suited for the mainland environment. A tightly knit business organization allows for quick decision making in a
fast-changing market, as well as flexibility in an environment where rule by law
has not been established. Networks provide information and contacts without
which it is difficult to do business in China.

NOTES

1. Milton J. Esman, *Ethnic Politics* (Ithaca: Cornell University Press, 1994), 9–16.

2. Donald L. Horowitz, *Ethnic Groups in Conflict* (Berkeley: University of California Press, 1985), 51–64.

3. Frank Dikötter, *The Discourse of Race in Modern China* (Stanford: Stanford University Press, 1992).

4. Quoted in ibid., 124.

5. Frank Dikötter, "Racial Discourse in China: Continuities and Permutations," in
The Construction of Racial Identities in China and Japan, ed. Frank Dikötter (London:
Hurst, 1997), 12–33. See also Lucian W. Pye, *The Spirit of Chinese Politics: A
Psychocultural Study of the Authority Crisis in Political Development* (Cambridge, Mass.:
MIT Press, 1968), 54–57; and idem, *Asian Power and Politics: The Cultural Dimension
of Authority* (Cambridge, Mass.: Harvard University Press, 1985), 185.

6. Xiang Dayou, "Lun Zhongguo gaige kaifeng yu hua zitou xiang qushi" ("On the
Reform and Opening of China and the Investment Inclination of Overseas Chinese"),
Bagui qiao shi (*Overseas Chinese History of Bagui*), 1994, no. 1: 5.

7. Sun Xingcheng, "Guanyu mingan wenti" ("Regarding Sensitive Issues"), in
Huaren jingji nianjian 1997–1998 (*Yearbook of the Ethnic Chinese Economy
1997–1998*) (Beijing: Shehui kexue wenxian chubanshe, 1997), 226–27.

8. Lincoln Kaye, "Quality Control," *Far Eastern Economic Review* (hereafter
FEER), 13 January 1994, 22.

9. Lynn Pan, *Sons of the Yellow Emperor: A History of the Chinese Diaspora* (Boston: Little, Brown, 1990), 10–11, 245.

10. George Yeo, "Asian Civilization in the Pacific Century," in *World Chinese Entrepreneurs Convention*, ed. Singapore Chinese Chamber of Commerce and Industry (Singapore, 1991), 32.

11. Ibid., 38.

12. Ibid., 40.

13. Edward Friedman, "Ethnic Identity and the De-Nationalization and Democratization of Leninist States," in *The Rising Tide of Cultural Pluralism*, ed. Crawford Young (Madison: University of Wisconsin Press, 1993), 234–37.

14. Yu Chung-Hsun, "Japan's Role in Southeast and East Asia during the Post-Cold War Era: In Relation to the Expanding Economic Power of the Ethnic Chinese," *Proceedings of Research Institute for Asian Development International Symposium 1992* (Research Institute for Asian Development, International University of Japan, 1993), table 1, 110. For a discussion of *guiqiao* and *qiaojuan*, see Wang Gungwu, *China and the Chinese Overseas* (Singapore: Times Academic Press, 1991), 227–30.

15. An excellent source on Chinese dialect groups is East Asia Analytical Unit, Department of Foreign Affairs and Trade, Commonwealth of Australia, *Overseas Chinese Business Networks in Asia* (Canberra: Commonwealth of Australia, 1995), 19–33. See also Lynn Pan, ed., *The Encyclopedia of the Chinese Overseas* (Cambridge, Mass.: Harvard University Press, 1999), 24–25.

16. See Bertil Lintner, "The Third Wave," *FEER*, 24 June 1999, 28–29.

17. Yu, "Japan's Role," 105–6.

18. "News Digest—Outward Investment by Asian Groups Plummets," *Financial Times* (London), 3 August 1999, Internet edition.

19. George Hicks, ed., *Overseas Chinese Remittances from Southeast Asia 1910–1940* (Singapore: Select Books, 1993), 137.

20. Victor Purcell, *The Chinese in Southeast Asia*, 2nd ed. (London: Oxford University Press, 1965), 83, 540, 563.

21. Marcus W. Brauchli and Dan Biers, "Asia's Family Empires Change Their Tactics for a Shrinking World," *Wall Street Journal*, 19 April 1995, A1.

22. Murray Weidenbaum and Samuel Hughes, *The Bamboo Network* (New York: The Free Press, 1996), 25.

23. S. Gordon Redding, *The Spirit of Chinese Capitalism* (Berlin: Walter de Gruyter, 1993), 3.

24. Louise do Rosario, "Network Capitalism," *FEER*, 2 December 1993, 17.

25. Alex Kuo, "The Engine of Asia," *World Today*, June 1997, Internet edition.

26. "Inheriting the Bamboo Network," *Economist*, 23 December 1995–5 January 1996, 79.

27. Walter Fernandez, "Indonesia in Need of Chinese Businessmen," *Straits Times* (Singapore), 4 December 1998, Internet edition.

28. For example, see Denny Roy, *China's Foreign Relations* (Lanham, Md.: Rowman and Littlefield, 1998), 180.

29. Henny Sender, "Inside the Overseas Chinese Network," *Institutional Investor*, September 1991, 37.

30. Lee Kam Hing, "Malaysian Chinese: Seeking Identity in Wawasan 2020," in *Ethnic Chinese as Southeast Asians*, ed. Leo Suryadinata (New York: St. Martin's Press, 1997), 102.

31. "The Overseas Chinese: A Driving Force," *Economist*, 18 July 1992, 21.

32. Andrew B. Brick, "The Emergence of Greater China: The Diaspora Ascendant," *Heritage Lectures*, no. 411 (1992), 3. However, another report claims that ethnic Chinese-owned companies have 35 percent of the sales of all domestically owned businesses in the Philippines. See "China's Diaspora Turns Homeward," *Economist*, 27 November 1993, 33.

33. Roy, *China's Foreign Relations*, 180.

34. For more detailed studies of Chinese capital, see Yoshihara Kunio, *The Rise of Ersatz Capitalism in South-East Asia* (Singapore: Oxford University Press, 1988), chapter 3; and Yuan-li Wu and Chun-hsi Wu, *Economic Development in Southeast Asia: The Chinese Dimension* (Stanford, Calif.: Hoover Institution Press, 1980), 52–88.

35. Jamie Mackie, "Economic Systems of the Southeast Asian Chinese," in *Southeast Asian Chinese and China*, ed. Leo Suryadinata (Singapore: Times Academic Press, 1995), 40.

36. Zhao Heman, "Huaqiao huaren jingji yu Zhongguo dui wai kaifeng" ("The Overseas/Ethnic Chinese Economy and China's Opening to the World"), *Bagui qiao shi* (*Overseas Chinese History of Bagui*), 1994, no. 1: 8–10.

37. United Nations Conference on Trade and Development, *World Investment Report 1998* (New York: United Nations, 1998), 36–38.

38. A good description of traditional Chinese business practices is found in East Asia Analytical Unit, *Overseas Chinese*, 131–52.

39. Redding, *Spirit.*

40. Ibid., 2.

41. Rupert Hodder, *Merchant Princes of the East* (Chichester, England: John Wiley, 1996).

42. Ibid., 297.

43. Rajeswary Ampalavanar Brown, "Introduction: Chinese Business in an Institutional and Historical Perspective," in *Chinese Business Enterprise in Asia*, ed. Rajeswary Ampalavanar Brown (London: Routledge, 1995), 1–26.

44. Victor Simpao Limlingan, *The Overseas Chinese in ASEAN: Business Strategies and Management Practices* (Manila: Vita Development Corporation, 1986).

45. John Kao, "The Worldwide Web of Chinese Business," *Harvard Business Review* (March/April 1993): 24–36.

46. For a case of an ethnic Chinese business introducing Western management techniques, see "Re-engineering in Thailand," *Economist*, 11 October 1997, 83–84.

47. Linda Y. C. Lim, "Chinese Business, Multinationals and the State: Manufacturing for Export in Malaysia and Singapore," in *The Chinese in Southeast Asia*, vol. 1, ed. Linda Y. C. Lim and L. A. Peter Gosling (Singapore: Maruzen Asia, 1983), 245–74. See also in the same volume Linda Lim, "Chinese Economic Activity in Southeast Asia: An Introductory Review," 1–29.

48. Lim, "Chinese Business," 245.

49. Cai Renlong, "'Diyi Taipingyang qiye jituan' chutan" ("Approach to the 'First Pacific Enterprise Group'") *in Nanyang yanjiu lunwenji* (*Essays on Southeast Asian Research*), ed. Xiamen daxue Nanyang yanjiusuo (Xiamen: Xiamen daxue chubanshe, 1992), 231–32.

50. Paul E. Doremus, William W. Keller, Louis W. Pauly, and Simon Reich, *The Myth of the Global Corporation* (Princeton, N.J.: Princeton University Press, 1998).

51. Sender, "Inside," 39.

52. Li Guoliang, "Comment to 'Japan's Role in Southeast and East Asia during the Post-Cold War Era: In Relation to the Expanding Economic Power of the Ethnic Chinese,' " *Proceedings of Research Institute for Asian Development International Symposium 1992* (Research Institute for Asian Development, International University of Japan, 1993), 118–19; see also Kunio, *Ersatz Capitalism,* especially 111–18, where he argues that Southeast Asia's development is "technologyless."

53. See William McGurn, "Prophet of Profit," *FEER,* 21 November 1996, 72–74.

54. See, for instance, Constance Lever-Tracy, David Ip, and Noel Tracy, *The Chinese Diaspora and Mainland China: An Emerging Economic Synergy* (New York: St. Martin's Press, 1996); and John Naisbitt, *Megatrends Asia* (New York: Simon and Schuster, 1996).

55. Milton J. Esman, "The Chinese Diaspora in Southeast Asia," in *Modern Diasporas in International Politics,* ed. Gabriel Sheffer (London: Croom Helms, 1986), 132.

56. Jessica Lipnack and Jeffrey Stamps, *The Networking Book: People Connecting with People* (New York: Routledge and Kegan Paul, 1986), 2.

57. See do Rosario, "Network Capitalism," *FEER,* 17.

58. See Hong Liu, "Old Linkages, New Networks: The Globalization of Overseas Chinese Voluntary Associations and Its Implications," *China Quarterly,* no. 155 (September 1998): 582–609.

59. The address of this site is http://www.cbn.com.sg.

60. http://www.huaren.org/body.shtml.

61. Peter Engardio, "The Chinese Dealmakers in Southeast Asia," *Business Week,* 11 November 1991, 61.

62. Hicks, ed., *Overseas Chinese,* xi.

63. Kao, "Worldwide Web," 32.

64. Lever-Tracy, Ip, and Tracy, *Chinese Diaspora and Mainland China.*

65. Janet T. Landa, "The Political Economy of the Ethnically Homogenous Chinese Middleman Group in Southeast Asia: Ethnicity and Entrepreneurship in a Plural Society," in *The Chinese in Southeast Asia,* vol. 1, ed. Linda Y. C. Lim and L. A. Peter Gosling (Singapore: Maruzen Asia, 1983), 87.

66. See Janet Tai Landa, *Trust, Ethnicity, and Identity* (Ann Arbor: University of Michigan Press, 1994), especially chapter 5.

67. Lucian Pye, *Chinese Commercial Negotiating Style* (New York: Quorum Books, 1992), quoted in Eric W. K. Tsang, "Can Guanxi be a Source of Sustained Competitive Advantage for Doing Business in China?" *Academy of Management Executive* 12, no. 2 (May 1998).

68. For a discussion of ethnic Chinese transaction costs in China, see Samuel P. S. Ho and Ralph W. Huenemann, *China's Open Door Policy: The Quest for Foreign Technology and Capital* (Vancouver: University of British Columbia Press, 1984), 178–81; and Chengze Simon Fang, "Why China Has Been Successful in Attracting Foreign Direct Investment: A Transaction Cost Approach," *Journal of Contemporary China* 7, no. 17 (March 1998): 21–32.

CHAPTER 3

Overseas Chinese Remittances and Investments in China: A Historical Survey

Before examining recent contributions of ethnic Chinese to China's development, it is useful to review overseas Chinese[1] investments and remittances in the past in order to place the current period in historical perspective. After determining what is unique about the contemporary period and what is a continuation of long-term trends, we will be in a better position to analyze the contributions of Asia's Chinese in the post-1978 period. It will become clear that with the exception of the Cultural Revolution, successive Chinese governments beginning in the late nineteenth century have attempted to tap the economic resources of the overseas Chinese. However, while overseas Chinese remittances did play an important economic role in southern China, the potential contribution of the overseas Chinese to China's development was never fully realized before the reform era.

THE QING AND REPUBLICAN PERIODS

Chinese contacts with Southeast Asia began centuries ago. Interactions with Malaysia go back to the fourth century B.C., while contacts with Indonesia date to the Han period (202 B.C.–A.D. 220). Chinese communities first began to be established in Southeast Asia from about the thirteenth century, generally in order to facilitate trade, although most Chinese settlements were founded within the past 350 years.[2] Before 1850, merchants made up the majority of migrants to Southeast Asia. After 1850, Chinese laborers swelled the ranks of overseas communities, responding to both poor economic conditions in China and the demand for labor in Southeast Asia that stemmed from colonial policies to exploit the region's resources. Over two million Chinese emigrated between 1848 and 1888.[3]

For many years the Chinese government frowned upon Chinese migration and overseas Chinese communities. Overseas Chinese practiced illegal trade (in that it was outside government control), and those who left the motherland were considered to be unfilial. Thus, laws on emigration and trade during the Ming Dynasty (1368–1644) were unfavorable, while the Qing (1644–1912) banned all such activities and even ordered the abandonment of coastal areas due to piracy and attacks by Ming loyalists. However, in the nineteenth century Qing policies began to change.[4] A clause in the Treaty of Nanking in 1842 recognized the right of Chinese to emigrate, opening the way for large-scale migration of laborers in the so-called coolie trade. In the mid-1860s, China for the first time demonstrated interest in the welfare of the overseas Chinese, signing a convention with Britain and France on regulating Chinese emigrant labor in 1866. The next year a movement began to establish Chinese consulates abroad, the purpose being to both protect the overseas Chinese and begin tapping into their wealth and skills.

By the 1890s, the campaign to attract the wealth and resources of the overseas Chinese was in full swing due to the Qing's recognition of the need to modernize. Thus, in 1893, China formally rescinded the prohibition against emigration, marking "a turning point in Ch'ing [Qing] policy and the symbolic beginning of a new campaign to attract the active support of overseas Chinese capitalists."[5] In 1909, the Qing adopted a nationality law containing the principle of *jus sanguinis*, making every ethnic Chinese a Qing subject regardless of place of birth or residence.

After belatedly recognizing its need for investment and industrialization and the potential contribution of overseas Chinese capital and experience, the Qing government tried to attract overseas Chinese investment in several ways. First, it offered ranks and titles to merchants who made large investments or other important contributions. In some cases merchants were given actual authority in government. A second tactic was to cooperate in setting up chambers of commerce throughout China and Southeast Asia to encourage new business activity. For example, the Qing government sent a representative to establish the Singapore Chinese Chamber of Commerce in 1906, a period of Chinese cultural revival in Singapore. The Chamber, officially linked to the Qing government, raised investment capital for China and provided political support for the government. However, it never became an active antirevolutionary force as desired by the Qing.[6]

Third, some efforts were made to improve China's investment environment and protect investors from corrupt local officials. For instance, in the first decade of the twentieth century, early commercial codes were established in an effort to protect merchants through law instead of leaving them to rely on the patronage of officials. The new chambers of commerce were also designed to play a protective role. Fourth, the Qing sent numerous special missions to Southeast Asia to collect funds for specific projects, such as railroad lines or steamship companies. Occasionally such missions would travel on Chinese naval vessels, being met with great ceremony by the overseas Chinese communities.

One overseas Chinese entrepreneur who became heavily involved in China's effort to modernize was Zhang Bishi, also known as Thio Thiau Siat. Zhang made his fortune in Southeast Asia before becoming involved in business and government service in China. Starting as Chinese first vice consul in Penang, he became consul-general for Nanyang (Southeast Asia) in Singapore in 1894. In 1895, Zhang founded the Zhang Yu (Chang Yü) Pioneer Wine Company in Yantai (Chefoo). Zhang also invested in railroads and banks in China, raised further funds in Southeast Asia for such ventures, as well as invested in manufacturing, mining, and construction. As a result, he was appointed to the directorship of China's railroads, later being granted the highest Qing rank and becoming vice president of China's Board of Trade. In 1903, Zhang became the Empress Dowager's personal consultant.[7]

Zhang believed that the overseas Chinese could lead China's modernization drive through their capital and business skills. He therefore planned various projects for southern China that would interest the overseas Chinese, and personally led fund-raising drives for such projects. As a Qing mandarin he also opened an office in Guangzhou to protect merchants from criminals and corrupt local officials who might prey upon them. Several other overseas Chinese also became interested in projects in China at this time. For example, Foo Choo Choon, who became wealthy through mining projects in the Malay States, began mining operations in Fujian and Hainan, being appointed the director of mining in both areas by the Chinese government. Lin Erjia introduced telephone service to Xiamen (Amoy) in 1907. Money was also raised among Southeast Asia's Chinese community for various railway lines in Fujian and Guangdong provinces.[8]

However, the successful completion of major projects using overseas Chinese funds was the exception rather than the rule, and in the end the Nanyang capitalists could save neither the Qing nor China. Many of the projects for which money was raised, most notably the railroads, were aborted, were left incomplete, or were in other ways financially unsuccessful. This was by no means a complete disaster for the Nanyang capitalists, however. As Michael Godley notes, although the profit motive and nationalism did play a role, "it was filial piety, provincialism and the search for status that really motivated the majority of overseas Chinese" who invested in southern China.[9] All three goals could be fulfilled even if a project was not financially successful. Indeed, most money sent to China from Southeast Asia was used for family expenses, home-building, land purchases, or schools rather than investment. Most Nanyang capitalists easily made the transition to the Republic after its initiation in 1912, with Zhang Bishi becoming the advisor of Yuan Shikai, the president who tried to make himself emperor.

Ironically, a great deal of overseas Chinese money was also raised for the purpose of overthrowing the Qing. Dr. Sun Yat-sen, for example, spent his time in exile raising funds from overseas Chinese of all social strata for revolutionary activities. Sun used patriotic appeals tapping anti-Manchu sentiment to raise support, promising a modern China that would overcome the humiliations suffered under Qing rule. Thus, the overseas Chinese played an important role in the overthrow of the Qing through their financial contributions. Reformers such as Kang Youwei and Liang Qichao also solicited contributions overseas to promote their visions of constitutional monarchism,[10] and various governing factions in South China were supported by competing Hong Kong merchant groups in the years surrounding the 1911 revolution.[11]

During the Republican period (1912–49), the various Chinese governments continued to emphasize links with the overseas Chinese. The Guomindang (KMT), the Nationalist Party, sent teachers to Southeast Asia to promote Chinese nationalism, while the Guomindang nationality law of 1929 reaffirmed the principle of *jus sanguinis* adopted by the Qing. Although the Guomindang had many reasons for promoting ties with the overseas Chinese, the primary motivation was to bring in funds. As Stephen Fitzgerald notes, "If education was the crucial factor in preserving the close association between the Overseas Chinese and China, the purpose of maintaining this link was primarily financial."[12] Thus, the Guomindang crafted special legislation giving overseas Chinese favorable investment terms and incentives, such as the Law to Encourage the Effectuation of Overseas Chinese Enterprise in the Homeland and the Overseas Chinese Incentive Ordinance. Government institutions, such as the Overseas Chinese Affairs Commission, were created to court the overseas Chinese.

Investments in China from the overseas Chinese thus continued during the Republican period. These investments had an important effect on a handful of southern cities in areas from which emigrants came, especially Xiamen. Approximately 60 percent to 70 percent of investments in Xiamen's industries were made by overseas Chinese, while about 60 percent of total investment in land and buildings from 1929 to 1934 similarly came from Nanyang. For example, Chinese from the Philippines organized the Xing Ye (Hsing Yeh) Corporation, purchasing 334 acres of land in Xiamen, where they built modern homes in the New Village of the Great South primarily for returned overseas Chinese. In 1931, land in Xiamen was selling at three to four times its previous value due to overseas Chinese purchases. Furthermore, in 1935 four of Xiamen's fourteen banks were financed entirely by overseas Chinese capital. Remer noted in 1933 that Xiamen's economy as well as the economies of other cities of China's southern coast were greatly impacted by the overseas Chinese.[13]

Looking at Guangdong, Shantou's (Swatow's) waterworks and electric company were organized by an overseas Chinese named Gao Zhengji (Kao Cheng Chi), while Au Boon Haw located a plant producing his famous Tiger Balm Medicine in Shantou. The Zhanglin-Shantou push car trolley, tugboat companies working the Han River, and bus companies in southern China also were funded by overseas Chinese.[14] One study of the Chaozhou-Shantou area found that from 1889 to 1949 overseas Chinese invested 79.77 million yuan in 4,062 ventures.

This comprised 11.4 percent of all overseas Chinese investments in China for the period. Approximately 70 percent to 80 percent of the funds came from Southeast Asia, particularly Thailand. Real estate absorbed almost 40 percent of the capital; commerce, 19 percent; and manufacturing, 6 percent.[15]

However, overseas Chinese investments again did not make a significant impact on China's overall development. The Guomindang government admitted this in the early 1940s, when Foreign Minister Liu Wei complained that "overseas Chinese investment in China is usually small while large investments are rare."[16] One of the most important reasons for the lack of wide-scale investment was China's political uncertainty. With the Republican period being characterized by instability, large investments in China were simply too great a risk. This is reflected in the fact that many Nanyang Chinese who invested in China lost money. For example, bus lines in southern China bore losses due to heavy taxation, banditry, and army confiscations. Similarly, companies that provided water and electricity suffered from illegal diversions, especially by government units.

Summarizing investments during the late Qing and Republican periods, Lin Jinzhi reports the total amount of investment by overseas Chinese from 1862 to 1949 at US$128 million. Ninety percent of this money was invested in Guangdong province, Fujian province, and Shanghai. Approximately 85 percent to 90 percent of these funds came from overseas Chinese in Southeast Asia, the United States, and Australia, with 10 percent to 15 percent of funds coming from Hong Kong or Macao. About 42 percent of overseas Chinese investments went into real estate, 16 percent into commerce, and 15 percent into industry.[17]

However, lack of investment does not mean that money from abroad was not flowing into China. China received millions of dollars in remittances during this era. The vast majority of remittances went to Guangdong or Fujian provinces, with most passing through Hong Kong. Many scholars have attempted to determine the amount of such remittances. Although all estimates are subject to error and in some cases estimates vary widely, they do provide an indication of the flow of funds.[18] Table 3.1 summarizes estimates of these remittance amounts, approximately 40 percent to 45 percent of which came from Southeast Asia.

The importance of these remittances can best be understood by viewing their benefits. One important function of remittances was the provision of currency to help balance China's international payments. C. F. Remer estimated in 1933 that the amount that China had paid out on returns for foreign investment in China was compensated by the amount of overseas remittances it had received.[19] Viewed in another way, remittances also helped China sustain trade deficits throughout the period. Lin Jinzhi reports that from 1868 to 1936 China ran a cumulative trade deficit of US$5 billion, while remittances were approximately half that level. From 1936 to 1940, remittances exceeded the trade deficit.[20]

Remittances were also vital for the families that received them. In many instances all or some of the men of families from parts of southern China went

Table 3.1
Estimates of Average Overseas Chinese Remittances to China

Years	Average Amount/Year
1902–13[a]	118–150 million yuan
1914–30	172–200 million yuan
1931–38	371–373 million yuan
1939–41	650–1,081 million yuan

[a]The 118 million yuan figure is an estimate for the years 1905–13.

Sources: Li Guoliang, Lin Jinzhi, and Cai Renlong, *Huaqiao huaren yu Zhongguo geming he jinshi (Overseas Chinese/Ethnic Chinese and Chinese Revolution and Construction)*, ed. Lin Jinzhi (Fuzhou: Fujian renmin chubanshe, 1993), 228–29; C. F. Remer, *Foreign Investments in China* (New York: Macmillan, 1933), 188–89; and George L. Hicks, ed., *Overseas Chinese Remittances from Southeast Asia 1910–1940* (Singapore: Select Books, 1993), 148, 331.

abroad to work, leaving the women, children, and elderly dependent on remittances to provide for their daily necessities. In a study of the sources of income of one hundred emigrant families, Ta Chen found that over 75 percent of the average total monthly income per family came from overseas remittances. This heavy dependence on funds from abroad was experienced by those in the highest and lowest income brackets.[21]

Remittances to China were also used for philanthropic purposes. For example, a 1943 report noted that 17 out of 39 primary schools in Xiamen had ties to overseas Chinese contributors, while 5 of 11 secondary schools had such links.[22] It has been estimated that 15 percent to 20 percent of remittances both before and after 1949 were used to support community institutions.[23] In addition to education, money was also donated to relieve disasters, build temples, establish libraries and hospitals, and support the war against Japan. One of the most noted overseas Chinese philanthropists was Tan Kah Kee. A businessman who made his fortune in the rubber industry in Singapore, Tan established or helped build 29 schools in Singapore and China, including Xiamen University and the Jimei Navigation College. Tan also raised money to assist China's war effort against Japan and provide for Chinese war refugees. He eventually moved back to China after the war, where he died in 1961.[24]

As was previously discussed, some remittances were used for investments. Overseas Chinese living in Southeast Asia and elsewhere came to appreciate the importance of infrastructure and industrialization for the well being of a country and saw potential applications for their knowledge and capital in China. Furthermore, the fact that they were not foreigners gave them an important edge in public acceptance of their investments. However, serious obstacles to investment existed in China at the time. These included instability, militarism, government corruption and greed (especially at the local level), and opposition to modernization. As a result, only a small percentage of remittances was invested. Chun-Hsi Wu reports that before World War II, 84.5 percent of remittances was used for family support, while 15.5 percent went to new enterprise capital or was used for other purposes.[25] Li Guoliang, Lin Jinzhi, and Cai Renlong estimate that from 1862 to 1949 only 3.65 percent of remittances was used for investment purposes.[26]

Finally, it is important to emphasize that throughout the late Qing and Republican periods a sense of Chinese nationalism was developing among the overseas Chinese. The overseas Chinese gave their primary loyalties to their families and native villages. However, as a struggling China appealed to its overseas citizens during this period, a new sense of Chinese national identity and political activism swept the overseas communities, manifesting itself in remittances and donations and reflected in slogans such as "once a Chinese always a Chinese." This nationalism worried the colonial powers. Paradoxically, it fueled overseas Chinese contributions both to China and to the early-twentieth-century revolutionary movements attempting to overthrow China's government as immigrants came to realize that their own status overseas was tied to the strength and prestige of the Chinese state.

1949–1977

When the Communist Party gained control of China in 1949, the international situation was very different from that faced by the Qing and Guomindang governments in earlier years. Southeast Asian nationalism was blooming, reinforcing suspicions of overseas Chinese in the minds of indigenous Southeast Asians. Furthermore, the ideological assumptions of the Communists (especially in regard to class and internationalism) led them to view the overseas Chinese with some misgivings. Nevertheless, the communist government still maintained an interest in the overseas Chinese, especially in tapping their resources, and had to deal with the legacy of previous Qing and Guomindang policies.[27]

In a manner similar to the Guomindang, the communist government established an Overseas Chinese Affairs Commission (OCAC) as a governmental unit to deal with overseas Chinese affairs, along with various committees, offices, bureaus, sections, and work groups. Because overseas Chinese work had both foreign and domestic aspects, one of the main functions of the OCAC was coordination with other governmental agencies that dealt with the overseas Chinese.[28] The leading party organization for overseas Chinese affairs was the United Front Work Department of the Communist Party Central Committee. A mass organization, entitled the All-China Returned Overseas Chinese Association, was also established to deal with domestic overseas Chinese affairs. Finally, several service organizations were set up specifically for the overseas Chinese, such as bank departments for handling remittances, special retail purchasing stores, and the Overseas Chinese Travel Service.[29]

There are various phases in pre-1978 PRC policy toward the overseas Chinese.[30] Shifts occurred as the result of contradictions among the principles underlying Chinese policy. One such principle, perhaps the central one, was continuing interest in obtaining hard currency. Stephen Fitzgerald declares that "In the seventeen years from 1949 to the end of 1965, the one concern which remained constant in Overseas Chinese policy was the necessity to attract foreign exchange."[31] Such foreign exchange was important for China's economic development. Due to Western hostility and economic sanctions, China had few ways to earn hard currency.

However, the desire to gain hard currency came in conflict with China's efforts at domestic socialist transformation and socialist principles of equality. In order to attract overseas remittances, China had to provide better living conditions for returned overseas Chinese and the dependents of overseas Chinese. If better conditions were not provided, remittances would dry up. As a result, the government built special stores where difficult-to-find goods could be purchased by domestic overseas Chinese only with remittances. Such favorable treatment created inequalities and resentments, and violated basic Chinese socialist tenets.[32]

Another principle of Chinese policy was protection of the overseas Chinese. To the mainland government this was a matter of pride, a sovereign right, and an arena of competition with the Guomindang regime in Taiwan, which also tried to win overseas Chinese support. The 1954 PRC Constitution declared: "The People's Republic of China protects the just rights and interests of Chinese residents abroad." Subsequent constitutions have maintained this commitment to protect the overseas Chinese. The Chinese government in actuality had little capability to enforce this pledge, although at times the PRC was able to repatriate those who were suffering severe discrimination. Furthermore, protection sometimes conflicted with other foreign policy goals.

For example, during the Bandung period (1954–57), China strove for good relations with Southeast Asia. As a result, Premier Zhou Enlai negotiated a treaty with Indonesia (not fully ratified until 1960) that would end dual citizenship for Chinese in Indonesia. He also offered to sign a nonaggression treaty with the Philippines and assured Thailand that China had no ill intentions in setting up a Thai Autonomous Zone in Yunnan province. China's general line during this period was to establish solidarity with the countries of Latin America, Asia, and Africa, as well as promote the Five Principles of Peaceful Coexistence (mutual respect for sovereignty and territorial integrity, mutual nonaggression, noninterference in each others' internal affairs, equality and mutual benefit, and peaceful coexistence). In subsequent periods, such as the break with the Soviet Union and the effort to establish a united front against the influence of the United States, China continued to press for good relations with Southeast Asia.[33]

Nevertheless, during the years prior to 1978 China faced a dilemma of attempting to balance state-to-state ties with Southeast Asian countries while at the same time supporting communist movements, often committed to insurgency, throughout the region. During phases when Beijing strove for good government-to-government relations (based on the international environment, China's national interests, and Beijing's own internal politics), communist parties were urged to engage in united front tactics wherein they attempted to obtain power through peaceful means. During other phases, Beijing provided arms, training camps, and propaganda support for armed struggle. Prior to the 1980s, Beijing found it necessary to maintain links with communist parties in order to legitimize its claims to the ultimate universal triumph of Chinese communist ideology.[34]

During periods in which China valued good ties with Southeast Asia, China ignored ill-treatment of the overseas Chinese. For example, Beijing disregarded the persecution of Chinese in Indonesia during the Sukarno regime.[35] When China did make an issue of the treatment of overseas Chinese, it was generally triggered by some other factor that caused relations with the offending state to deteriorate. This occurred when China protested Vietnam's treatment of overseas Chinese in the late 1970s. The primary issue was Vietnam's deepening ties with the Soviet Union. Thus, China's relationship with the overseas Chinese after 1949 was subordinated to its broader foreign policy goals.

China's desire for good relations with Southeast Asia led it to strive to settle the question of the nationality of overseas Chinese. During the postwar period there were fears throughout Southeast Asia and the West that China would use the overseas Chinese in its alleged ambitions to take control of Southeast Asia.[36] In order to calm fears that the PRC wished to use Chinese abroad as a fifth column, China was willing to abandon the principle of *jus sanguinis* adopted by the Qing and Guomindang governments and in doing so reject the notion of dual citizenship. However, although it urged overseas Chinese to take local citizenship, China insisted that they have the right to make their own choice. The highlight of China's efforts to settle the nationality issue was the negotiation of the Sino-Indonesian Treaty of Dual Nationality in 1955.

From 1956 until the Cultural Revolution, China attempted to disassociate itself from the overseas Chinese by urging their assimilation into the societies where they lived, encouraging overseas Chinese to choose local citizenship, closing the door to most overseas Chinese students who desired an education in China, and discouraging Chinese education in Southeast Asia. However, China still wished to maintain economic ties with the overseas Chinese and continue receiving their remittances and investments. Fitzgerald labeled this policy as a type of "decolonization."[37] From China's perspective, however, this label was a misnomer. China had suffered from imperialism just as the Southeast Asian nations, and was never a colonizing power at any point in time. The fact that large numbers of Chinese lived in Southeast Asia was due to Chinese weakness before 1949 and the policies of the former colonial powers, most notably the Dutch and British.

The Cultural Revolution brought great changes to China's overseas Chinese policy, as well as its broader policies toward Southeast Asia.[38] On the foreign front, Chinese embassy officials encouraged Chinese chauvinism and radicalism among the overseas Chinese in Burma, North Vietnam, and Cambodia, damaging China's foreign relations. On the domestic front, actions were taken against the so-called reactionary bourgeois influence of domestic overseas Chinese (dependents of overseas Chinese and returned overseas Chinese). Overseas Chinese investment corporations were closed down, special retail stores were locked up, homes built with overseas Chinese funds were confiscated or sacked, domestic overseas Chinese were persecuted for their "foreign" connections, and the government's apparatus for overseas Chinese affairs was dismantled following intense criticism of overseas Chinese policies. Although Cultural Revolution policies had moderated somewhat by the early 1970s, especially in regard to foreign relations, it was not until 1977 that the government began to address seriously the damage done to overseas Chinese affairs during the Cultural Revolution.

Similar to the late Qing and Republican periods, remittances played an important role from 1949 to 1977. Lin Jinzhi estimates that from 1950 to 1975 a total of US$4.6 billion was sent to China, with 85 percent to 90 percent of remittances going to Fujian and Guangdong provinces. Lin divides this period into four phases. In the first phase, 1950–57, overseas Chinese sent $1.170 billion in remittances (an average of $146 million a year), compared to a total trade deficit in that period of $1.38 billion. Thus remittances played an important part in making up for China's deficit. During the second period (1958–62), remittances dropped to $450 million (averaging $90 million a year) due to China's leftist policies reflected in the Great Leap Forward. However, the trade deficit also dropped to $498 million. During the third period (1963–65), remittances recovered somewhat, reaching $454 million (averaging $151 million per year). At the same time the trade deficit rose to $963 million. The last phase is 1966–75, the Cultural Revolution, with remittances reaching $2.523 billion. The average yearly remittance during this period was $252 million, although this average hides the fact that for the first three years of the period remittances fell but then steadily rose for the next seven years. During this time China also experienced a favorable balance of trade.[39]

Chun-hsi Wu's estimates of remittances to China between 1950 and 1964 are much lower. Wu calculates that overseas remittances to China in those years totaled US$667.7 million,[40] compared to Lin's figure of $1.8953 billion. Similarly, Wu's and Lin's figures on China's trade balance for the same years are quite different.[41] Wu further estimates that from 1950 to 1964, just over 50 percent of remittances to China came from Southeast Asia, as opposed to 40 percent before World War II. Hong Kong residents provided 27 percent, while 10 percent came from the Americas and Australia.[42]

The role of Hong Kong in funneling remittances merits closer examination. After 1949, as before, most remittances to China went through Hong Kong. More important, after the victory of the Communists, Hong Kong became the final destination of the majority of remittances. Wu calculates that after 1949 approximately 30 percent of remittances to Hong Kong were passed on to the mainland, while 70 percent remained in the colony, both to support Chinese relatives who had moved there and for investment purposes. Investment funds came largely from Southeast Asia and played a major role in developing Hong Kong's economy. Between 1950 and 1964, overseas Chinese made approximately HK$4.455 billion in business investments in Hong Kong, ranging from a low of HK$135.96 million in 1950 to a high of HK$598.81 million in 1957.[43]

In spite of continued remittances to the mainland, overseas Chinese business investment in China was minimal after 1949. This was not because the Chinese government was oblivious to overseas Chinese investments. Beginning in the early 1950s, eleven provinces and cities established overseas Chinese investment companies to attract capital. The most significant of these were in Fujian and Guangdong provinces, which between them took in approximately 75 percent of all overseas Chinese investments. In 1957, the State Council promulgated a law on such companies which stipulated that those overseas Chinese and domestic overseas Chinese who invested in them would receive an 8 percent annual return, half of it payable in hard currency. After twelve years the investment could be paid back in *renminbi*, the Chinese currency. Furthermore, provisions would be made for investors or their family members to work in the companies which received such funds.

Altogether, approximately 200 million yuan *renminbi* was raised by these companies (or about US$100 million), a relatively small amount. The money was used to expand existing production facilities or build new plants in sectors such as sugar processing, textiles, cooking oil production, paper production, and other light industries. However, the overseas Chinese investment companies were closed down during the Cultural Revolution.[44] Thus, between 1949 and 1977, overseas Chinese investments in China were small, and, consistent with earlier periods, made up only a fraction of total remittances. Nevertheless, the overseas Chinese investment corporations did provide communist officials with valuable lessons regarding foreign investment, lessons that were put to use later in the post-1978 open door policy.[45]

SUMMARY AND CONCLUSIONS

In viewing late Qing, Republican, and PRC policies before the Cultural Revolution, there are common patterns in China's relationship with the overseas Chinese that will be useful for comparison with the current period. First, successive Chinese governments have been eager to tap overseas Chinese resources in the form of remittances, charitable donations, and investments. However, while remittances and charitable donations played an important role for families, communities, and the provision of hard currency, investments for profit were much more limited. While investment did contribute to the development of specific cities, its economic importance for China as a whole was minimal, especially in terms of the growth of commerce and industry. Those who did invest were usually motivated more by psychological factors than a quest for profit.

The main reason for the lack of investment during all three periods was political instability and a poor investment environment. During the Qing and Republican periods, warfare, banditry, and corruption made any venture risky. During none of the periods in question was a legal foundation credibly established for the protection of investments. Furthermore, communist ideology, shifting policies, and difficulties in obtaining hard currency greatly limited investments for profit after 1949. Those who did invest in the overseas Chinese investment corporations generally did so for reasons other than personal financial gain.

Geographically, with few exceptions, most major investments were located in Guangdong, Fujian, or Shanghai. The vast majority of remittances also went to Guangdong and Fujian. However, with the passage of time Hong Kong played an increasingly important role. Initially, in line with its entrepôt status, Hong Kong served as a transit point for remittances from other locations. After 1950, when China was closed off from much of the rest of the world, the importance of this role increased. At the same time Hong Kong became the second largest contributor of remittances to China. Even more important, it became the final destination of a major portion of remittances by overseas Chinese, as well as an important recipient of overseas Chinese investment.

Finally, overseas Chinese remittances and investments have never been encouraged by the governments of Southeast Asia. During the late Qing and Republican periods, colonial rulers in Southeast Asia allowed remittances but were sometimes alarmed by the enthusiasm and loyalty that overseas Chinese demonstrated toward China. After gaining independence, the new Southeast Asian nation-states, attempting to develop national identities, build their economies, and cope with the cold war, were even less tolerant.

However, there are also significant differences between the Qing/Republican era and the post-1949 period. First, while the Qing gave government positions with real authority to overseas Chinese, the post-1949 government did no such thing outside of overseas Chinese affairs, and actually was suspicious of overseas Chinese. Second, while Chinese nationalism in Southeast Asia increased during the Qing and Republican periods, it decreased during the post-1949 period. Third, and relatedly, Chinese government policy changed. The post-1949 government encouraged overseas Chinese to accept local citizenship and made efforts toward uncoupling its policy of extracting economic gains from Southeast Asia's ethnic Chinese from significant political ties. Nevertheless, Beijing's stated intention of protecting overseas Chinese still conflicted with its broader foreign policy goal of good relations with Southeast Asia that China held for much of this period.

In closing, before the 1980s, the Chinese diaspora was not able to play the role that many from the late Qing onward hoped it might in significantly aiding China's development and advancing economic integration in Asia. This is summed up well in the words of C. F. Remer, a longtime observer of China's interactions with the overseas Chinese. Writing in the mid-1960s, Remer stated, "At an earlier time . . . it seemed to me that the overseas Chinese might come to play a significant part, through their skill in international trade and finance, in the economic integration of East and Southeast Asia. This appears now to have been no more than an insubstantial dream."[46] However, as later chapters illustrate, Remer was perhaps premature in relinquishing his dream. The 1980s and 1990s saw an explosion of ethnic Chinese investment in China, with major consequences for China and Asia.

NOTES

1. For the balance of this chapter, the term "overseas Chinese" will be used. For most of the period in question, the ethnic Chinese abroad were in fact *huaqiao*.

2. For details on early Chinese contacts with Southeast Asia, see Victor Purcell, *The Chinese in Southeast Asia*, 2nd ed. (London: Oxford University Press, 1965), chapters 2–3; and C. P. Fitzgerald, *The Third China: The Chinese Communities in Southeast Asia* (Vancouver: University of British Columbia, 1965), 3–5.

3. For an examination of patterns of Chinese migration, see Wang Gungwu, *China and the Chinese Overseas* (Singapore: Times Academic Press, 1991), chapter 1. The 2 million figure comes from Lynn Pan, *Sons of the Yellow Emperor: A History of the Chinese Diaspora* (Boston: Little, Brown, 1990), 42.

4. Much of the detail on the Qing era in this section comes from Michael R. Godley, *The Mandarin-Capitalists from Nanyang: Overseas Chinese Enterprises in the Modernization of China 1893–1911* (Cambridge: Cambridge University Press, 1981).

5. Ibid., 78.

6. See Yen Ching-hwang, "Ch'ing China and the Singapore Chinese Chamber of Commerce, 1906–1911," in *Southeast Asian Chinese and China*, ed. Leo Suryadinata (Singapore: Times Academic Press, 1995), 133–60.

7. Zhang's story is told throughout Godley, *Mandarin-Capitalists*. See especially chapters 4 and 5.

8. For other overseas Chinese who made important investments in China in the late Qing and Republican periods, see Li Guoliang, Lin Jinzhi, and Cai Renlong, *Huaqiao huaren yu Zhongguo geming he jinshi (Overseas Chinese/Ethnic Chinese and Chinese Revolution and Construction)*, ed. Lin Jinzhi (Fuzhou: Fujian renmin chubanshe, 1993), 404–69.

9. Godley, *Mandarin-Capitalists*, 169.

10. See C. Martin Wilbur, *Sun Yat-sen: Frustrated Patriot* (New York: Columbia University Press, 1976); Robert A. Scalapino and George T. Yu, *Modern China and Its Revolutionary Process: Recurrent Challenges to the Traditional Order, 1850–1920* (Berkeley: University of California Press, 1985); and Yen Ching Hwang, *The Overseas Chinese and the 1911 Revolution: With Special Reference to Singapore and Malaya* (Kuala Lumpur: Oxford University Press, 1976).

11. Stephanie Po-yin Chung, *Chinese Business Groups in Hong Kong and Political Change in South China, 1900–25* (New York: St. Martin's Press, 1998).

12. Stephen Fitzgerald, *China and the Overseas Chinese: A Study of Peking's Changing Policy, 1949–1970* (Cambridge: Cambridge University Press, 1972), 8.

13. C. F. Remer, *Foreign Investments in China* (New York: Macmillan, 1933), 187.

14. Many examples of investments are found in Ta Chen, *Emigrant Communities in South China*, ed. Bruno Lasker (New York: Institute of Pacific Relations, 1940), 205–24; and George L. Hicks, ed., *Overseas Chinese Remittances from Southeast Asia 1910–1940* (Singapore: Select Books, 1993), 200–13, 245–48.

15. Lin Jinzhi, "Haiwai huaren zai Chao-Shan diqude touzi" ("Overseas Ethnic Chinese Investment in the Chaozhou-Shantou Area"), *Nanyang wenti yanjiu* (*Southeast Asian Affairs*), 1994, no. 1:18–19, 21–22.

16. Hicks, ed., *Overseas Chinese Remittances*, 213. Of course, it was unrealistic to expect large investments during wartime.

17. Lin Jinzhi, "1979–1992 nian haiwai huaren zai Zhongguo dalu touzide xianzhuang ji qi jinhou fazhan qushi" ("The Current Situation and Future Trends in the Investments of Overseas Ethnic Chinese on the Chinese Mainland, 1979–1992"), *Huaqiao huaren lishi yanjiu* (*Overseas Chinese and Ethnic Chinese Historical Research*), 1993, no. 1:3–5. For greater detail, see Li, Lin, and Cai, *Huaqiao huaren yu Zhongguo*, 343–403. This source puts total overseas Chinese investment for the period at approximately 700 million yuan *renminbi*.

18. For a description of the difficulty in estimating remittances, see J.A.C. Mackie, "Introduction," in Hicks, ed., *Overseas Chinese Remittances*, xxv–xxxii; and Chun-Hsi Wu, *Dollars, Dependents and Dogma: Overseas Chinese Remittances to Communist China* (Stanford, Calif.: Hoover Institution, 1967), 15–20. For estimates of remittances from numerous scholars for various years, see Hicks, 146–47; and Wu, 167–68.

19. Remer, *Foreign Investment*, 225–28.

20. Lin Jinzhi, "Qiaohui dui Zhongguo jingji fazhan yu qiaoxiang jianshede zuoyong" ("The Role of Remittances of Overseas Chinese in the Economic Development of China"), *Nanyang wenti yanjiu* (*Southeast Asian Affairs*), 1992, no. 2:21–24; the same figures are given in Li, Lin, and Cai, *Huaqiao huaren yu Zhongguo*, 260–64. See also Hicks, ed., *Overseas Chinese Remittances*, 172–76.

21. Chen, *Emigrant Communities*, 83. Chen goes on to demonstrate how this source of income improved their lives in numerous respects and made them better off than others who did not have overseas relatives.

22. Hicks, ed., *Overseas Chinese Remittances*, 210.

23. Lynn Pan, ed., *The Encyclopedia of the Chinese Overseas* (Cambridge, Mass.: Harvard University Press, 1999), 109.

24. For details on Tan's life, see C. F. Yong, *Tan Kah-Kee: The Making of an Overseas Chinese Legend* (Singapore: Oxford University Press, 1987).

25. Wu, *Dollars*, 22.

26. Li, Lin, and Cai, *Huaqiao huaren yu Zhongguo*, 364.

27. For a view from Taiwan describing this period, see Ku Ch'ang-yung, "Cong zhengzhi jingji cengmian lun Zhonggongde Dongnan Ya huaqiao zhengce" ("Economic and Political Perspectives on Peking's Policy Regarding Overseas Chinese in Southeast Asia"), *Zhongguo dalu yanjiu* (*Mainland China Studies*) 37, no. 9 (September 1994): 15–25.

28. There are two broad categories of overseas Chinese: those who are abroad and domestic overseas Chinese, who include dependents of overseas Chinese (*qiaojuan*) and returned overseas Chinese (*guiqiao*).

29. For details on these organizations, see Fitzgerald, *China and the Overseas Chinese*, chapter 2.

30. For a listing of phases, see Wu, *Dollars*, chapter 3; and Milton J. Esman, "The Chinese Diaspora in Southeast Asia," in *Modern Diasporas in International Politics*, ed. Gabriel Sheffer (London: Croom Helms, 1986), 134–39. See also Zhuang Guotu, "The Policies of the Chinese Government Towards Overseas Chinese (1949–1966)," in *The Chinese Diaspora: Selected Essays*, vol. 1, ed. Wang Ling-chi and Wang Gungwu (Singapore: Times Academic Press, 1998), 14–28.

31. Fitzgerald, *China and the Overseas Chinese*, 124. See also Chan Ngor Chong, "PRC Policy on the Overseas Chinese," in *ASEAN and China: An Evolving Relationship*, ed. Joyce K. Kallgren, Noordin Sopiee, and Soedjati Djiwandono (Berkeley: Institute of East Asian Studies, University of California, 1988), 126.

32. For a description of Beijing's shifting policies toward the domestic overseas Chinese, see Fitzgerald, *China and the Overseas Chinese*, chapter 4. For a variety of laws concerning the overseas Chinese, see Wu, *Dollars*, appendix C, 169–85.

33. For a study of the phases of Chinese foreign policy, see Michael B. Yahuda, *China's Role in World Affairs* (New York: St. Martin's Press, 1978).

34. See Jay Taylor, *China and Southeast Asia: Peking's Relations with Revolutionary Movements*, 2nd ed. (New York: Praeger, 1974).

35. For analysis of the role of overseas Chinese in the PRC's relations with Indonesia, see Robert S. Ross, "China and the Ethnic Chinese: Political Liability/Economic Asset," in *ASEAN and China: An Evolving Relationship*, ed. Joyce K. Kallgren, Noordin Sopiee, and Soedjati Djiwandono (Berkeley: Institute of East Asian Studies, University of California, 1988), 149–52, 158; Leo Suryadinata, *China and the ASEAN States: The Ethnic Dimension* (Singapore: Singapore University Press, 1985), 34–38; and Purcell, *Chinese in Southeast Asia*, part 7.

36. For a work that portrays the overseas Chinese as serving the "communist conspiracy" to take over Southeast Asia, see Robert S. Elegant, *The Dragon's Seed: Peking and the Overseas Chinese* (New York: St. Martin's Press, 1959).

37. Fitzgerald, *China and the Overseas Chinese*, chapter 8.

38. For details on China's policies toward overseas Chinese during the Cultural Revolution, see Fitzgerald, *China and the Overseas Chinese*, chapter 9; and Theresa Chong Cariño, *China and the Overseas Chinese in Southeast Asia* (Quezon City, Philippines: New Day Publishers, 1985), chapter 4.

39. Figures taken and calculated from Lin Jinzhi, "Qiaohui dui Zhongguo," 27–31. The same figures are repeated in Li, Lin, and Cai, *Huaqiao huaren yu Zhongguo*, 267–73.

40. Calculated from Wu, *Dollars*, table 47, 142. Wu also notes how during difficult times in the PRC food parcels were sent by overseas Chinese rather than cash remittances.

41. It is outside the scope of this work to attempt to rectify these estimates. However, it can be said that the estimates were made at different time periods (with Wu working during the height of the cold war). Furthermore, Wu used mainly source country data and data from Hong Kong, while Lin relies on mainland sources. Wu lists estimates by fourteen different authors of remittances to China during the 1950–62 period, and the variances between them are sometimes greater than the variance between Wu and Lin. See Wu, *Dollars*, 18.

42. Wu, *Dollars*, 93, 160. For details on specific countries, see 93–134. For various restrictions placed on remittances by countries of origin, see appendix A, 166.

43. Wu, *Dollars*, 85–93.

CHAPTER 4

China's Reform Era Policies Toward Ethnic Chinese and the Ethnic Chinese Response

CHINA'S REFORM ERA POLICIES TOWARD ETHNIC CHINESE

China's policies toward ethnic Chinese went through radical changes during the Cultural Revolution and then ceased to exist as the institutions that formed and implemented such policies were dismantled. The first public sign that Beijing was again interested in Asia's ethnic Chinese came on 29 September 1977. On that day Deng Xiaoping commented that overseas Chinese[1] affairs should be put back on China's agenda as he met with a delegation of ethnic Chinese, both Chinese citizens and foreign nationals, visiting China for National Day. Then on 4 January 1978, the *Renmin ribao* (*People's Daily*) carried an editorial on work among the overseas Chinese and an article by Liao Chengzhi, director of the State Council's Overseas Chinese Affairs Office (*qiaowu bangongshi*). These two articles authoritatively set forth China's new policy toward overseas Chinese.[2]

The *Renmin ribao* editorial proclaimed that good relations with the overseas Chinese were important for advancing the Four Modernizations (modernization of industry, agriculture, science and technology, and the military), expanding the "patriotic united front" against those who opposed the PRC, and improving relations between China and countries with large populations of overseas Chinese. It went on to state that "overseas Chinese ardently love the motherland and have made big contributions" to China, and "the vast majority of the overseas Chinese are patriotic." Therefore, the "gang of four," under whose influence the domestic overseas Chinese (dependents of overseas Chinese and returned overseas Chinese) were persecuted and overseas Chinese were considered capitalist enemies during the Cultural Revolution, had made grave errors. The editorial further called for rectification of the violations of overseas Chinese policy committed by the gang of four, special consideration for the domestic overseas Chinese because of their "special needs," protection of remittances, help in arranging travel, and the provision of good conditions for overseas Chinese students. The editorial also encouraged overseas Chinese to take on the nationality of their countries of residence, but noted that those who do so "are still our kinfolk and friends," regardless of nationality. Finally, foreign governments were asked to "protect the legitimate rights and interests of overseas Chinese and respect their national traditions, customs and habits."

Similarly, Liao attacked the policies of Cultural Revolution leader Lin Biao and the gang of four, especially their assertions that overseas connections were reactionary. Liao thus laid the ideological groundwork for the reincorporation of the overseas Chinese into respectable political standing. He also commented that "those who have chosen the nationality of their country of residence are still our kinfolk even though they are no longer Chinese citizens." Such people will "continue to maintain close contacts with us." As for those Chinese who maintain Chinese nationality, Liao stated that "we should welcome their choice, and the motherland has the duty to protect their legitimate rights and interests."

Thus, in the late 1970s, China renewed important aspects of its pre–Cultural Revolution policy toward ethnic Chinese abroad. As such it called on ethnic Chinese to assist China in its modernization, a historic theme of the government's overseas Chinese policy. It also called on overseas Chinese to adopt the nationality of their place of residence, but promised to protect those overseas Chinese who maintained Chinese citizenship, a policy that can be traced to the 1950s. Ethnic Chinese were further called upon to join the international united front against hegemonism, highlighting continued fears of the Soviet Union and foreshadowing worsening relations with Vietnam, where the treatment of overseas Chinese was becoming an important issue. As a restoration of previous policy, China also revived its organs for dealing with the overseas Chinese, renewed privileges for the domestic overseas Chinese and Chinese abroad, as well as took steps to amend the wrongs committed during the Cultural Revolution.[3]

Other statements throughout 1978 continued the same themes, with special emphasis on countering Soviet charges that China would exploit the overseas Chinese for its own political purposes. Thus, Lien Kuan, vice director of the Overseas Chinese Affairs Office, claimed that "the founding of New China has improved the position of overseas Chinese who are no longer 'overseas orphans.' This is why they love their socialist motherland more dearly than ever." Furthermore, he asserted that Chinese living abroad are "filled with patriotism and showing great concern for the modernization of China." However, Lien did not in any way acknowledge this as a problem for China's international relations because with the carrying out of the Party's new policy, "the masses of overseas Chinese will surely make still greater contributions to the development of relations of friendship and co-operation between their motherland and the countries of their residence."[4]

Following the third plenum of the 11th Chinese Communist Party (CCP) Central Committee meeting in late 1978—a watershed in moving China down the path of reform—those offices responsible for overseas Chinese work began to devote their attention primarily to mobilizing Asia's ethnic Chinese to assist in China's modernization. Other areas of overseas Chinese work were downplayed, although competition with Taiwan for the loyalty of ethnic Chinese, which is linked to economic competition for ethnic Chinese trade and investments, still played an important role. In Beijing's terms, the work of overseas Chinese affairs shifted to a focus on "socialist modernization."

As sources of capital and expertise for aiding China in its development, Asia's ethnic Chinese were unmatched for two reasons. First, the ethnic Chinese held major resources and were willing to use them in China, if only on a small scale early on. Second, because of their ethnicity, the involvement of overseas Chinese in China's economy was more acceptable than that of non-Chinese foreigners. Throughout the twentieth century China strove for development that was both socialist and true to Chinese cultural values, with cultural values being of highest importance.[5] The use of ethnic Chinese in development helped maintain an appearance of faithfulness to such values.

This emphasis on "Chineseness" was especially important in light of China's history. At the beginning of the century foreign investment was seen by many as a symbol of foreign invasion, and thus was a catalyst for nationalism.[6] This nationalism contributed to the overthrow of the Qing government. After the establishment of "New China" in 1949, the Party emphasized self-reliance, an important element of Maoist dogma. During the Cultural Revolution foreign contacts were especially vilified. Thus, as the Chinese government began reforms in 1978, ethnic Chinese proved to be an important bridge in moving from self-reliance to a more open policy.[7]

This is demonstrated in the initiation of special economic zones, one of the centerpieces of early reform efforts. China's four original special economic zones of Xiamen, Shenzhen, Zhuhai, and Shantou, located in the southeastern provinces of Fujian and Guangdong, were chosen largely because of their links with Chinese living outside the mainland. For instance, an estimated 230,000 Hong Kong Chinese have family ties with residents of Shenzhen. Approximately 70 percent of Taiwan's population has roots in southern Fujian, and Fujian and Guangdong residents have kinship ties throughout Southeast Asia.[8] China has developed its policies in order to attract investments from Taiwan, Hong Kong, and Southeast Asian Chinese and has been successful in this regard.

Moving now to look more broadly at the post-1978 reform period, several features of China's policy toward ethnic Chinese stand out. First, throughout this time period China has continued to appeal to ethnic Chinese throughout Asia and the world to contribute to its development. It has done so through the use of various institutions devoted to the "overseas Chinese," referring to both Chinese nationals and foreign citizens throughout the world.[9] When China revived its pre–Cultural Revolution policy in 1978, the defunct government and Party offices for dealing with overseas Chinese affairs were resurrected as well. Thus, the Overseas Chinese Affairs Commission (*qiaowu weiyuanhui*) returned in 1978 as the Overseas Chinese Affairs Office (*qiaowu bangongshi*). Under the State Council, the Overseas Chinese Affairs Office was headed by Liao Chengzhi until his death in 1983. The All-China Federation of Returned Overseas Chinese (*quanguo guiqiao lianhehui*) was also brought back in 1978 as a mass organization for returned overseas Chinese. Various offices and committees were reestablished at the provincial and local levels as well. Later, in 1983, the National People's Congress (NPC) established a committee on overseas Chinese affairs.

The main purpose of the various offices related to overseas Chinese affairs has been to encourage ethnic Chinese to contribute to China's modernization. This was reflected early in the reform period when in 1981 the Fujian Provincial Federation of Returned Overseas Chinese reported that it and its branches had "actively assisted departments concerned in importing foreign and Overseas Chinese's capital and science and technology and have taken the initiative in helping overseas businessmen hold talks on compensatory trade and on agreements to have their raw material processed in Fujian."[10] The report further noted that the federation had set up processing enterprises and workshops employing over 3,000 dependents of returned overseas Chinese. The vice chairman of the All-China Federation of Returned Overseas Chinese, Huang Junjun, claimed that in the first ten years of work after the initiation of reforms, overseas Chinese offices at various levels directly participated in attracting one-fifth of China's total foreign investments, contributing to over 35,000 enterprises.[11] In early 1996, Zhejiang province officials claimed that overseas Chinese affairs bodies in the province received 8,700 visitors in the previous two years. Partially as a result of their work, the province is home to 700 enterprises funded by ethnic Chinese.[12]

The continuing focus of overseas Chinese affairs work on economic development was reflected in the choice of Guo Dongpo to head the State Council Overseas Chinese Affairs Office in 1997. Guo's background was in international commerce, having spent twenty years working at the China Association for the Promotion of International Trade. He also served for five years as the head of the Xinhua Macao branch, making him the highest ranking mainland official in Macao and providing him with experience in dealing with issues related to Hong Kong, Taiwan, and Macao.

Not surprisingly, the various overseas Chinese organizations have changed their roles as China's economic reforms have progressed, moving from promoting business with ethnic Chinese by sponsoring trade fairs, establishing contacts, and sending businesspersons abroad to developing consulting offices, conducting follow-up services, and setting up firms. This movement by overseas Chinese affairs organizations into actual enterprise management is reminiscent of the overseas Chinese investment corporations of the 1950s and reflects wider trends by Chinese government organs during the reform period. Shifting from merely assisting overseas Chinese to operating enterprises advanced most rapidly in Guangdong. Overseas Chinese affairs departments there set up at least 450 firms in areas such as construction, foreign currency markets, shopping centers, and industrial towns.[13] However, in late 1998, Beijing ordered all military, government, and Party units to give up their business enterprises. Presumably this has affected companies run by overseas Chinese affairs offices as well.

There have also been changes in the structure of overseas Chinese organizations. In 1990, the China Overseas Exchanges Association was established as a nongovernmental organization. Its duties include "disseminating and showcasing China's achievements in reform, opening up, and economic construction; in carrying out work to promote unity and friendship with overseas Chinese and foreign nationals of Chinese descent; and in developing cooperation and exchanges with overseas Chinese and foreign nationals of Chinese descent in various fields."[14] The Overseas Chinese Affairs Committee of the National People's Congress has received some attention, reflecting the greater role in Chinese politics played by the NPC. The All-China Federation of Returned Chinese has expanded its branches as well. For instance, in 1998, the All-China Federation of Returned Overseas from Vietnam, Laos, and Cambodia was established under the auspices of its parent organization. Nevertheless, the lead organization in overseas Chinese affairs is the State Council Overseas Chinese Affairs Office. The importance of the work of these institutions and overseas Chinese work in general is reflected in the high level of attention that such work receives. For example, the 1999 national work conference on overseas Chinese affairs was addressed by Jiang Zemin himself, China's president and number one individual in the Communist Party hierarchy.

Official organs involved in overseas Chinese affairs work are backed by academic institutions focusing on Asia's ethnic Chinese. For example, Xiamen University is host to the Center for Southeast Asian Studies, which focuses heavily on Chinese in Southeast Asia. Similar institutions exist in other southern provinces. Various periodicals are devoted to diaspora Chinese, such as *Huaren* (*Ethnic Chinese*), *Bagui qiao shi* (*Overseas Chinese History of Bagui*), *Huaqiao huaren yu qiaowu* (*Overseas Chinese, Ethnic Chinese, and Overseas Chinese Affairs*), *Huaqiao yu huaren* (*Chinese Overseas*), *Hua sheng* (*Chinese Voice*), and *Huaqiao gongzuo yanjiu* (*Research on Overseas Chinese Work*). A study in a mainland journal found 213 articles on ethnic Chinese issues in 1996.[15]

Chinese leaders and overseas Chinese affairs organizations use a variety of means to attract ethnic Chinese investors. One is official contacts via trips abroad by high-level government officials. When Chinese leaders travel abroad they often meet with ethnic Chinese business leaders. For example, President Jiang Zemin met with ethnic Chinese on his trip to the Philippines in 1996 and Canada in 1997. The director of the Overseas Chinese Affairs Office has traveled to Thailand, meeting the Thai prime minister, and various governors have traveled to Southeast Asia to seek Southeast Asian Chinese investment. Southeast Asian leaders have taken Chinese entrepreneurs from their countries on visits to China as well.

Overseas Chinese affairs organizations and local governments also work with ethnic Chinese voluntary associations and individual entrepreneurs. For example, the Chinese National Association for Overseas Liaisons was established in May 1997, with leaders of ethnic Chinese voluntary associations asked to serve as founding members.[16] Other techniques used to attract ethnic Chinese money include sending delegations abroad to discuss investment opportunities, promoting ethnic Chinese hometowns as advantageous places to invest in, using traditional Chinese festivals to foster friendship with ethnic Chinese, hosting visiting delegations, and establishing working groups to negotiate with investors and help provide for their needs.[17] Furthermore, efforts have been made to lure scientific talent to China. For instance, in 1999, Xinhua announced that China would attempt to attract ethnic Chinese scientists to China with grants totaling 600 million yuan over the following three years. One special target for luring scientific expertise is mainland Chinese students who studied in the West and stayed there.

One type of enticement to ethnic Chinese used by various officials and institutions, the so-called patriotic appeal, has been aimed to foster and manipulate the love for the motherland supposedly felt by all Chinese. There are many examples of patriotic appeals to ethnic Chinese, most notably during the early years of reform. For example, Guangdong Provincial CCP Committee First Secretary Ren Zhongyi, speaking at a provincial conference on overseas Chinese affairs in 1981, said, "The Overseas Chinese love our motherland. No matter how poor the motherland, no matter what painful events the Overseas Chinese suffered in their native villages, no matter what corner of the globe they have drifted to, and no matter how many generations they have lived overseas, the Overseas Chinese still unswervingly love the motherland and their native village. This is a national characteristic of China."[18] Similarly, in 1983, the *Renmin ribao* proclaimed, "The overseas Chinese and Chinese people of foreign nationality who are living abroad are all the yellow race" and have an "enthusiastic love for the motherland and their native places."[19] At times China has even portrayed itself as being dependent upon the overseas Chinese. A 1986 broadcast reported that Fujian Governor Hu Ping remarked that "Fujian's dominant role in using foreign funds relies on the millions of Overseas Chinese who serve as bridges in Fujian's efforts to open to the outside world and as a prime force in invigorating Fujian."[20]

These emotional appeals to Asia's ethnic Chinese for funds continued into the 1990s as well, sometimes taking on an almost bizarre character. For example, the government built "homeland gardens of the Chinese nation" across China, selling shares to ethnic Chinese who wanted to buy a "piece of the motherland."[21] Official pronouncements continue to put forth an emotional appeal. At a forum on overseas Chinese affairs in 1998, vice premier and Politburo member Qian Qichen claimed that overseas Chinese institutions have "provided all sorts of services for overseas Chinese; won their hearts; and further mobilized the enthusiasm of overseas Chinese. . . . They have stepped up contact with and cultural and publicity work among overseas Chinese and ethnic Chinese to enhance their attachments for and understanding of China . . . and to enhance unity of patriotic forces and isolate separatist forces in the cause of motherland reunification."[22] Similarly, in a speech to ethnic and overseas Chinese in Canada, China's president Jiang Zemin was paraphrased by Xinhua as saying, "no matter how long they are separated from the motherland, ethnic and Overseas Chinese always cherish deep feelings toward their native land."[23]

China's emphasis on patriotism in its appeals to ethnic Chinese has not been without controversy in China. Some analysts comment that using patriotism was understandable in the early 1980s, when officials were not yet confident in the new open door policy or wanted to attract capital quickly. However, they argue that today an emphasis on patriotism is no longer appropriate, largely because most ethnic Chinese abroad are rooted where they live and are loyal to their countries of residence. Appeals based on patriotism toward China are unrealistic as well as harmful toward Chinese diplomacy. Instead, appeals for investment must be based on a profitable investment climate.[24]

Those who write on ethnic Chinese investments tend to emphasize the objective reasons for investing in China. Nevertheless, appeals to sentiment and racial ties are still commonly found. In a 1994 article on investments in the Chaozhou–Shantou area, Lin Jinzhi credits ethnic Chinese investments to stable Chinese policies, a good investment environment, careful work by various overseas Chinese affairs offices, as well as the growth of ethnic Chinese businesses. However, he also attributes investments by ethnic Chinese to "the ardent love like a newborn baby that the ethnic Chinese have for their former land," further noting that "the foundation of China's open policy is vigorous promotion of the Chinese nationality (Zhonghua minzu)."[25] Similarly, Xiang Dayou gives a reasoned analysis of how ethnic Chinese should determine where to invest their money, based on security, rate of return, and local conditions. He further notes that race should not be a monopolizing condition. However, he goes on to claim that "offspring of China both inside and outside the country, descendants of Yan and Huang, have identical nationality, ties of blood, the same language, a common culture, and emotional bonds. With this nationality and cultural background, every ethnic Chinese businessperson that comes to China to invest brings a special feeling of intimacy, an emotion of returning home."[26]

Related to the issue of appealing emotionally to ethnic Chinese is the matter of offering preferences not available to others, which have been common. Preferences can be broken down into two subsets: preferences to domestic overseas Chinese not available to ordinary citizens, and preferences to overseas Chinese investors.

Before the Cultural Revolution Beijing gave special treatment to domestic overseas Chinese. The purpose of such preferences was to attract remittances and investments from Chinese living abroad. Beginning in 1978, these privileges were restored to the domestic overseas Chinese and new ones were added. Privileges included provisions allowing the purchase of difficult-to-obtain materials with remittance receipts, the reopening of special stores for domestic overseas Chinese, allotments of grain and clothing, provisions allowing visiting family members to bring in televisions and radios, better access to education, and allowances for rural dwellers to move to cities. Perhaps more important, remittances could be used to start businesses and production materials could be received from abroad. Officials also made efforts to restore properties that had been confiscated in previous years.[27]

The purpose of providing privileges to domestic overseas Chinese was to attract funds from their relatives abroad. Although remittances were sought after, investment was particularly valued. Thus, a 1984 meeting attended by Hu Yaobang for directors of overseas Chinese affairs offices at various levels of government held that "support should be given those specialized households among the returned Overseas Chinese and the dependents of Overseas Chinese who are actively developing production with the help of their relatives living abroad so that they can become well off first."[28] Today the preferences are unnecessary, due to overall relaxed policies regarding foreign currency and the freedom given to all Chinese to invest in businesses.

Preferences also go to overseas Chinese investors who actually live overseas. This was noted explicitly in an interview by the Hong Kong paper *Wen wei po* in 1981 with executive secretary of the Fujian Provincial CCP Committee Xiang Nan:

Question: Do you offer different terms to Overseas Chinese and foreign investors who intend to make investments in Fujian? Will you offer more favorable terms to Overseas Chinese investors?

Answer: We will offer favorable terms to all foreign investors in Fujian and the terms for Overseas Chinese investors will be even more favorable. . . . Foreign investors might not be willing to invest in some projects and we will not invite them either. But no such restriction will be placed upon Overseas Chinese investors, because we treat them as the people of the mainland and regard them as our compatriots. They may put forth any investment plan they wish.[29]

One example of a specific law for overseas Chinese is the "State Council's Regulation on Encouraging Overseas Chinese, Hong Kong, and Macao Compatriots to Invest in the Mainland," issued in 1990. This law is designed for Chinese nationals, although in its local implementation it may apply to other ethnic Chinese as well. Its provisions are similar to those laid out for foreigners. However, the overseas Chinese are given added benefits, such as preferences regarding real estate. Guangzhou in 1984 promulgated "Temporary Preferential Measures Regarding Investments by Overseas Chinese and Hong Kong and Macao Compatriots in Guangzhou."[30] This law reduced land use fees, relaxed restrictions on the domestic market, provided special titles to those who make major contributions to Guangzhou, allowed relatives of investors to work in the new firms that are created, provided tax benefits, provided for relatives of investors to move from rural areas to the city, and established cash awards for domestic overseas Chinese who introduce investors to the city. Guangdong province has similar legislation. In 1998, a Fujian law gave overseas Chinese investors preferential treatment in taxation and infrastructure.

Furthermore, Zhuhai exempts the "house tax" for three years on property purchased by foreign investment enterprises. For overseas Chinese and compatriots from Hong Kong and Macao the exemption is five years.[31] Fujian gives five-year exemptions from enterprise income taxes for new contracts of ten years or more and a 50 percent reduction during the remaining years to overseas Chinese. It also grants special tax reductions to overseas Chinese who invest in low-profit industries or underdeveloped areas.[32] Guangdong's Meixian county government offers preferential policies to encourage ethnic Chinese investors as well.[33] Robert Ross calls this preferential treatment that is limited to overseas Chinese a "reminder of their ethnicity and of their responsibility to their fellow Chinese on the mainland."[34]

The amount of influence that preferential treatment has had in attracting overseas investors is unclear. Although it has played a role in bringing in investors, it is only one factor among many economic considerations. In looking beyond the economic realm, however, preferential policies have assured potential investors that they are welcome, providing a hospitable environment that was especially important after the ravages of the Cultural Revolution. In this regard, preferential treatment for domestic overseas Chinese has perhaps been even more important. Many of the earliest forms of assistance given by ethnic Chinese were contributions to relatives to begin small manufacturing operations. Improvements in the condition of those Chinese with relatives overseas laid the groundwork for the earliest wave of foreign capital investment in the reform period.[35] Even today support from overseas relatives is still important for many families in southern China engaged in the kinship mode of production.

However, preferential treatment given to ethnic Chinese, like patriotic appeals, is now controversial. Thus, one official from the Xiamen Foreign Investment Executive Committee, in a conversation with the author in 1994, asserted that the financial incentives for Westerners and overseas Chinese to invest in China are the same. Shen Hongfang goes so far as to argue that preferences are harmful to China's interests for three reasons. First, non-Chinese feel that China's preferential tax policies are discriminatory and do not conform to international conventions. International conventions are now especially important as China seeks to join the World Trade Organization (WTO). Second, much of the investment brought about by such preferences is small-scale and utilizes little advanced technology. Third, ethnic Chinese are sometimes used as fronts for other investors who merely want to obtain the preferences granted to overseas Chinese.[36]

Another theme in China's policy toward the overseas Chinese has been protection. During the Cultural Revolution domestic overseas Chinese suffered a great deal of persecution and discrimination at the hands of officials. Protecting the overseas Chinese against further discrimination, as well as redressing past wrongs, has been an issue in the post-1978 era at the national, provincial, and local levels.

For example, in 1983, a broadcast from Beijing reported that Fujian's Anxi county had "recently adopted effective measures to determinedly curb the malpractice of demanding money and materials from Overseas Chinese."[37] As we have seen from chapter 3, these illegal practices that Anxi attempted to curb are not new. One of Zhang Bishi's goals during the late Qing period was to eliminate the exploitation of overseas Chinese and demands for money made upon them by corrupt officials. However, after many years of the open door policy, problems continue. A symposium held by the All-China Federation of Returned Overseas Chinese reported in 1994 that there are four types of infringements on the rights of the overseas Chinese: housing confiscated before 1978 still has not all been returned; the interests of investors are trampled upon; overseas Chinese detained in lawsuits are held illegally; and returned overseas Chinese suffer from frame-ups.[38]

Several laws at various levels of government were passed in the 1990s to alleviate these injustices. For example, on 1 January 1991, a law entitled the "People's Republic of China Law on Protecting the Rights and Interests of Returned Overseas Chinese and of Family Members of Chinese Nationals Residing Abroad" went into effect after approval by the 15th session of the 7th National People's Congress Standing Committee. In 1993, the State Council issued thirty-one articles to implement this law, including provisions assisting businesses that provide jobs for returned overseas Chinese, allowing returned overseas Chinese to open enterprises in any part of the country, and providing for favorable consideration for the children of returned overseas Chinese in entering universities. In 1992, Guangdong issued "Regulations on Protection of the Rights and Interests of the Overseas Chinese," and in 1994, Beijing municipality approved similar regulations. In 1998, Fujian province passed legislation protecting the rights and interests of overseas Chinese investors, and in 1999, China's State Council announced new measures to protect overseas Chinese investors. However, these laws have evidently not been enforced properly or are insufficient, as evidenced by their continuing proliferation and reports in the 1990s that returned overseas Chinese still suffer difficulties, including discrimination at the hands of local officials.[39]

A final issue that arises in China's policy is the distinction between ethnic Chinese of foreign nationality and those living abroad who are stateless or maintain their Chinese citizenship. On one hand China needs to differentiate between Chinese citizens and noncitizens. Such a separation is important for China's relations with Southeast Asia and conformance with international norms. However, at another level, China sees little difference between Chinese nationals and foreign nationals in terms of their utility for contributing to China's development. All are ethnic Chinese with ties to China, and China is interested in having all contribute to its modernization. As David Yen-ho Wu notes, "In the Chinese mind the overseas Chinese or *huaqiao* (the Hua sojourners) are natural members of *zhonghua minzu* [the Chinese race] as well as *zhongguoren* [people of China]."[40] As a result, China's statements regarding ethnic Chinese sometimes seem ambiguous or confusing.

In a like manner, ambiguity in language creates confusion. In Chinese *huaqiao* generally indicates a Chinese national, while *huaren* indicates an ethnic Chinese (implying foreign nationality). However, Chinese officials stopped using the term *huaqiao* to refer to all ethnic Chinese only after Deng Xiaoping's visit to the ASEAN countries in 1978.[41] To add to the ambiguity, some argue that in addition to the narrow legal and political meaning of *huaqiao*, there is also a broader meaning entailing the Chinese race and culture.[42] In addition, the English term "overseas Chinese" has been used to translate both *huaqiao* and *huaren*. Thus, statements coming out of Beijing in English are sometimes unclear.

China's official policy in 1978 distinguished between ethnic Chinese with foreign citizenship and those with Chinese citizenship. A *Renmin ribao* editorial in 1978 stated, "Those of Chinese origin who have acquired the nationality of the host country are no longer 'overseas Chinese.' "[43] Nevertheless, the article went on to note the enduring ties of kinship and natural contacts with China enjoyed by ethnic Chinese regardless of citizenship. Party Chairman Hua Guofeng also stated that year that "the concern and preferential treatment extended to the relatives of Overseas Chinese will equally be extended to the relatives in China of foreign nationals of Chinese descent."[44] More ominous-sounding were the comments of Liao Chengzhi, director of the State Council's Overseas Chinese Affairs Office, in 1979, uttered as China's conflict with Vietnam intensified: "We still have not done what we should have done for many kinsmen who have voluntarily become naturalized citizens of their countries of residence. We deeply regret this."[45] Liao's comments appeared to give China some type of responsibility for foreign nationals of Chinese descent. Nevertheless, since then Beijing has tended to remain silent on the way in which other countries have treated their own citizens, whether Chinese or not. Thus it was surprising when Beijing protested to Indonesia over the violence committed against ethnic Chinese Indonesians in the May 1998 riots and rape incidents in which ethnic Chinese were the main victims.[46]

Many commentators in the late 1970s found China's policy ambiguous. David Bonavia noted that "Chinese official pronouncements on the level of responsibility which Peking accepts for its kin abroad have been kept deliberately vague."[47] Wang Gungwu said, "The main feature of the rhetoric now revived is not to distinguish between various kinds of Chinese abroad but to call all of them 'Overseas Chinese' and declare that 'they constitute part of the Chinese nation.' "[48] Wang lamented this new policy, noting it was not in the best interests of Asia's ethnic Chinese.

However, China was not unaware of the concerns of Southeast Asia, and in 1980, the PRC passed its first nationality law. This law codified former premier

Zhou Enlai's policy that any Chinese who voluntarily acquired foreign citizenship ceased being a citizen of the PRC. As already mentioned, the PRC also began to be more careful in its terminology when making pronouncements, although today many in China who refer to ethnic Chinese use the term *huaqiao-huaren*, a phrase some Southeast Asian scholars find ambiguous and disturbing because it again lumps all ethnic Chinese into one category.[49]

Since the early 1980s, Beijing has continued its two-track policy of officially separating Chinese nationals from foreign nationals but appealing to both groups to contribute to China's modernization, in spite of the fact that only about 5 percent of Chinese in Southeast Asia are Chinese nationals. A statement by an official in the Overseas Chinese Affairs Office is illustrative of the ambiguity in China's policy: "As for Chinese with foreign nationalities, it is necessary to strictly distinguish them from Overseas Chinese and to promote the friendly affection between them and China. We must endeavor with greater enthusiasm to help them carry out relevant matters in China, continue to carry out the various policies on Overseas Chinese affairs, and extend more care and assistance to their relatives in China."[50] Similarly, high Chinese officials make statements to both citizens and foreign nationals. For example, Chinese leaders routinely address New Year greetings to overseas Chinese, returned overseas Chinese, ethnic Chinese, and Chinese students abroad. Thus, China walks a fine line in its dual-track policy.

LEVELS OF ETHNIC CHINESE INVESTMENT

Turning to estimates of the amount of investments that ethnic Chinese have made in China, it is clear that the majority of foreign investment in China throughout the reform period has come primarily from ethnic Chinese, mostly those in Hong Kong but also Taiwan and Southeast Asia. In 1989, Xinhua reported that Chinese nationals living abroad, residents of Hong Kong, Macao and Taiwan, and foreign nationals of Chinese origin had invested more than $30 billion in China, providing over 70 percent of total foreign investment and establishing 80 percent of foreign-invested enterprises. Ten years later, Xinhua reported that ethnic Chinese investments remained at over 70 percent of direct foreign investment in China.[51] Others have set the figure even higher. A report from the government of Australia put investments by ethnic Chinese from 1979 to 1993 at almost 85 percent of foreign investments, with 69 percent coming from Hong Kong alone, although the report notes that ethnic Chinese investment did constitute less than 50 percent of total investment before 1985.[52]

The amount of investments coming from Southeast Asian Chinese is difficult to calculate. Before 1992, the figure was not comparatively high. Lin Jinzhi calculates that between 1979 and 1991, ethnic Chinese invested $17.9 billion in China, accounting for 67 percent of all utilized foreign investment. Of this $17.9 billion, $13.9 billion was from Hong Kong and Macao (51.8 percent of total foreign investment), $2.5 billion was from Taiwan (9.3 percent of the total), while

$1.5 billion (5.6 percent of the total) was from ethnic Chinese from other places, mainly Southeast Asia. This breakdown is very different from the pre-1966 period when most ethnic Chinese investments in China came from Southeast Asia.[53]

Lin's figure for investments from Southeast Asia are somewhat conservative when compared to others. For example, Xiang Dayou from the Guangxi Overseas Chinese Affairs Office wrote in 1994 that ethnic Chinese investments make up 80 percent of all foreign investments in China. Investments from Hong Kong and Taiwan formed two-thirds of the total, while investments from Southeast Asian Chinese comprised 10 percent to 15 percent. The *Economist* made the same estimate in 1992.[54] Other accounts in 1994 put the figure for Southeast Asian investment in China at $8 billion, compared to $40 billion for Hong Kong and at least $5.4 billion for Taiwan.[55]

In 1992, public investments from Southeast Asia began increasing rapidly as China's reforms deepened and its relations with Southeast Asia improved. (There are no figures kept specifically on Southeast Asian Chinese investments in China, so investments from Southeast Asia in general, most of which are from Chinese, must serve as a proxy.) For example, Singapore's utilized investments in China rose by more than 2-fold in 1992, while those of the ASEAN Four (Indonesia, Malaysia, the Philippines, and Thailand) rose almost 5-fold. Altogether the ASEAN Five's investments in China rose over 65–fold from 1990 to 1998, as shown in official Chinese statistics summarized in table 4.1. Actual figures for Southeast Asian investment in China are higher, due to the fact that many Southeast Asian Chinese investments are routed through Hong Kong or go unreported.[56]

Statistics for specific localities in southern China confirm the importance of ethnic Chinese investment, especially early in the reform period. For example, between July 1979 and December 1981, officials approved $15 billion in investments for joint ventures in Guangdong province. About 90 percent of this money reportedly came from ethnic Chinese.[57] In the Chaozhou–Shantou area of Guangdong, 80 percent to 90 percent of foreign-invested enterprises were reported to be funded by ethnic Chinese who have ancestral roots in the area. A significant number of these investments came from Southeast Asia, especially Thailand.[58] In 1984, Bonavia reported that 80 percent of the approved investments (by number of enterprises) in Xiamen were from overseas Chinese.[59] Hainan Island, due to its location, gets a significant degree of interest from Southeast Asian investors.

The dangers of China's heavy reliance on Asian Chinese capital were revealed with the onset of the Asian economic crisis in 1997. Although investments in China from Southeast Asia have gone up every year since 1990, as illustrated in table 4.1, if Singapore is excluded, investments decreased in 1997 and again in 1998. Even in Singapore's case, contracted investment, an indication of future investment trends, dropped in 1998 for the third consecutive year. In 1998, utilized investments from Hong Kong dropped 10 percent, while in-

Table 4.1
Utilized Direct Foreign Investment by Southeast Asian States in China[a]
(in million U.S. dollars)

Year	Indonesia	Malaysia	Philippines	Singapore	Thailand	Total	Minus Sing
1990	1.00	.64	1.67	53.28	7.52	64.11	10.83
1991	2.18	1.96	5.85	58.21	19.73	87.93	29.72
1992	20.17	24.67	16.55	125.93	84.32	271.64	145.71
1993	65.75	91.42	122.50	491.80	234.37	1,005.84	514.04
1994	115.70	200.99	140.40	1,179.61	234.87	1,871.57	691.96
1995	111.63	259.00	105.78	1,860.61	288.24	2,625.26	764.65
1996	93.54	459.95	55.51	2,247.16	328.18	3,184.34	937.18
1997	79.98	381.83	155.63	2,606.96	194.00	3,418.40	811.44
1998	68.97	340.57	179.27	3,403.97	205.38	4,198.16	794.19

[a]Includes direct foreign investment and other.

Source: Statistical Yearbook of China and the China Council for the Promotion of International Trade (www.ccpit.org).

vestments from Taiwan dropped 8.7 percent. The year 1999 started out even worse. In the first four months of 1999, investment from across Asia dropped again, by as much as 43.6 percent in the case of Taiwan and 23.3 percent in the case of Hong Kong.[60]

Having presented the foregoing estimates on ethnic Chinese investments over the past twenty years, it is important to note that they are only a rough approximation of the true numbers. In the first place, China's overall figures for foreign investment are too high. One analyst described figures for contracted investment as embodying "every letter of intent or memorandum of understanding scrawled on the back of an envelope after a few glasses of Maotai."[61] Figures on utilized investments also are beset by inaccuracies. For instance, the Chinese government's official figure for FDI in 1998 was $45.6 billion. However, a senior Chinese government economist said the correct number was probably around $30 billion, creating an overestimate of 50 percent.[62] One cause for overestimation is the high percentage of "foreign investment" coming from Hong Kong and Macao that actually originates in the mainland. Such money, after being transferred offshore, returns to China as "foreign investment" in order to receive preferential tax treatment. Up to 25 percent of stated investment from Hong Kong may have involved this type of transaction, although recently China has made concerted efforts to stop this practice. Another cause for error, as admitted by the head of China's State Statistical Bureau in 1999, is exaggeration of economic figures by local officials for the sake of political gain. Nevertheless, in spite of inaccuracies, investment statistics are useful for examining broad trends.

Distinguishing ethnic Chinese investment from other types of investment also presents a major difficulty. The Chinese government does not publish statistics on investments by ethnic Chinese. Thus, estimates must be made on the basis of country-level data, data provided by various overseas Chinese affairs offices, and press reports. Furthermore, country-level data that would be helpful in determining amounts of ethnic Chinese investment are often skewed. For example, Nanjing officials who kept joint venture data routinely listed ethnic Chinese business partners as being from Hong Kong, regardless of their true nationality or place of residence.[63] This is likely to have occurred in many other locations as well. Another reason for the difficulty in identifying the exact nature of ethnic Chinese investments in China is that many enterprises are funded by a mixture of capital from Southeast Asia, Hong Kong, and Taiwan.

A final cause of the difficulty in accurately estimating ethnic Chinese investment in China is the fact that much of it goes through Hong Kong. Hong Kong's importance to ethnic Chinese goes back to well before the reform period. Lynn Pan states that Hong Kong is "the largest node of the Greater Chinese network, its connections and influences extending across the seas like the circles of a pebble dropped in a pool, to kinsmen, classmates, friends, business partners, [and] fellow provincials."[64] Throughout the postwar period ethnic Chinese enterprises have shifted capital to Hong Kong, especially when Southeast Asian states have restricted the business activities of their ethnic Chinese entrepreneurs at home. Hong Kong has thus become both a final destination for the international flow of ethnic Chinese capital as well as a base from which to invest around the globe.

With the advent of reforms, Southeast Asian Chinese have used Hong Kong as a base for investing in China because of Hong Kong's dynamic environment and in order to hide the origin of their capital. Investing through Hong Kong has accelerated as reforms have progressed. Thus, many ethnic Chinese firms made small, low-profile investments in China during the early years of the country's reforms. When the investment climate proved to be satisfactory for larger investments, these firms invested through branches that had already been set up in Hong Kong. Thus, it is difficult to determine which investments coming out of Hong Kong are made by Southeast Asian Chinese, although Rajeswary Ampalavanar Brown estimates that over half of "Overseas Chinese" investments moved through Hong Kong, while a Beijing source suggests that two-thirds of Malaysian investment is funneled through the former colony.[65]

China itself has encouraged Southeast Asian Chinese both to invest in Hong Kong and to use Hong Kong as a base for investing in China. Xu Jiatun reports in his memoirs that as head of Xinhua's Hong Kong branch, Beijing's de facto representative office in Hong Kong until 2000, one of his duties was to assist Southeast Asian entrepreneurs in their investments on the mainland. Xinhua also cooperated with other organizations in this regard, including the Bank of China, mainland enterprises, and various business groups.[66]

There are many examples of Southeast Asian firms that invest in China through Hong Kong. Indonesian tycoon Liem Sioe Liong (Lin Shaoliang) bases his First Pacific Group there. Indonesia's Lippo Group uses Hong Kong companies to invest in China, as does Malaysia's Robert Kuok (Guo Henian), whose main holding is the Kerry Group. Other Malaysians investing out of Hong Kong are the Guo brothers and Golden Lion Group. Thailand's Charoen Pokphand Group, although investing openly in China, uses Hong Kong as an important base. The Philippines' Frank Chan also has money in Hong Kong through Eton Properties. However, to keep the issue in perspective, Southeast Asian business leaders use Hong Kong as a base for globalization, not just thrusts into China. Hong Kong has provided an environment conducive to establishing cooperation with foreign firms, raising money, and gathering information, although some fear that since the reversion to Chinese rule Hong Kong is beginning to lose some of its dynamism. Furthermore, multinational corporations from around the world also use Hong Kong as a base for their Chinese investments.

This examination of the difficulties of separating forms of ethnic Chinese capital illustrates the disconnect between economics and politics. From a political perspective, or perhaps more accurately from the perspective of sovereignty, it is useful to distinguish among overseas Chinese, Southeast Asian ethnic Chinese, and Chinese "compatriots" from Hong Kong, Macao, and Taiwan. Governments care where their citizens are investing for economic and security reasons. From an economic point of view, efforts to determine where capital "comes from" are artificial. Thus, in important respects the existence of the nation-state system and its emphasis on territoriality, security, and sovereignty is at odds with the economic and social realities of an interdependent world.

Although we cannot determine the exact amount of Southeast Asian Chinese capital that has flowed into China, we can look at companies owned by Southeast Asians that have invested in China. Arguably the most important of these companies is Thailand's Charoen Pokphand Group, or CP.[67] Started in 1921 in Bangkok by Chia Ek Chaw, an immigrant from Shantou, CP is chaired by Dhanin Chearavanont and controlled by the Chearavanont family. Although agribusiness is still the company's core concern, CP has diversified into telecommunications, manufacturing, retailing, property, and numerous other areas. With approximately 250 companies in 20 countries, CP had an annual turnover of $9 billion in 1997, two-thirds of it in agriculture.

CP was one of the first multinationals to invest in China with the advent of reforms, investing in Shenzhen in a joint venture with American firm Continental Grain in 1979. Since that time its investments in China have expanded rapidly, with China contributions to group operations rivaling those of Thailand itself. China operations are managed under Hong Kong-listed C. P. Pokphand Co. Ltd., with 30 percent of group turnover generated in China. CP has approximately 170 investments in China, located throughout the country but concentrated in

Guangdong, Liaoning, Shanghai, and Tianjin. Investments have been spread across agrolivestock, aquaculture, downstream petrochemical products, automobiles and motorcycles, beer brewing, and real estate. However, most investment is in agriculture, with over one hundred chicken feed mills located in China.

CP's successful expansion has been due partially to its savvy style of conducting business in China. One strategy is to make alliances with local officials, who are often hired by the company. For example, the manager of a Shanghai plant is the former Party secretary of Song Jiang County. Mr. Dhanin himself has access to top leaders, such as the mayor of Shanghai, and was one of only three non-Chinese nationals appointed to China's advisory group on Hong Kong. Large contributions also help smooth the way for business. In 1990, CP contributed HK$10 million to help China host the Asian Games, while later donating Rmb 12 million for flood relief and building schools and a hospital in Shanghai. CP also has pleased Chinese officials by bringing in technology through partnerships with multinationals such as Honda, Ford, Nynex, and Heineken.

However, CP has been hurt by the Asian financial crisis. Having borrowed heavily to fund its expansion in China, Thailand, and elsewhere, CP struggled to avoid default on a $100 million note in 1998 resulting from the fall of the Thai baht and slowed demand and subsequent losses in Asia and China. As a result, CP has been forced to restructure loans, reduce costs, obtain outside help, and cut back on non-core businesses. For instance, CP has sold off its Shanghai motorcycle factory and shares in its Shanghai brewery to raise capital. Other elements of the China business empire are for sale as well. Thus CP, considered by many to be China's largest foreign investor, is currently reducing its investments in China rather than expanding.

Ethnic Chinese from Indonesia have also invested in China, usually through Hong Kong. The Riady family's Lippo Group is one example. With global revenues of approximately $5 billion, 30 percent of which is generated in Indonesia, Lippo invests in Hong Kong and China through Hong Kong-based Lippo Limited. In this it has been assisted by Hong Kong's Li Ka Shing and mainland firm China Resources, owned by China's Ministry of Foreign Trade and Economic Cooperation. Both firms have significant holdings in various Lippo companies. Most of Lippo's investments are south of Putian in Fujian province, ancestral home of the Riady family. For instance, Lippo has been granted a lucrative franchise to develop Fujian's Meizhou Island. However, due to the Asian financial crisis, no new large-scale investments by the group are planned any time in the near future.[68]

Another Indonesian conglomerate with interests in China is Liem Sioe Liong's (Lin Shaoliang's) Salim Group, now run by son Anthony. Liem left China for Indonesia at the age of eighteen in 1937. Starting with nothing, he built up a business empire worth $20 billion, largely as a result of close ties with Indonesia's former president Suharto. Liem has invested hundreds of millions of dollars in his hometown of Fuqing in Fujian province, where he has put up a highway, apartment buildings, office buildings, factories, a hotel, and port facilities, as well as constructed much of the city's infrastructure. The Liem family's major vehicle in Hong Kong, First Pacific, was purchased in 1979 and does business around the world. First Pacific's holdings in China include cell phone companies Shenzhen Merchant Link and Fujian Telecom. Recently, however, the Liem empire has also been rocked by the Asian economic crisis. After riots in Indonesia in May 1998, in which Liem's home was destroyed, Salim-owned Central Bank Asia lost 42 percent of its deposits. This, coupled with the devaluation of the Indonesian rupiah, left Salim with $5 billion in bad loans. After a government takeover of the bank, Salim has been selling assets in a possible effort to recover the bank. First Pacific, however, remains relatively healthy, making further investments throughout Asia.[69]

There are other examples of Southeast Asian tycoons who do business in China. Chinese-Filipino Lucio Tan has beer and cigarette interests in China. Bangkok Bank, controlled by Thailand's Sophonpanich family, was moving into China in the mid-1990s, but has been badly hit by the Asian financial crisis. Malaysia's Robert Kuok (Guo Henian), now based in Hong Kong, has numerous investments in China as well, including Shangri-la hotels distributed across China, the China International Trade Center, and Coca Cola bottling. Indonesia's Sinar Mas Group, founded by Eke Tijpta Widjaja (Oei Ek Tjong), is another major investor in China.

These wealthy entrepreneurs who invest in China are not broadly representative of Southeast Asia's ethnic Chinese. Most tend to be first- or second-generation Chinese who speak Chinese and have had some Chinese education. Some also have sentimental ties with their hometowns. None of them has invested exclusively in China. In fact, only a minority of their holdings are in China. It remains to be seen how future generations, who grew up in Southeast Asia, deal with China differently than their fathers.[70]

MOTIVATIONS OF ETHNIC CHINESE INVESTORS

Ethnic Chinese investment in China has taken place in a broader global context where foreign direct investment (FDI) around the world in general and China in particular has vastly increased. Within this environment companies invest in China for a variety of reasons. Some, for instance, have sought low labor costs in order to establish an export platform. Other companies hope to tap into China's large but segmented domestic market. However, in the midst of this activity, the motivations of ethnic Chinese who invest in China have sometimes been an issue. The question of why ethnic Chinese invest is important. If investments are made primarily to earn a profit, ethnic Chinese investors are no different from other international investors. If investments are made primarily for sentimental or charitable reasons, ethnic Chinese, especially those from Southeast Asia, act differently from other investors and are open to suspicion and attack by Southeast Asian nationalists who ask why they do not invest in poor areas at home.[71] The question is not easily resolved. Nevertheless, the evidence that is available indicates that motives are mixed, although profit is primary.

Many insist that the main motivation of those who invest in China is profit. For example, an executive of CP states, "We invest in China as a business, not out of sentiment."[72] Chang Pao-Min from the National University of Singapore argues that most Southeast Asian Chinese, unlike previous generations, feel no identity with China. Therefore, appeals by China to ethnic or cultural factors will be unsuccessful. Those Southeast Asian Chinese who engage in business with China do so "purely out of utilitarian considerations rather than any sense of identification with or commitment to China."[73] This is an argument that most Southeast Asian Chinese feel is important to make for their own well being in Southeast Asia. While generally true, it clearly does not apply to all Chinese in Southeast Asia.

The main evidence for profit as being a major motivating factor for the vast majority of Southeast Asian Chinese investors is the scope and timing of investment in China. Large-scale investment did not occur until the early 1990s, once it became clear that investing in China was safe and profitable and political hurdles in Southeast Asia had been cleared. In fact, this was the first time in history that large-scale investment for profit by ethnic Chinese in China had occurred. Investing at this level for purely sentimental reasons would destroy entrepreneurs. Furthermore, there are other reasons for investing in China that are more plausible for businesspersons. No one claims that Motorola is investing for sentimental reasons when it puts hundreds of millions of dollars into China.

There is evidence that profit is indeed a major motivating factor from investment patterns in southern China. During the early days of reform, Guangdong's Shantou, which had family links with Southeast Asian Chinese, did not do as well as the Pearl River delta area closer to Hong Kong in attracting investments. This was due to several reasons, one of which was that Southeast Asian businesspersons who had roots in Shantou, while still having sentimental feelings toward the area, had little economic incentive to invest there because they had access to cheap labor in Southeast Asia.[74] Hong Kong investors, meanwhile, were searching for nearby cheap labor and invested more quickly. If sentiment had been more of a motivating force than profit for the Southeast Asians, the accessibility of cheap labor in Southeast Asia would not have been a factor and they would have invested immediately in China.

On the other hand, sentiment clearly plays at least a small role in ethnic Chinese investment. Some analysts take a strong position in this regard. For example, Roy Hofheinz Jr. and Kent Calder claim the overseas Chinese "are willing to take a smaller piece of the action in order to benefit the motherland," while John Garver claims the "Overseas Chinese" invested in China for patriotic reasons.[75] However, these judgments were made before the massive investments of the 1990s. Although investing for sentimental purposes may occur with a limited number of investors, it is no longer possible on a widespread basis. It is ironic that the tone of Beijing's appeals to ethnic Chinese for investment would lead one to suspect that ethnic Chinese invest mainly out of sentiment. However, this type of suspicion is dangerous for Southeast Asia's ethnic Chinese because it questions their belonging in Southeast Asia.

Nevertheless, there are emotional awards for investing. For example, Victor Fung, a Hong Kong executive whose family has invested in his ancestral village and donated schools, describes a visit to China: "About a year ago, I was greeted by several hundred schoolchildren, a parade, firecrackers. It was like a royal visit. It was quite an emotional experience. You can multiply this story 10,000 times."[76] Quek Peck Lim, head of research at Morgan Grenfell Asia Securities in Singapore, describes similar experiences for Southeast Asian Chinese: "Coming home is immensely important. The overseas Chinese have had to battle everybody and everything. They have had to change their names, their whole cultural style. Imagine what it means for them to be able to return to whatever dirt town in China and be proclaimed the tycoon of the town, the local boy made good."[77]

Chinese officials also acknowledge the role of sentiment in investments by ethnic Chinese. An official in Fujian province emphasized that at the beginning of the reform period sentimental attractions had some impact in attracting investors. However, with the passing of time, more attention was paid to business aspects. In line with this, early in the reform period investments were often made in ancestral hometowns. The hometown was the locus of sentiment and relatives could be used to manage an enterprise.[78]

Investing in ancestral hometowns illustrates the complexity of separating the profit motive from issues of sentiment. Any emotion toward China that might be held by ethnic Chinese entrepreneurs is directed mainly toward the ancestral hometown rather than China as a whole. This is illustrated most clearly in the links established between Chinese voluntary associations in Asia (based on dialect, surname, or ancestral area) and the Chinese hometowns connected with such associations. Thus, investing in hometowns may indicate a degree of sentiment.[79] However, investing in ancestral homes can have sound economic reasons too, such as good connections with officials, a knowledge of conditions, an understanding of the dialect, favorable investment policies, or relatives to manage an enterprise or help with the work.

There is evidence of such investments in hometowns. For example, Lin Jinzhi reported that 80 percent to 90 percent of foreign invested enterprises in Guangdong's Chaozhou–Shantou area are from ethnic Chinese who have roots in that region. The figure rises to 90 percent for the Shantou Special Economic Zone. Lin interprets this as providing evidence of the overseas Chinese love of China.[80] Li, Lin, and Cai discuss investments by ethnic Chinese from throughout Asia (including Hong Kong) in locations that are the traditional hometowns of the overseas Chinese. Thus, for example, Guangdong's Five Cities, Fujian's Quanzhou City, Fujian's Jinjiang county, Fujian's Anxi county, Zhejiang's Yongjia county, as well as other areas of historically high emigration are now experiencing rapid gains in employment and income due to investments from ethnic Chinese whose families came from those places. All of these regions historically have been very poor but now have greatly improved standards of living.[81] In a survey reported by the government of Australia, relatively high percentages of investors in Guangdong and Fujian provinces had roots in the local area.[82]

Liem Sioe Liong and Djuhar Sutanto (Lin Wenjing) are two tycoons who have invested heavily in their ancestral town of Fuqing. When asked to characterize the investments, Mr. Sutanto stated, "I did not do this for profit. . . . Our aim was to do something for our home town, provide work for its people and raise living standards" by providing infrastructure and employment. If indeed this statement is true, this type of investment is affordable by only a few. Moreover, direct investment that should in reality be characterized as a donation may open the door for lucrative future investments by creating goodwill with officials.[83]

Instances of investment in hometowns indicate that more than just a profit versus sentiment calculation is at work when making investments in China. Dialect and locality ties, family links, as well as concern for the lives of those "left behind" also play a role when investors decide where to locate their enterprises, involving both the profit motive and emotion. It is also at this level that appeals by officials are made most effectively.

REMITTANCES, DONATIONS, AND ADVISING

The previous chapter demonstrated how remittances have been important to China throughout the past century, especially for balancing its foreign exchange accounts. Remittances also played an important role at the beginning of the reform period. The Chinese government reinstated its preferential policies for domestic overseas Chinese in order to attract funds from abroad after its renewed focus on overseas Chinese work began in 1978. As a result, the bank accounts of those with overseas relatives grew and visiting family members spent money in China and carried in consumer goods. In 1979, Fujian received much more in remittances than in investments.

However, during the reform period the character and importance of remittances changed. Officially recorded remittances that pass through banks have fallen. From an all-time high of over $715 million in 1979, remittances dropped steadily to only $95 million in 1988, the lowest level since 1962. There were two important reasons for this drop in remittances. First, as a result of reforms there have been a host of new channels for remittances, whereas in the past remittances were required to go through banks or government offices. Second, China's distorted official exchange rate throughout the 1980s made exchanges on the black market much more attractive than official channels. Thus throughout the 1980s actual remittances were much higher than statistics indicate.[84]

Nevertheless, remittances have decreased in importance throughout the reform period. Remittances used to be a major source of foreign exchange and were necessary for balancing China's trade deficits. Currently they constitute only a small fraction of the amount of hard currency brought in by trade and investment in China and are relatively insignificant from a macroeconomic perspective. Much of the money that is sent from abroad goes into charitable projects in ancestral hometowns, such as the building of hospitals and schools. In short, the conditions that made remittances so important in the past no longer exist in China today.

However, remittances still play a major role in certain regions of China. For instance, residents of the western Pearl River delta in Guangdong can be divided into three categories: those without overseas relatives, those with distant relatives overseas, and those with close relatives overseas. Those without relatives tend to be laborers. Those with distant relatives generally receive remittances, using them to establish enterprises and become deeply involved in the local economy. Those with close relatives abroad live well due to the remittances they receive. Nevertheless, many in this group expect to someday leave China, and therefore avoid investing in the local economy.[85]

Charitable donations by ethnic Chinese continue to play a role in the reform period too, although it is again difficult to separate Southeast Asian money from that of Hong Kong or Taiwan. Donations are usually made to ancestral hometowns and thus tend to be concentrated in southern China, although contributions also go to high-profile national projects such as flood relief. At times such donations may be difficult to distinguish from investments. At other times they lay the groundwork for more attractive investments in that they make a favorable impression on local officials or create necessary infrastructure. Usually donated money goes to build schools, hospitals, roads, bridges, or temples.

For example, ethnic Chinese, both individuals and voluntary associations, have contributed money for universities in Guangdong's Five Cities area, Shandong province, Shantou, and Hainan province. Hong Kong's Li Ka-shing has been a very important donor to his hometown of Shantou, building a university, church, bridge, and hospital.[86] Thai Chinese built the library at Hainan University. In addition, ethnic Chinese have donated money for various projects in Guangdong's Taishan, including a middle school addition, a library, a museum, a science institute, an educational television station, a television university, and an amusement center.[87] Substantial donations have also been made in Fujian's Jinjiang county and Zhejiang's Yongjia county for schools, roads, bridges, and other facilities.

Statistics from 25 ethnic Chinese hometowns and counties in Fujian indicate that from 1977 to 1982, overseas Chinese donated over 53 million yuan for schools, building 450,000 square meters' worth of classrooms.[88] More recent figures are noteworthy as well. Xinhua reported that by the end of 1992, overseas Chinese had donated 9 billion yuan to Guangdong for building 1,353 hospital rooms, 15,000 classrooms, 470,000 meters of floor space for kindergartens, 360,000 square meters of floor space for cinemas and libraries, over 15,000 kilometers of highways, and 3,381 bridges.[89] In 1997, it was reported that donations from overseas Chinese totaled $3.6 billion from 1979 to 1995.[90]

Thus, some ethnic Chinese entrepreneurs return a portion of their profits to their ancestral hometowns as donations. Although with China's rapid economic growth donations do not play a critical role in China's overall development, they are important in specific localities. Moreover, they raise the status of the donor and help smooth the way for future business deals.

Finally, some of Southeast Asia's ethnic Chinese have also served as economic and political advisors to the Chinese government. Advisors are not nearly as powerful as those overseas Chinese who served the Qing dynasty early in the twentieth century. Nevertheless, they provide outside information to China's policymakers and are important symbolically.

Dhanin Chearavanont has served as an advisor on Hong Kong affairs. Several Singaporeans have been named as advisors to China as well, most notably former first deputy prime minister Goh Keng Swee, named as advisor to China's special economic zones. Other Singaporeans include Member of Parliament (MP) Fong Sip Chee and former chief planner of Singapore Liu Thai Ker (advisors to Tianjin), and MP and trade unionist John Chen (advisor to Chengdu). Malaysia's Robert Kuok was involved in discussions with China's president Jiang Zemin on the appointment of Hong Kong's first chief executive. In these roles ethnic Chinese have moved from the economic sector to the explicitly political realm.

CONCLUSIONS

This chapter has examined China's policies toward ethnic Chinese since the end of the Cultural Revolution as well as the response of Asia's ethnic Chinese. Although the investments of Southeast Asia's Chinese are difficult to measure and are overshadowed by those of Hong Kong, they have played an important role in the early years of reform in testing the waters, establishing contacts, and proving that entrepreneurs can make money in China. These investments increased in the 1990s as China's economic environment improved and its relations with Southeast Asia got better, although the Asian economic crisis has reduced investment in China from all of Asia's ethnic Chinese and will continue to do so for the foreseeable future.

There is evidence that Beijing may now be reducing the priority it gives to efforts to attract ethnic Chinese investments due to the character of such investments in terms of scale and technology. (This will be discussed in the next chapter.) Nevertheless, China has by no means retreated in its appeals to ethnic Chinese around the world to help develop China economically. In fact, China is becoming bolder as its power grows. Thus, in sending Chinese New Year's greetings to ethnic Chinese outside the mainland, former premier Li Peng proclaimed, "The Chinese people are a great nation." Li continued by expressing a belief that "the channels of reporting must be extended so as to let the overseas Chinese and people of the Chinese origin feel the care and expectations of their motherland and the people."[91] Li's language expresses the continuing bond the

Chinese government feels with ethnic Chinese abroad, a bond that the Chinese government is not likely to sever.

NOTES

1. In the context of China's policies and institutions, "overseas Chinese" generally refers to both Chinese citizens and Chinese with local citizenship.

2. The editorial is in *Peking Review*, 20 January 1978, 14–16; Liao's remarks are in "Text of Liao Cheng-Chih Overseas Chinese Policy Article," Peking NCNA in English (4 January 1978), Foreign Broadcast Information Service (hereafter FBIS) *DR/PRC*, 5 January 1978, E11–E21.

3. For analyses of China's policy at this time, see Wang Gungwu, "China and the Region in Relation to Chinese Minorities," *Contemporary Southeast Asia* 1, no. 1 (May 1979): 36–50; and C. Y. Chang, "Overseas Chinese in China's Policy," *China Quarterly*, no. 82 (June 1980): 281–303.

4. Lien Kuan, "History of Overseas Chinese and Their Glorious Tradition," *Peking Review*, 26 May 1978, 12–17.

5. Suzanne Ogden, *China's Unresolved Issues: Politics, Development, and Culture*, 2nd ed. (Englewood Cliffs, N.J.: Prentice-Hall, 1992).

6. Chi-ming Hou, *Foreign Investment and Economic Development in China 1840–1937* (Cambridge, Mass.: Harvard University Press, 1965), 134.

7. Stephen Fitzgerald, "Peking's New Pull at the Purse-Strings," *Far Eastern Economic Review* (hereafter *FEER*), 16 June 1978, 19–20.

8. Xiangming Chen, "China's Growing Integration with the Asia-Pacific Economy," in *What Is in a Rim? Critical Perspectives on the Pacific Region Idea*, ed. Arif Dirlik (Boulder: Westview Press, 1993), 102.

9. For an overview of Chinese institutions and policies regarding the overseas and ethnic Chinese, see Fang Xiongpu, "Haiwai qiaotuande fazhan yanbian ji qi xiangguan zhengce" ("The Development and Changes in Overseas Chinese Mass Organizations and Related Policies"), *Huaqiao huaren lishi yanjiu* (*Overseas Chinese and Ethnic Chinese Historical Research*), 1997, no. 1:8–11.

10. "Fujian Federation of Overseas Chinese Meets," Fuzhou Fujian Provincial Service in Mandarin (23 April 1981), FBIS *DR/China*, 24 April 1981, O4.

11. Li Guoliang, Lin Jinzhi, and Cai Renlong, *Huaqiao huaren yu Zhongguo geming he jinshi* (*Overseas Chinese/Ethnic Chinese and Chinese Revolution and Construction*), ed. Lin Jinzhi (Fuzhou: Fujian renmin chubanshe, 1993), 493–95.

12. "Zhejiang Work with Overseas Chinese Viewed," Beijing Xinhua in English (31 January 1996), FBIS, 31 January 1996.

13. "Overseas Chinese Affairs Departments Role Viewed," Beijing Zhongguo Xinwen in Chinese (3 May 1993), FBIS *DR/China*, 18 May 1993, 24; and "Overseas Chinese Enterprises Develop in Guangzhou," Beijing Xinhua in English (9 December 1992), FBIS *DR/China*, 10 December 1992, 45.

14. "Qian Qichen Addresses Overseas Association Meeting," Beijing Xinhua Domestic Service in Chinese (18 February 1994), FBIS *DR/China*, 28 February 1994, 32–33.

15. "1996 nian guonei baokan youguan huaqiao huaren yanjiu wenzhang yao mu" ("Selected Contents of Articles on Overseas Chinese Studies Published in Domestic Newspapers and Periodicals in 1996"), *Huaqiao huaren lishi yanjiu* (*Overseas Chinese and Ethnic Chinese Historical Research*), 1997, no. 2:75–80.

16. See Hong Liu, "Old Linkages, New Networks: The Globalization of Overseas Chinese Voluntary Associations and Its Implications," *China Quarterly*, no. 155 (September 1998): 595–98.

17. For details, see Lu Shouwei, "Jiceng qiaowu gongzuo yu yinjin qiao zi" ("Grassroots Overseas Chinese Affairs Work and the Importation of Overseas Chinese Capital"), *Huaqiao yu huaren* (*The Chinese Overseas*), 1995, no. 2:26–27, 33; and Zhang Xiaowei, "Bawo 'wu ge zhuanwan,' fazhan qiao xiang youshi" ("Grasp the 'Five Turns,' Develop the Advantage of Overseas Chinese Hometowns"), *Huaqiao yu huaren* (*The Chinese Overseas*), 1995, no. 2: 14–16.

18. "Guangdong's Ren Zhongyi Speaks on Overseas Chinese," Guangzhou Guangdong Provincial Service in Mandarin (2 August 1981), FBIS *DR/PRC*, 5 August 1981, P2.

19. "*Renmin Ribao* Editorial," Beijing *Renmin Ribao* in Chinese (3 January 1983), FBIS *DR/China*, 5 January 1983, K21–K22.

20. "Fujian Governor on Overseas Chinese Investment," Beijing in Mandarin to Taiwan (18 October 1986), FBIS *DR/China*, 20 October 1986, O3.

21. " 'Piece of the Motherland' Sales Campaign Begins," Beijing Xinhua in English (26 April 1993), FBIS *DR/China*, 27 April 1993, 25.

22. "Qian Qichen at Forum on Overseas Chinese Affairs," Beijing Xinhua in Chinese (19 June 1998), FBIS, 19 June 1998.

23. "Jiang Calls on Consulate Personnel, Overseas Chinese," Beijing Xinhua in Chinese (26 November 1997), FBIS, 26 November 1997.

24. For details regarding this debate, see Guo Liang, "Zhan hou Dongnan Ya huaren rentong, tonghua wenti yanjiude jizhong guandian" ("Some Views on the Identification and Assimilation of Ethnic Chinese in Postwar Southeast Asia"), *Nanyang wenti yanjiu* (*Southeast Asian Affairs*), 1992, no. 2:18–19; and Mu-Heng Wang, "Current Situation of Southeast Asian Studies in Mainland China," *RIAD Bulletin* 1 (March 1992): 6–7. The author is also indebted to scholars interviewed at the Center for Southeast Asian Studies, Xiamen University, in 1994.

25. Lin Jinzhi, "Haiwai huaren zai Chao-Shan diqude touzi" ("Overseas Ethnic Chinese Investment in the Chaozhou-Shantou Area"), *Nanyang wenti yanjiu* (*Southeast Asian Affairs*), 1994, no. 1: 20–21, 26.

26. Xiang Dayou, "Lun Zhongguo gaige kaifang yu hua zitou xiang qushi" ("On the Reform and Opening of China and the Investment Inclination of Overseas Chinese"), *Bagui qiao shi* (*Overseas Chinese History of Bagui*), 1994, no. 1:1–3, 5.

27. Sources on the preferences given to domestic overseas Chinese include "*Hsin Wan Pao* Reports on Overseas Chinese Affairs Policy," Hong Kong *Hsin Wan Pao* in Chinese (10 May 1978), FBIS *DR/PRC*, 11 May 1978, N4–5; "Privileges of Overseas Chinese Being Restored," Paris AFP in English, FBIS *DR/PRC*, 18 August 1978, E1; and Yuen-Fong Woon, "Family Strategies of Prosperous Peasants in an Emigrant Community in South China," *Canadian Journal of Developmental Studies* 15, no. 1 (1994): 21–22.

28. "Hu Yaobang Speaks at Overseas Chinese Meeting," Beijing Xinhua Domestic Service in Chinese (22 April 1984), FBIS *DR/China*, 23 April 1984, K8.

29. "Xiang Nan on Fujian Policies for Overseas Chinese," Hong Kong *Wen Wei Po* in Chinese (1 November 1981), FBIS *DR/China*, 5 November 1981, O2.

30. Guangzhou shi dui wai jingji maoyi weiyuanhui and Guangzhou shi zhengce yanjiushi (Guangzhou City Foreign Economy and Trade Commission and the

Guangzhou City Policy Research Office), *Guangzhou touzi zhinan* (*Guide to Investment in Guangzhou*), undated.

31. Zhuhai City International Communication Office, *Zhuhai Special Economic Zone of China*, October 1983, 12.

32. "Overview of Investment Incentives," *China Business Review*, May/June 1986, 20–23.

33. "Guangdong Attracts Overseas Chinese Investors," Beijing Xinhua in English (8 May 1998), FBIS, 8 May 1998.

34. Robert S. Ross, "China and the Ethnic Chinese: Political Liability/Economic Asset," in *ASEAN and China: An Evolving Relationship*, ed. Joyce K. Kallgren, Noordin Sopiee, and Soedjati Djiwandono (Berkeley: Institute of Southeast Asian Studies, University of California, 1988), 168. Not surprisingly, there are also preferences given to Taiwanese investors. See Eliza Rosenbluth, "Preferential Treatment for Taiwan Investors," *China Business Review*, September/October 1990, 36–37.

35. Ezra Vogel, *One Step Ahead in China: Guangdong under Reform* (Cambridge, Mass.: Harvard University Press, 1989), 350.

36. Shen Hongfang, "Jiushi niandai Dongnan Ya guojia yu woguode waizi touzi huanjing bijiao" ("A Comparison of the Foreign Investment Environments of China and the Southeast Asian States in the 1990s"), *Nanyang wenti yanjiu* (*Southeast Asian Affairs*), 1994, no. 2:54–55.

37. "Fujian Curbs Abuses Against Overseas Chinese," Beijing Zhongguo Xinwen She in Chinese (21 August 1983), FBIS *DR/China*, 6 September 1983, O1.

38. "Seminar Discusses Rights of Overseas Chinese," Beijing Zhongguo Xinwen She in English (15 December 1994), FBIS *DR/China*, 16 December 1994, 26.

39. See Sheila Tefft, "Repatriates Transform Economy, Yet Endure Persistent Resentment," *Christian Science Monitor*, 30 March 1994, 11–12; and "NPC to Safeguard Rights of Returnees," *China Daily*, 5 June 1996, 1.

40. David Yen-ho Wu, "The Construction of Chinese and Non-Chinese Identities," *Daedalus* 120, no. 2 (Spring 1991): 163.

41. This is described by Leo Suryadinata, *China and the ASEAN States: The Ethnic Chinese Dimension* (Singapore: Singapore University Press, 1985), 3–4.

42. Ku Ch'ang-yung, "Cong zhengzhi jingji cengmian lun Zhongguode Dongnan Ya huaqiao zhengce" ("Economic and Political Perspectives on Peking's Policy Regarding Overseas Chinese in Southeast Asia"), *Zhongguo dalu yanjiu* (*Mainland China Studies*) 37, no. 9 (September 1994): 16.

43. "China's Policy is Open, Aboveboard, Consistent," *Peking Review*, 7 July 1978, 24.

44. "State Council Official Explains Policy on Overseas Chinese," Peking NCNA in English (5 April 1978), FBIS *DR/PRC*, 6 April 1978, E7.

45. "Liao Chengzhi Addresses New Year Message," L2.

46. See Michael Vatikiotis, Matt Forney, and Ben Dolven, "Compatriot Games," *FEER*, 20 August 1998, 20–23.

47. David Bonavia, "The Overseas Chinese," *FEER*, 16 June 1978, 18.

48. Wang, "China and the Region," 40.

49. See Wang Gungwu, "Upgrading the Migrant: Neither *Huaqiao* nor *Huaren*," in *The Last Half Century of Chinese Overseas*, ed. Elizabeth Sinn (Hong Kong: Hong Kong University Press, 1998), 26.

50. "Overseas Chinese Policy 'Will Never Be Changed,' " Beijing Domestic Service in Mandarin (17 July 1989), FBIS *DR/China*, 18 July 1989, 26.

51. "Report Details Investments by Overseas Chinese," Beijing Xinhua in English (7 October 1989), FBIS *DR/China*, 19 October 1989, 42; and "New Measures to Protect Overseas Chinese Investors," Beijing Xinhua in English (17 March 1999), FBIS, 17 March 1999.

52. East Asia Analytical Unit, Department of Foreign Affairs and Trade, Commonwealth of Australia, *Overseas Chinese Business Networks in Asia* (Canberra: Commonwealth of Australia, 1995), 197–98.

53. Lin Jinzhi, "1979–1992 nian haiwai huaren zai Zhongguo dalu touzide xianzhuang ji qi jinhou fazhan qushi" ("The Current Situation and Future Trends in the Investments of Overseas Ethnic Chinese on the Chinese Mainland, 1979–1992"), *Huaqiao huaren lishi yanjiu* (*Overseas Chinese and Ethnic Chinese Historical Research*), 1993, no. 1:1–4, 12.

54. Xiang Dayou, "Lun Zhongguo gaige," 6; and "The Overseas Chinese: A Driving Force, *Economist*, 18 July 1992, 24.

55. George Hicks and J.A.C. Mackie, "A Question of Identity," *FEER*, 14 July 1994, 47; and "Don't Question Loyalty of Overseas Chinese: MCA," *Straits Times* (Singapore), 8 August 1994, 21.

56. For example, one estimate of Indonesian investment in China in 1994 was over $800 million, seven times greater than the official figure. See Sheila Tefft, "Chinese Investors Face Scrutiny as Indonesia Vies in Asian Economy," *Christian Science Monitor*, 6 April 1994, 13.

57. Suryadinata, *China and ASEAN*, 95.

58. Lin Jinzhi, "Haiwai huaren zai Chao-Shan," 19–21. See also Huang Qiwen, "Shantou kai bu yilaide huaqiao touzi yu jinhoude yin zi" ("Overseas Chinese Investment in Shantou after Its Opening and Its Future Attraction of Investment"), *Huaqiao yu huaren* (*Chinese Overseas*) 1996, no. 2: 40–43.

59. Bonavia, "Investing," 50–51.

60. See Colin Galloway, "Fall in FDI Tests Economic Resolve," *South China Morning Post* (Hong Kong), 10 June 1999, Internet edition; "Singapore Direct Investment Jumps 30.4 Percent," *Inside China Today*, 15 February 1999, Internet edition; and official Chinese statistics.

61. "Number Crunching," *Business China*, 2 May 1994, 6.

62. "China Promises Measures to Improve Investment Environment," *Inside China Today*, 29 March 1999, Internet edition.

63. Richard Pomfret, *Investing in China: Ten Years of the Open Door Policy* (Ames: Iowa State University Press, 1991), 108–13.

64. Lynn Pan, *Sons of the Yellow Emperor: A History of the Chinese Diaspora* (Boston: Little, Brown, 1990), 372.

65. Wang Gungwu, "Greater China and the Chinese Overseas," *China Quarterly*, no. 136 (December 1993): 930–31; Rajeswary Ampalavanar-Brown, "Overseas Chinese Investments in China—Patterns of Growth, Diversification, and Finance," *China Quarterly*, no. 155 (September 1998): 612; and Lin Wuguang, "Malaixiya huashang dui Zhongguo dalu touzide xianzhuang yu tedian" ("Investment on the Mainland of China by Overseas Chinese Businessmen in Malaysia and Its Characteristics"), *Huaren jingji nianjian 1997–1998* (*Yearbook of the Huaren Economy 1997–1998*) (Beijing: Shehui kexue wenxian chubanshe, 1997), 286–87.

66. Xu Jiatun, *Xu Jiatun Xianggang huiyilu* (*Xu Jiatun's Memoir of His Hong Kong Experience*), vol. 1 (Taipei: Lianhe bao, 1993), especially 240–43.

67. For accounts of CP, see Yong Pow Ang, "An Ongoing Romance," *Singapore Business*, February 1992, 44–50; "The Growth Machine," *Asiaweek*, 23 June 1993, 54–58; Michael Vatikiotis, "Trouble at the Mill," *FEER*, 28 May 1998, 60–62; Ampalavanar-Brown, "Overseas Chinese"; and Dan Biers and Michael Vatikiotis, "Back to School," *FEER*, 8 April 1999, 10–14.

68. For details on the Lippo Group, see "Enter the Lippo-potamus," *Economist*, 16 July 1994, 61–62; Jay Solomon, "Happy at Home," *FEER*, 3 April 1997, 42–44; and Salil Tripathi, "Banking on Recovery," *FEER*, 18 June 1998, 55–56.

69. For details on the Salim Group, see James McGregor, "Overseas Chinese Quietly Invest at Home," *Wall Street Journal*, 16 June 1992, A10; Gary Silverman, "Almost Family," *FEER*, 17 November 1994, 85–86; Dorinda Elliott, "The Fall of Uncle Liem," *Newsweek*, 15 June 1998, 20; Rigoberto Tiglao and Kathy Wilhelm, "Blue-Chip Ambitions," *FEER*, 17 December 1998, 10–13; and Mark Landler, "An Asian Empire Still on a Seesaw," *New York Times*, 28 April 1999, Internet edition.

70. For a list of Southeast Asian entrepreneurs who have invested in China and a discussion of their characteristics, see Leo Suryadinata, "China's Economic Modernization and the Ethnic Chinese in ASEAN: A Preliminary Study," in *Southeast Asian Chinese and China*, ed. Leo Suryadinata (Singapore: Times Academic Press, 1995), 202–4, 209–15.

71. For details of the debate in China on whether the motivation of overseas Chinese in investing in China is profit or "patriotism," see Li Guoliang, "Chinese Scholars' Studies on the Changes of Overseas Chinese and Their Descendants after World War II," *RIAD Bulletin*, no. 2 (March 1993): 129–31.

72. Carl Goldstein, "Full Speed Ahead," *FEER*, 21 October 1993, 67.

73. Chang Pao-Min, "China and Southeast Asia: The Problem of a Perception Gap," *Contemporary Southeast Asia* 9, no. 3 (December 1987): 190–91.

74. Vogel, *One Step*, 158, 241.

75. Roy Hofheinz Jr. and Kent E. Calder, *The Eastasia Edge* (New York: Basic Books, 1982), 201; and John W. Garver, *Foreign Relations of the People's Republic of China* (Englewood Cliffs, N.J.: Prentice-Hall, 1993).

76. Paul Blustein, "Forging 'Greater China' " *Washington Post*, 1 December 1992, A1, A30.

77. Michael Selwyn, "Southeast Asian Chinese Head for Home," *Asian Business*, April 1993, 25.

78. Interview by author, 1994.

79. See, for instance, Li Hongjie, "Haiwai Anxiren dui jiaxiang jianshede gongxian" ("The Contribution by the Overseas Anxi People for their Hometown Construction"), *Bagui qiao shi* (*Overseas Chinese History of Bagui*), 1997, no. 3:44–48.

80. Lin Jinzhi, "Haiwai huaren zai Chao-Shan," 19–21.

81. Li, Lin, and Cai, *Huaqiao huaren yu Zhongguo*, 525–37. See also General Office, Jiangmen People's Government, "A Booming Hometown of Overseas Chinese," *China's Foreign Trade*, June 1990, 51.

82. East Asia Analytical Unit, *Overseas Chinese*, 226–28.

83. Mark O'Neill, "Overseas Fortunes Help Out the Motherland," *South China Morning Post* (Hong Kong), 6 April 1997, 4.

84. Lin Jinzhi, "Qiaohui dui Zhongguo jingji fazhan yu qiaoxiang jianshede zuoyong" ("The Role of Remittances of Overseas Chinese in the Economic Development of China"), *Nanyang wenti yanjiu (Southeast Asian Affairs)*, 1992, no. 2:29–32.

85. Graham E. Johnson and Woon Yuen-Fong, "The Response to Rural Reform in an Overseas Chinese Area," *Modern Asian Studies* 31, no. 1 (1997): 47–51.

86. Jasper Becker, "Born to be the King of Shantou," *South China Morning Post* (Hong Kong), 19 June 1997, 21.

87. Laura Li, trans. Brent Heinrich, "Taishan: Wellspring of the Chinese Diaspora," *Sinorama*, July 1994, 30.

88. Yu Chung-Hsun, "Xin Zhongguo jingji quan yu huan Taipingyang jingji" ("The New Chinese Economic Groupings and Links with the Pacific Economy"), in *Huaqiao huaren wenti lunwenji (Essays on the Question of Overseas Chinese and Ethnic Chinese)*, ed. Chen Bisheng (Nanchang: Jiangxi renmin chubanshe, 1989), 148–49.

89. "Guangdong Receives Aid from Overseas 'Compatriots,'" Beijing Xinhua in English (28 October 1993), FBIS *DR/China*, 2 November 1993, 67.

90. "Law to Regulate Donation Process," *Beijing Review*, 25–31 August 1997, 6.

91. "Li Peng Sends Greetings to Overseas Chinese," Beijing Xinhua in English (28 January 1995), FBIS *DR/China*, 30 January 1995, 20, 21.

The source of foreign investment in China is predominantly Asia's ethnic Chinese. Approximately 70 percent of foreign investment has come from ethnic Chinese, mostly from Hong Kong and Taiwan but also with a significant amount coming from Southeast Asia. Thus, China is a unique example of a country that has received large-scale foreign investment with the vast majority coming from newly industrialized or developing countries rather than large MNCs based in the West or Japan.

The fact that ethnic Chinese have been the predominant source of China's foreign investments has important economic implications. The benefits that China has enjoyed from foreign investment, including expanded trade, greater employment, and more productive capital, can be attributed primarily to ethnic Chinese investors. Thus, investment has improved the daily lives of numerous people, especially in poor towns and villages in coastal China that have boomed as a result of foreign contact. Ethnic Chinese firms tend to be smaller than most MNCs, with lower levels of technology, but have some advantages in terms of the ability to transfer technology and in the appropriateness of their technology for China. However, reliance on ethnic Chinese firms for a high percentage of capital has also made China vulnerable to shocks such as the Asian economic crisis.

Ethnic Chinese capital has been important in serving as a catalyst for investment in China. This catalyst role can be analyzed in terms of both scale and national origin of investments. Small-scale ethnic Chinese investment and assistance to relatives in China in the earliest days of reform stimulated larger-scale investments later. Ethnic Chinese investment also paved the way for investors from Japan and the West who saw that investing in China could be successful.

In regard to the first type of role, many of the earliest foreign investments in China consisted of assistance given by ethnic Chinese to relatives in China as a result of changed government policies. Thus, in regard to Guangdong, Ezra Vogel notes that "the improvement in the lot of those with overseas connections created conditions for the first wave of foreign capital investments in China since 1949." This wave consisted of compensation trade and processing agreements implemented in Guangdong throughout 1978 and 1979, with foreign investors providing equipment and receiving a share of the output. Numerous garment factories and other small workshops were also set up.[3] Thus, many small investors, making remittances and building businesses in the 1980s, provided the capital and gained the experience that led to the burst of investments in the 1990s.[4] This role as catalyst has been recognized by the Chinese government. An official of the State Council called ethnic Chinese and Chinese nationals who invested in China "pioneers" who built bridges linking China with foreign countries.[5]

One way ethnic Chinese have served as bridges is by being the first investors to deal with Chinese officials. In the early days of reform ethnic Chinese dealt with bureaucrats who were unfamiliar with the needs of entrepreneurs and helped familiarize them with market-oriented ways of doing business. Ethnic Chinese investors have also demonstrated that money could be made in China in spite of the lack of a coherent legal framework. As Wei and Frankel note, "If it were not for the overseas Chinese, the lack of property rights protection and contract laws could well have resulted in only a trickle of foreign investment going into China."[6] Furthermore, ethnic Chinese investors formed partnerships with Western companies that wished to invest in China. For example, Thailand's Charoen Pokphand has been linked with Nynex, an American telecommunications company, as well as Honda, Ford, and Heineken, while Coke turned to Malaysian Robert Kuok for assistance in expanding into China.

There are many reasons for Western firms to enter into partnerships with ethnic Chinese companies when seeking to invest in China. Doing business in China has numerous potential pitfalls. Problems include changing rules and laws, shifting tax policies, currency exchange controls, numerous fees at the local level, contract violations, corruption, bureaucratism, intellectual property violations, and the predominance of personal relations over rule by law.[7] Ethnic Chinese firms face the same problems, but are often better-equipped to deal with them. For this reason many have thrived in China and make good partners for Western firms.

One cultural trait shared by both mainlanders and the ethnic Chinese that smooths business transactions is a utilization of *guanxi*. Ethnic Chinese entrepreneurs have forged numerous connections among themselves and mainlanders that are crucial for doing business in China. Personal ties are so important because of the lack of a consistent legal system. Almost every aspect of joint ventures covered by Chinese law is open to bargaining and negotiation with local officials. In a study of joint ventures in China, Michael Roehrig notes, "The most important source of variation in bargaining between the joint venture and local policy implementers is the nature of the personal relationships that the enterprise has."[8] A senior executive of a large ethnic Chinese company makes a similar point: "Who I know in China and whether I have some network there is exclusive information. I hardly make it known even to my closest friends."[9]

Mainland officials make use of *guanxi* to attract ethnic Chinese investors. This is evident in the calling of ethnic Chinese "kin" and the appeals by hometown officials to those who have emigrated. Xu Jiatun further describes how Xinhua's Hong Kong office (the de facto representative of the PRC government in Hong Kong prior to 2000) used *guanxi* to persuade wealthy Southeast Asian entrepreneurs to invest in China.[10] In fact, Chinese law even makes provisions for the workings of *guanxi*. The "Provisional Preferential Measures in Guangzhou City for the Overseas Chinese, Hong Kong, and Macao Investments" stipulates that friends and relatives of investors have priority for employment in invested enterprises. In addition, ethnic Chinese investors can invite a mainland relative or friend to serve as legal representative.[11]

The process of establishing *guanxi* is difficult for Westerners because of cultural and language barriers.[12] Establishing *guanxi* also requires that a certain amount of time be spent in the country by executives. One particular challenge is understanding the boundaries of ethical behavior in establishing connections.

For example, it is customary for entrepreneurs in China to have closer contacts with local officials than what businesspersons in the United States are accustomed to. These contacts may include shared meals and occasional gift giving. However, knowing what the Chinese themselves consider to be crossing the line into corruption requires a great deal of experience.

As a result of being able to operate through *guanxi* networks, ethnic Chinese entrepreneurs are better able to operate in an environment such as China that does not have a well-developed legal framework. As Singapore's senior minister Lee Kuan Yew told delegates of the Second World Chinese Entrepreneurs Convention in 1993, *guanxi* is a major advantage for ethnic Chinese businesses, and "can make up for a lack in the rule of law, and transparency in rule and regulations. This *guanxi* capability will be of value for the next 20 years at least."[13] Similarly, a Hong Kong businessman explained, "Foreign investors ask me about the lack of a commercial-law system, but being Chinese, I can work on a handshake basis. In fact, I prefer that."[14] However, this latter viewpoint is not representative of all ethnic Chinese. Many, including Lee Kuan Yew, are striving to help China improve its legal environment. It is likely that as China's commercial law develops and transparency increases (a necessity if China joins the WTO) *guanxi* will become less important. Nevertheless, *guanxi* continues to be important to doing business.

Another advantage held by the most important ethnic Chinese entrepreneurs is access to top officials in China. For example, Hong Kong's Gordon Wu, head of Hopewell Holdings, is a member of the Chinese People's Political Consultative Conference and an advisor to the State Council. Thus, it was no surprise that Hopewell's CEPA was the first company given permission to build a power plant in China in 1994 after a long period when no approvals were given due to a dispute over rates of return. Another example is Malaysian Teh Soon Seng. His company, Granite Industries, was granted a twenty-year contract with Heilongjiang province to supply slot machines and assist in running parlors, the first slot machine contract in China. This came about through Teh Soon Seng's close ties with provincial officials. As a result of these connections, brokerage firm Credit Lyonnais told investors, "We highly rate the management's ability to secure similarly lucrative leisure-related businesses."[15]

The disadvantages that ethnic Chinese face can be seen as mirror images of the advantages. Mainlanders do not view ethnic Chinese as foreigners, making it easier for ethnic Chinese entrepreneurs to establish relations and do business in China. However, at the same time, the greater familiarity mainlanders feel with ethnic Chinese also makes it easier for the unscrupulous to abuse them. For instance, the Hong Kong government has documented numerous cases where businessmen with Hong Kong links have been detained in China without charges or have disappeared. Many more cases go unreported. Examples of reported cases include Lok Yuk-shing, a Hong Kong resident held for sixteen months in Inner Mongolia without charge regarding a business dispute and released in October 1999; Chong Kwee-sung, a Hong Kong resident and American citizen held in Henan province without charge for thirty months before being released; Philip Cheng, U.S.-passport holder and Hong Kong resident, also held without charge for seven months over a business dispute; and James Peng, an Australian kidnapped in Macao in 1993, held in China in spite of court rulings that there was insufficient evidence against him, eventually sentenced to a lengthy jail sentence and finally freed in 1999.[16] On occasion this type of mistreatment is also inflicted on non-Chinese businesspersons, although this is less common.[17]

Other areas in which ethnic Chinese investors contribute to China's development are technology and management. Technology is "a new and more efficient way of achieving gains that facilitate or even revolutionize economic developments." Broadly defined it embodies products, processes, and people, and thus includes hardware, software, and supporting activities.[18] One of the main reasons the Chinese government has sought foreign investment is to gain technology and management skills. Thus, China gives special tax advantages to those joint ventures that are "technologically advanced." However, technology transfer is a complicated process. Not only are there cultural and technical barriers to such transfers. Investing companies often attempt to protect their technology and prevent it from being transferred.[19] Thus, the Chinese government and investing firms may have different interests in regard to technology transfers. We look first at the engineering side of technology and then move on to management aspects.

From a theoretical viewpoint, ethnic Chinese firms should be in the best position to transfer technology to mainland joint ventures because cultural sensitivity plays a major role in the process of technology transfer. Holstius has found that "technology transfer is always a people-oriented phenomenon, and therefore cultures are an integral part of the transfer and its success depends on close interrelationships between the parties involved."[20] From a cultural perspective, cross-national joint ventures are actually the most difficult form of collaboration, as international technology transfers within joint ventures require adjustments among participants in terms of national, corporate, and business cultures. In many joint ventures, cultural conflicts over decision making, worker standards, and other areas have created serious problems. However, such problems are less likely among joint ventures in China set up by ethnic Chinese.

Nevertheless, in spite of lower cultural barriers, technology transfers from ethnic Chinese, whether from Hong Kong, Taiwan, or Southeast Asia, have so far been modest. Most ethnic Chinese investment in China has been relatively small-scale. For instance, while U.S., Japanese, and European investments have averaged $3.63 million per venture, Hong Kong investments have averaged $1.56 million while Singapore projects have averaged $2.14 million.[21] Oftentimes investments are in labor-intensive processing, assembly operations, or the service sector. For instance, Taiwan investments in China have been in labor-intensive light manufacturing, although there have been some large-scale projects. Hong Kong firms similarly moved labor-intensive operations for export into

China to escape high costs in Hong Kong, and have also been involved in infrastructure projects and real estate development. Malaysian, Singaporean, and Thai firms shifted low-end manufacturing jobs into China during the 1990s as a result of rising costs in those countries too, although Southeast Asian investors have differed from Taiwan and Hong Kong investors in that they tend to be motivated by consumer demand in China, invest more in primary industries and infrastructure, and are less involved in export processing.[22]

Small-scale investments have provided quick returns at relatively low risk, and have been well suited for China's environment, especially early in the reform period. Thus, one reason for the lower technical level of ethnic Chinese investments has been the economic climate on the mainland, with underdeveloped infrastructure and an abundance of cheap labor. As Ezra Vogel remarks regarding Guangdong, "As much as Guangdong wanted to acquire modern technology, the brutal fact was that its most promising niche in the world economy in the late 1980s was in labor-intensive industry."[23]

Another important reason for the lack of high-technology investment in China by ethnic Chinese companies is the technical limitations of such companies themselves. Although ethnic Chinese firms are advancing rapidly in some high-tech areas, notably computer technology, broadly speaking, they do not have a base in heavy industry, advanced electronics, or high-technology ventures. Kunio goes so far as to call industrialization in Southeast Asia, where Chinese capital predominates, inefficient and "technologyless."[24] Even in Singapore Chinese entrepreneurs have not developed a dynamic industrial capitalism. As *Singapore Business* stated bluntly, "Singaporeans have relatively little manufacturing know-how to offer" China.[25] As a result, observers such as Singapore's senior minister Lee Kuan Yew have stated that if China relies too heavily on ethnic Chinese capital, its growth will be slowed due to technological limitations.[26]

Nevertheless, technology has indeed been transferred to China through ethnic Chinese investments. One study found that while Hong Kong and Taiwanese technology invested in China is not much more sophisticated than mainland technology, it is much more likely to be transferred than the higher technology found in Japanese firms.[27] Moreover, the technological level of ethnic Chinese firms is growing over time. This is reflected in their investments in China, which in the 1990s began to lean more heavily toward capital- and research-intensive industries. For instance, projects in infrastructure have increased, such as Gordon Wu's power plants and expressway in Guangdong. Singapore firms have set up various factories in China to produce buses, holographs, helicopters, and repair aircraft. Thai firms have invested in petrochemicals, plastics, mobile phones, and agribusiness, while a Malaysian firm has invested in an engine plant. An increasing amount of Taiwan's information technology production is moving to the Chinese mainland as well. Nevertheless, the potential for expansion of ethnic Chinese-based high-technology investments is limited, at least in the short to medium run.

The issue of technology ultimately should be assessed in terms of the level of technology most appropriate for China. Chinese officials want the highest technology possible, but this level of technology may not always be most productive. According to the flying geese pattern of shifting comparative advantage, China's advantage will be in lower-technology industries.[28] However, China is a unique case in this regard. Although its standard of living resembles that of developing countries, China also has well-trained personnel and high technology in specific areas. One example is China's satellite-launching capabilities. China has been attempting to "catch up" with advanced technology since the Opium War and is unwilling to passively accept only middle-level technology.

Nevertheless, China may be best suited for investments utilizing middle-level technology. In a study of foreign investment in China, Pomfret concluded that joint ventures have experienced the most problems when they have been farthest from producing goods in which China has a comparative advantage, that is, when they have invested in capital-intensive heavy industry.[29] When U.S. firms offer their most advanced technologies for joint ventures with Chinese companies, the deals can fall through after Japanese or European firms offer lower technology at more competitive prices. When the highest technology is provided, it has sometimes proven too advanced to be effectively utilized.[30] Similarly, Tsang describes four major problems that make technology transfers to joint ventures in China difficult: a shortage of highly skilled personnel, a lack of managerial skills, high training costs, and government requirements to purchase locally produced components.[31] Thus, in spite of China's economic advances, it will be many years before it can compete on a broad scale in the realm of high-technology products.

Regarding management skills, ethnic Chinese companies are from a cultural perspective the optimal investors for passing management techniques to China. Lucian Pye lays the theoretical groundwork for this assertion by discussing the difficulty of cross-cultural learning. Technology transfer, broadly defined as including management, involves cultural diffusion, which is slow and exacts social costs. This is especially true in regard to superior-subordinate relations. People learn early in life the mechanisms for guarding against the powerful and extracting benefits from them. Such mechanisms are bound in culture. Attempts to change these norms and bring in new types of authority relations thus are often met with hostility, limiting the utility of cross-cultural models.[32]

Many ethnic Chinese, however, operate from a cultural context similar to that of mainland Chinese. The extent of the similarity, of course, depends on a variety of factors, including what country specific investors call home, the extent of their adoption of local cultures, and their Chinese language skills. Ethnic Chinese can bring effective management techniques and organizational skills that may differ in some respects from those of their Western counterparts and are more easily adopted on the mainland.[33] As one Chinese official asserted, it is easier to get used to ethnic Chinese management.[34] As a result, ethnic Chinese managers are highly sought after in China by all types of firms that have invested there.

In fact, the most important transfers of technology to China have been not in hardware but in software—management, marketing, and workplace techniques, transfers that are in some respects more difficult than hardware transfers. A recent example of this type of skills transfer is the large industrial park being built in Suzhou by a Singapore consortium. Both the Chinese and Singaporean sides have emphasized the transfer of public administration software that is taking place as Singapore trains Chinese managers and officials in running an industrial park. The fact that Singapore in frustration reduced its shares in that project in 1999 illustrates the difficulties involved.

An important issue regarding management is how transferable the management techniques of most ethnic Chinese investors are for use in running large-scale organizations like state-owned enterprises. Certainly some large ethnic Chinese firms utilize trained managers. However, many smaller companies are run in a paternalistic fashion, with tight control maintained by the family patriarch and company boss. The entrepreneurial thinking of small ethnic Chinese companies is difficult to combine with professional management.[35] Nevertheless, mainland enterprises can learn from small, patriarchal companies, especially in terms of attributes such as work ethic, flexibility, understanding markets, customer service, marketing, and networking.

Some analysts have lauded the role played by diaspora Chinese investment in China's economic transformation. For instance, Lever-Tracy et al. describe a synergy between diaspora entrepreneurs and China's smaller cities, townships, and villages, with diaspora entrepreneurs fueling China's export growth, teaching mainlanders successful business practices through their examples, and in general, driving China's economic growth. Large Western and Japanese MNCs, on the other hand, are said to focus on China's domestic market and have done comparatively little to develop China's economy, due partially to their bureaucratized nature.[36]

Nevertheless, there are disadvantages to China's heavy reliance on ethnic Chinese capital. The chapter has already touched on lower levels of technology and management techniques that may not be suitable for large-scale organizations. A second issue for China is that most of the low-wage assembly operations in Hong Kong and Taiwan have already moved to China. Thus, one-time gains have already been taken advantage of. A third problem is heightened vulnerability to economic shocks. This came to haunt China during the Asian economic crisis, when outward foreign investment from Asian countries fell sharply. Even before the crisis began, there was evidence that China's investment boom was slowing.[37] In 1998, foreign investment from Asian countries, much of which goes to China, fell by a quarter, with sharp declines registered by Taiwan, Hong Kong, Singapore, Malaysia, and Thailand. In 1999, investments from Taiwan, Hong Kong, and Macao dropped 6.2 percent, while investments from Asia fell 10.3 percent. China's overall foreign investments in 1999 fell almost 10 percent.

Even more ominous for China, it is estimated that 1998 saw a near-halving in the asset value of the top five hundred overseas Chinese companies.[38] This suggests that the main source of foreign investment in China will be unable to supply large-scale investment for the foreseeable future. Falling exports to Asia and concerns by foreign bankers over loan repayments by Chinese companies have compounded the problem, as has a serious slump in the township and village enterprises in China's countryside.

Therefore, some voices in China have called for limitations on ethnic Chinese investments and greater efforts to attract Western MNCs. Li Yanlong of China's Northeast Finance and Economics University argued forcefully in 1995 that too high a concentration in investments from Hong Kong, Macao, and Taiwan has led to overinvestment in certain fields, overconcentration in projects with small to medium amounts of capital, and relatively low levels of technology. In fact, he referred to capital from Hong Kong and Taiwan as "quasi-foreign capital," noting that others call it "national capital in a special form." Li stated that China needs to put greater effort into attracting capital from medium to large transnational corporations (TNCs) from developed countries. These TNCs will supply larger-scale investments with higher technology.[39] Shen Hongfang likewise argued that regulations that encourage investment by Hong Kong, Macao, Taiwan, and ethnic Chinese investors discourage investments from other countries, lead to small-scale and low-technology investments, and create competition for domestic enterprises. He, too, urged greater striving to expand the sources of foreign investment.[40]

In response to the Asian economic crisis, attempts to attract more American and European investments intensified. In 1998, Minister of Foreign Trade and Economic Cooperation Shi Guangsheng promised greater efforts to attract investors from developed nations. When China's prime minister visited the United States in 1999, Zhu Rongji tirelessly courted business executives. Even after the North Atlantic Treaty Organization (NATO) bombing of the Chinese embassy in Belgrade in 1999, Chinese officials strove to prevent Chinese protests from damaging the investment environment.

Evidence indicates that Western investment is beginning to play a more important role in China. U.S. direct investment in China has risen steadily, reaching approximately $4 billion in 1998 (although falling in 1999). Political and Economic Risk Consultancy Ltd. predicted in late 1998 that American and European firms would take over as the main source of foreign investment in the Greater China area from overseas Chinese and Japanese companies. There is clearly a great deal of potential, as U.S. Bureau of Economic Analysis figures show U.S. investments in China totaling only $6.3 billion in 1998 out of total worldwide investment from the United States, on a historical cost basis, of $980.6 billion.[41] (Chinese figures show $17.5 billion as of 1997.) In 1998, U.S. capital outflows to China were only 1.2 percent of total U.S. capital outflows. EU investments in China are similarly comparatively low. However, barriers to investment continue to plague Western companies, such as low profits in China and political tensions between China and the United States.

POLITICAL RAMIFICATIONS OF ETHNIC CHINESE INVESTMENT

Ethnic Chinese investment has also had effects on China's political realm. There are two broad points of view regarding the political consequences of ethnic Chinese investments. The first camp asserts that investments in China contribute to the development of rule by law and promote democracy. The second camp argues that ethnic Chinese investment in China leads to corruption and disintegration. Both positions will be characterized and evaluated.

Investments Contributing to Political Pluralism

Those who believe that investments in China help create a more open political environment, albeit in an indirect manner, start with the assertion that investment and trade contribute to development, and development leads to democracy. This is an argument often used by the American business community in fending off economic sanctions that would limit its dealings with China, and is also a pillar of the Clinton administration's policy of engagement. This logic is supported by research that demonstrates a high correlation between indicators of development and democracy. Seymour Martin Lipset, for example, argues, "that all the various aspects of economic development—industrialization, urbanization, wealth, and education—are so closely intertwined as to form one major factor which has the political correlate of democracy."[42] Samuel Huntington suggests that economic development has contributed to the most recent "third wave" of democratization by shaping people's values, increasing levels of education, and spreading greater resources among social groups, thus alleviating conflicts, opening societies to international influences, and expanding the middle class.[43]

There are several ways in which increased investment leading to greater wealth and development might work to promote democracy and rule of law. Investors in general, including many ethnic Chinese, insist on clear laws that will be enforced in a fair manner. Thus, in order to attract investments, especially those that are large and technologically sophisticated, China has had to improve on its record of rule by law, at least in the commercial sector, and there is some evidence that this is spilling over into the civil sector as well. For instance, the number of lawyers in China has expanded, and there are reports that criminal suspects will soon gain the right to remain silent during questioning and a jury system will be instituted in Chinese courts. Suits against both foreign and Chinese companies have increased, and ideological struggles have even gone to court. However, at the same time the application of law is uneven and power and money often trump the legal system. There continues to be in China a fundamental disconnect between party or personal rule and rule by law.

Another common argument is that increasing wealth leads to the creation of a civil society that will assert its own interests independent of the state. The formation of such a civil society is linked to the rise of a middle class and newly rich entrepreneurs who have sources of power outside the regime.[44] According to the theory, this new middle class will establish independent organizations that will demand their own space in society and press for the promotion of specific interests. Ethnic Chinese investments can play a part in this process, as managers rise to middle-class status and mainland relatives, business partners, and suppliers gain their own wealth, interests, and influence.

Another view is that ethnic Chinese themselves will present a model that ultimately results in the transformation of China's political-economic system. One version of this model is that of a rational authoritarian state that is well organized and well run, and promotes economic growth. Singapore's senior minister Lee Kuan Yew has forwarded this vision. In a speech to the first World Chinese Entrepreneurs Convention in Singapore in 1991, Lee proclaimed, "Successful Chinese communities overseas are a spur to action in China. China's leaders have been studying them." Lee also asserts that "just by being ourselves, making progress in our lives, Chinese abroad become a powerful pull factor in China's evolution forward. We are living examples of Chinese people, imbued with Chinese culture doing immensely better because we work under a different system."[45]

Taiwan also presents itself as an example to mainland China, although a more democratic model than what Lee Kuan Yew envisions. The Taiwan government has called for the economic and political transformation of the mainland, hoping the mainland will follow a path similar to that traversed by Taiwan itself. In fact, Taipei insists that reunification with the mainland can proceed only after democratization has occurred in the PRC. Taiwan has thus promoted people-to-people contacts with the mainland and allowed (or acquiesced to) major Taiwanese investment on the mainland in order to promote such transformation. Nevertheless, this vision is greatly constrained by Taiwan's reluctance to become economically dependent on the mainland as well as the aversion of China's leaders to such a transformation.

Ethnic Chinese as a Destabilizing Force

Another view on the role of ethnic Chinese has been put forward and is summarized by the *Christian Science Monitor*: "Western and Asian observers contend the growing overseas Chinese presence in China . . . feeds the growing instability in China. Their secretive, backroom dealings fuel corruption in the Communist Party and the government. And their privileged status makes them a target of local resentment."[46] This resentment was made manifest when a group of residents of Fuzhou, displaced from their homes by a 15-acre development by wealthy Chinese-Indonesian Liem Sioe Liong (Lin Shaoliang), protested the development every Sunday for four months, questioning why a foreigner should be allowed to develop prime property. Other complaints centered around Liem's acquisition of land at extremely low prices.[47] Surprisingly, even a Fuzhou official admitted that ethnic Chinese have obtained real estate at low prices and stricter rules are needed in this regard.[48]

In a similar vein, ethnic Chinese-capitalized enterprises, especially small firms funded from Hong Kong and Taiwan, are often charged with labor abuses. One observer has described endless Hong Kong- and Taiwan-owned textile, shoe, and toy factories located along the Guangdong and Fujian coasts, "extremely polluted, ugly, unsanitary, and unsafe." Teenagers work ten to fifteen hours, six to seven days a week in such factories, with numerous accidents, no leave or breaks, cramped living quarters, and poor food.[49] As a result, the central government has called for the unionization of workers at foreign-funded enterprises. However, there is unlikely to be any major changes, as both the central and local governments are eager to continue to attract investors.

Another charge brought against ethnic Chinese investors is that they foster regionalism. One analyst claims that Beijing must "continue dealing with the potential erosion of its power monopoly that may come from Taiwanese and *huaqiao* [overseas Chinese] investment throughout the PRC territory."[50] Since the beginning of the reform area, coastal regions in China have clearly benefited economically vis-à-vis central and western areas.[51] This was seen by reformers as an unavoidable consequence of opening up to the outside world. However, regionalism also manifests itself in provincial and local governments ignoring Beijing's wishes. For instance, local governments continue to offer unauthorized tax breaks to lure foreign investors. Ethnic Chinese may contribute to regionalism more than other investors because of their ties with local and provincial officials in China.

Assertions concerning the ethnic Chinese contributions to regionalism in China take place in a more general context of ambiguous central-provincial relations. Beijing has been at loggerheads with China's most prosperous provinces over the percentage of revenues that go to Beijing and the optimal rate of growth of their economies, as taxes given to Beijing by the provinces lag behind rates of economic growth and provincial officials refused to implement Beijing's austerity plans during times of economic overheating. In fact, the south of China has developed at such a rate that some think it is forming a separate identity, perhaps a "proto-community" that "reaches out from southern and coastal China to embrace the Chinese diaspora."[52] There has even been discussion of China dividing into parts or disintegrating.[53] As a result of ambiguous central-provincial relations, interprovincial relations have also suffered. Various provinces have exercised "economic warlordism," with localities guarding their producers with protectionist measures.

One sign of regional disparities in China is the uneven distribution of foreign investments. Since the early 1980s, approximately 90 percent of foreign investment has been directed toward coastal provinces. From 1983 to 1996, Guangdong received 30.2 percent of FDI, Jiangsu 11.3 percent, Fujian 10.4 percent,

Shanghai 8.6 percent, and Shandong 6.7 percent. In 1998, Guangdong was again the largest recipient of investment, receiving 26.4 percent of the national total, followed by Jiangsu, Shanghai, Fujian, and Liaoning. In fact, foreign investment in the central and western parts of China was actually down in 1998.[54] These differing investment levels are reflected in the fact that foreign capital contributes a large proportion of the coastal region's industrial output, reaching over 60 percent in Guangdong and 40 percent in Hainan and Shanghai. With the exception of Sichuan, the contribution of foreign capital in the central and western regions is negligible.

What has changed during the reform period is a decrease in the percentage of investments being attracted by Guangdong, although not the absolute dollar figures (see table 5.1). For instance, Guangdong received 58.4 percent of all foreign investment through 1987. By 1993, it received only 27.2 percent; 26.4 percent in 1998. Guangdong's drop in percentage of investments has been made up, however, by other coastal provinces. Especially noteworthy is the rise in the rankings of the Yangtze valley, especially Shanghai and Jiangsu, beginning around 1992. More northern coastal provinces are doing better as well. This shift to areas outside Guangdong reflects market forces, as costs rise in the south but the interior remains too remote, and government policy.

Furthermore, provincial statistics do not reveal the distribution of investment within a province. Even those provinces that have high levels of investment con-

Table 5.1
Utilized Direct Foreign Investment in Selected Coastal Provinces of China as a Percentage of National Total

Province	Through 1987	1995–97[a]
Guangdong	58.4%	26.2%
Fujian	5.6%	9.3%
Beijing	12.0%	3.2%
Tianjin	2.8%	4.7%
Shanghai	6.9%	8.4%
Jiangsu	1.7%	12.0%
Liaoning	2.7%	4.2%
Zhejiang	1.2%	3.2%
Shandong	1.9%[b]	6.1%

[a] Includes direct foreign investment and other.
[b] Percentage of total contracted investment.

Sources: Calculated from Richard Pomfret, *Investing in China* (Ames: Iowa State University Press, 1991), table 5.1, 75; and State Statistical Bureau, People's Republic of China, *Statistical Yearbook of China* (Beijing: China Statistical Publishing House, 1997 and 1998).

tain areas that lag behind due to geography, infrastructure, leadership, population characteristics, or migration patterns. For example, in Guangdong there are disparities between the coastal inner Pearl River delta area and the mountain counties, as well as between the eastern and western delta. Jiangsu provides another example, where in September 1991 Suzhou had 313 approved contracts for foreign investments while Huaiyin's total was only 12.[55] This disparity within and between provinces in investment rates leads to intense competition for investments. This is one reason why local governments often ignore central regulations establishing conditions for investments, tax rates, and other business-related stipulations.

Ethnic Chinese investments play some role in the regional character of foreign investment, due to the ethnic linkages that exist with southern China as well as the economic characteristics and stage of development of ethnic Chinese companies. Mainland writers emphasize the expanding geographic location of ethnic Chinese investments.[56] However, half of ethnic Chinese investments are located in Guangdong and Fujian, with most of the rest positioned in other coastal areas.[57] If the argument in the previous chapter was correct that connections, dialect, and hometown considerations play at least some role in ethnic Chinese decisions on where to invest, these factors favor the south. Qu and Green term these types of factors "social distance."[58] Geographic proximity to Hong Kong remains important for export-oriented companies, as do favorable government policies that have benefited the south since the institution of reforms. Western firms, by contrast, tend to be more interested in China's domestic market. Thus they emphasize technical and industrial capabilities, as well as population size, when deciding where to invest. As a consequence they tend to favor large cities and their investments are more widely dispersed.

Another way to assess the geographic impact of ethnic Chinese investments is to look not at their provincial location but at the size of the political units in which they are located. Some have argued that the key to ethnic Chinese success has been to minimize problems by investing away from established industrial areas, focusing instead on smaller political units with cooperative local officials.[59] Thus, ethnic Chinese have invested in small towns and villages where others have not, spreading the benefits of reform. Fujian and Guangdong have offered many such localities, as both provinces were economically neglected during the Maoist era due to security and ideological concerns.

In discriminating between ethnic Chinese investments, Southeast Asian projects have a slightly different character than those of Hong Kong and Taiwan. First, the original hometown areas of China, although overlapping, are not the same. Thus, for example, many Chinese in Thailand have ancestors from the Chaozhou–Shantou area, while other Southeast Asian Chinese have roots in Fujian. Thus, Southeast Asians have propensities to invest in ancestral hometowns that, although still in southern China, are different from the Guangdong hometowns of most Hong Kong Chinese. Second, Southeast Asian Chinese businesses have a different character from those of Taiwan or Hong Kong, being less involved in labor-oriented manufacturing for export. This tends to result in greater geographical dispersion in their investments. For example, Thailand's CP, which produces primarily agricultural products for the Chinese domestic market, has enterprises throughout China.

This chapter has discussed the argument that ethnic Chinese contribute to regionalism in China. Some go even further, asserting that the Chinese periphery (comprising Hong Kong, Taiwan, Singapore, and Southeast Asian Chinese) is now the driving force behind Chinese culture and economics, not the mainland itself. Harvard's Tu Wei-ming is a proponent of this view, claiming:

Although the phenomenon of Chinese culture disintegrating at the center and later being revived from the periphery is a recurring theme in Chinese history, it is unprecedented for the geopolitical center to remain entrenched while the periphery presents such powerful and persistent economic and cultural challenges. Either the center will bifurcate, or, as is more likely, the periphery will come to set the economic and cultural agenda for the center, thereby undermining its political effectiveness.[60]

As a result, Tu sees that the "Hong Kongization" of certain parts of China has occurred, while the "Taiwanization" and "Singaporization" of regions and social strata of China are also possible. This is another form of regionalism that is a consequence of a state being driven by the values and political/economic system of its diaspora. The main challenge to mainland intellectuals then "is not the modern West per se but the modern West mediated through industrial East Asia."[61]

This is an argument that does indeed have some evidence behind it. For example, during the spring and summer of 1989 many in Guangdong questioned the government's actions at Tiananmen. Beijing had to send envoys to Guangdong to negotiate with the army there at that time.[62] At a societal level, ethnic Chinese have pressured local officials into restoring lineage organizations that had earlier been disbanded by the government.[63] China has also taken many lessons from the ethnic Chinese in reforming its economy. Nevertheless, the issue of who is on the cutting edge of an ancient culture is extremely complex, and a longer historical perspective will be necessary for the issue to be properly evaluated.

Assessment

Stepping back, how can we assess the arguments that, first, ethnic Chinese investments indirectly contribute to pluralism in China and second, ethnic Chinese foster corruption and disintegration? Relevant to both questions is the fact that a major divide still separates ethnic Chinese ways of thinking and doing business from the state ideology of China. While the ethnic Chinese entrepreneur places high value on money-making, flexibility, personal initiative, property rights, and free enterprise, the Chinese state is still dedicated to a moral order dictated by the center. This is demonstrated by the way in which private businesses are treated in China. In spite of a constitutional amendment in 1999 declaring private business "an important component of the socialist market economy," mainland entrepreneurs face discrimination in securing loans, using land, and obtaining government contracts. They are also kept out of the Communist Party and are underrepresented in government institutions.[64] This divide focuses our question on the political effects of ethnic Chinese investment. Can the state manage the effects of investment? Will the state change to adjust to new realities, and if so, what will be the pace and direction of change?

In regard to whether ethnic Chinese investment indirectly promotes democratic change, there is evidence that foreign investment has indeed contributed to rationalization in China. In spite of the fact that ethnic Chinese are best equipped to develop channels of *guanxi*, many still have pressed for greater rule by law. This is especially true in the case of Singaporeans. Consequently, rule by law, although far from perfect, has advanced in China. Ethnic Chinese entrepreneurs have also taught mainlanders a great deal about market-oriented business methods, and through their initial investments have helped Chinese officials come to understand what environmental conditions are necessary for joint ventures to succeed.

We can go beyond rationalization to consider what relationship investments might have for greater pluralism. The thesis that increasing wealth contributes to a more open political system is powerful, even if the mechanisms through which this occurs have not been satisfactorily described. There is evidence that the family members in China of Chinese living abroad have, with the financial backing of their relatives, become an independent elite that is not beholden to cadres and the state. Such "domestic overseas Chinese" thus have an independent base of power and may contribute to the formation of a civil society.[65]

Looking more broadly, there has been a significant increase in nongovermental interest and social groups in China. In 1998, there were two hundred thousand officially registered organizations, with numerous unregistered groups as well. Although the Party attempts to organize and supervise such groups, and in fact plays an important role in maintaining the environment in which such associations develop, some are still pushing their own agendas. Included among these are entrepreneurs who have formed organizations to promote business interests and develop networks with other businesspersons.[66] China's middle class is also growing in numbers and rising in affluence, and understands what goes on outside China's borders. Again, this is due partially to the spillover effects of foreign investment. Members of this class may soon demand an increasing say in politics as a complement to their economic influence.

On the other hand, there is no reason to expect imminent political opening in China, and there are even some discouraging signs regarding the prospects for the influence of civil society to promote pluralism. For example, Margaret Pearson, in a study of Chinese managers in Western and Japanese firms, found little support for the proposition that marketization leads to democratization because the new business elite is apolitical. The state has set up various institutions to control economic interests, a system Pearson describes as socialist corporatism, while at the same time clientelism defines the interaction of business elites with the state.[67] China's private sector also places high value on stability, wary of new uncertainties. Furthermore, much of China's growth has been spurred by collectives, enterprises led by local officials. Profits from such enterprises serve to strengthen entrenched elites rather than raise up competing elites. Those enterprises funded by ethnic Chinese are also characterized by close relationships between entrepreneurs and officials. Thus, at least in the medium term, there is no necessary link between economic reform and democratization. This is confirmed by the case of Singapore, which adheres to rule by law and is extremely rational but is not democratic.

In the short to medium run, the most likely scenario for China's political future continues to be what Robert Scalapino labels authoritarian-pluralism. Such a system is characterized by restraints on freedom and a single dominant party. Nevertheless, the political order does have some flexibility, with the boundaries of what is permissible always being tested. Furthermore, there is a certain degree of pluralism in the social and economic spheres,[68] although as the 1999 crackdown on the Falun Gong sect demonstrates, the Party will not tolerate any organization that it believes threatens its rule.

What about the charge that ethnic Chinese are leading to the ruin of China? This is overblown. Certainly corruption is a major problem in China. General Secretary Jiang Zemin has made a reduction in corruption a major party goal, as is evidenced by the sacking of Politburo member Chen Xitong on corruption charges and a massive investigation of officials in Xiamen. However, as these examples indicate, corruption in China is a problem endemic to the system. Its prevalence is a result of a loss of norms as well as systemic issues related to China's political-economic structure. If some ethnic Chinese entrepreneurs take advantage of the climate of corruption, they are not the driving force behind the problem.

The issue of regionalism is more directly related to ethnic Chinese investments. This is especially true with investments from Hong Kong and Taiwan, due to their geographic proximity with the areas in which their investments are concentrated. For example, because of Fujian's many exchanges with Taiwan, the province has stronger interests in good cross-Strait relations than Beijing. In a study of Chinese regionalism, Simon Long thus asserts that in Fujian there exists "the germs of a . . . contradiction between central government policy and local trading interests."[69] Fujian officials themselves admit that "they have hitched their fortunes to Taiwan."[70] Furthermore, the central government continues to have difficulty collecting taxes from the coastal provinces. In sum, coastal provinces have achieved a great deal of autonomy, by both policy design and the movement of events, a level of autonomy that is damaging to the center.

Ethnic Chinese entrepreneurs have contributed to this situation by investing primarily in the coastal provinces, especially those in the south. The wealth that they have helped create gives leverage to local officials in their dealings with

Beijing. In addition, the economic and political systems of Taiwan, and even Hong Kong to some extent, may provide a model for southern provinces that contains elements unacceptable to Beijing. Again, ethnic Chinese investors have not set out to create regional strains. In fact, investors desire stability to preserve their assets. Nevertheless, regionalism is one consequence of investors following their own economic interests.

However, China's difficulties regarding central-provincial relations can by no means be attributed mainly to ethnic Chinese investors. Decentralization was a goal of Deng Xiaoping's reforms. Policies were designed by Beijing to favor the coastal provinces with the knowledge that regional economic disparities would result. Furthermore, the problem of central-local relations in China existed in the Maoist era and before, although it has been exacerbated in the reform period. Indeed, it is an issue for all large states. If decentralization and the ensuing regionalism have gone too far, it is due to long-standing difficulties in finding the optimal division of power in China rather than a problem caused by ethnic Chinese investors. Furthermore, as ethnic Chinese entrepreneurs begin to engage in cross-investing in numerous provinces, they serve as a unifying force in China, connecting various regions economically.[71] Thus, the relationship between ethnic Chinese investors and regionalism in China is actually very complex.

Perhaps a more fruitful way to look at the problem of regionalism is to step outside the framework of ethnic Chinese investment and look at it from the broader perspective of China's numerous international contacts. The Chinese economy can be conceptualized as consisting of a series of economic zones, each connected with particular international partners. As one observer describes it, "There are relatively distinct spatial boundaries that encircle and envelop parts of China and neighboring or geographically proximate countries into economic subregions." These subregions "not only contain internal flows of trade and investment, but constitute a division of labor reflecting economic dynamics at the global and Asia-Pacific regional levels."[72] Examples of such areas are the South China Economic Zone, including Guangdong, Fujian, Hong Kong, and Taiwan; the Yellow Sea Economic Zone, or Bohai Circle, including Liaoning, Shandong, South Korea, and Japan; the Shanghai-Pudong Economic Zone, or Yangtze Circle, defined as the Yangtze River delta; the Tumen River region at the border of China, Russia, and North Korea; the Northwest Circle of western China, Russia, and the Central Asian Republics; and the Mekong River Economic Area, consisting of China, Burma, Vietnam, Laos, Kampuchea, and Thailand.[73] Thus, ethnic Chinese investors are part of a larger framework in which various parts of China are included. Nevertheless, the most dynamic element of this larger framework is China's coastal areas, tying the coast economically more closely to Asia and the world than China's interior. What this means for governance is being played out.

In reference to the framework developed in the first chapter, this section has reviewed a dynamic relationship between the Chinese state and ethnic Chinese investment. Investment contributes indirectly to greater pluralism, provides opportunity for corruption, and has a bearing on the regionalism question. Yet in all of these areas state policies play a major role as well. Investments are made in China at the invitation of the state. State policy made investing in the coast attractive, and now promotes investment in the hinterland as well. Corruption is tied to the political-economic structure fostered by the state, as well as a vacuum in ideology and moral framework. Furthermore, the state has options on how it will manage the pressures for pluralism, stifling such pressures in a way that eventually leads to economic decline and hostility within society toward the state, or adapting to pressures in a manner that will allow greater citizen participation in state decisions and a healthier balance between the center and the provinces.

NOTES

1. These figures come from State Statistical Bureau, People's Republic of China, *China Statistical Yearbook 1998* (Beijing: China Statistical Publishing House, 1998); and the China Council for the Promotion of International Trade, www.ccpit.org.

2. United Nations Conference on Trade and Development, *World Investment Report 1998* (New York: United Nations, 1998), 11.

3. Ezra Vogel, *One Step Ahead in China: Guangdong under Reform* (Cambridge, Mass.: Harvard University Press, 1989), 350.

4. See Wang Gungwu, "Greater China and the Chinese Overseas," *China Quarterly*, no. 136 (December 1993): 930.

5. "Report Details Investment by Overseas Chinese," Beijing Xinhua in English (7 October 1989), Foreign Broadcast Information Service (hereafter FBIS) *DR/China*, 19 October 1989, 42.

6. Shang-Jin Wei and Jeffrey Frankel, "A 'Greater China' Trade Bloc?" *China Economic Review* 5, no. 2 (1994): 188.

7. Some of the many articles that describe the difficulty of doing business in China include Pamela Yatsko, "Rethinking China," *Far Eastern Economic Review* (hereafter *FEER*), 18 December 1997, 52–57; Henny Sender, "Not for the Faint-Hearted," *FEER*, 12 January 1995, 64–65; and "Hong Kong's Li Criticizes China's Market Policies," *Wall Street Journal*, 25 November 1994, A4.

8. Michael Franz Roehrig, *Foreign Joint Ventures in Contemporary China* (New York: St. Martin's Press, 1994), 91. Throughout the book Roehrig consistently discusses the importance of bargaining for the success of joint ventures in China. See also S. Gordon Redding, *The Spirit of Chinese Capitalism* (Berlin: Walter de Gruyter, 1993), chapter 5.

9. Louis Kraar, "The Overseas Chinese: Lessons from the World's Most Dynamic Capitalists," *Fortune*, 31 October 1994, 106–8.

10. Xu Jiatun, *Xu Jiatun Xianggang huiyilu* (*Xu Jiatun's Memoir of His Hong Kong Experience*), vol. 1 (Taipei: Lianhe bao, 1993), 240–45.

11. Guangzhou shi dui wai jingji maoyi weiyuanhui and Guangzhou shi zhengce yanjiushi (Guangzhou City Foreign Economy and Trade Commission and the Guangzhou City Policy Research Office), *Guangzhou touzi zhinan* (*Guide to Investment in Guangzhou*), undated, 15–16.

12. See Eric W. K. Tsang, "Can Guanxi Be a Source of Sustained Competitive Advantage in Doing Business in China?" *Academy of Management Executive* 12, no. 2 (May 1998): 64–73.

13. Louise do Rosario, "Network Capitalism," *FEER*, 2 December 1993, 17.

14. Joel Klein, "Why China Does It Better," *Newsweek*, 12 April 1993, 23.

15. "Granite's Big Bet on China," *Asiaweek*, 13 July 1994, 39.

16. See Kam Wong, "Law Holds Little Help for Businessmen," *South China Morning Post*, 5 November 1999, Internet edition; Louise do Rosario, "Risky Business," *FEER*, 26 January 1995, 20–21; and Martin C. M. Lee, "Why China Needs Hong Kong's Legal System," *Wall Street Journal*, 28 December 1994, A11.

17. For example, American Troy McBride was held in Hefei in 1995 over a commercial dispute. Afterward McBride remarked, "I knew that if you are an ethnic Chinese they don't care which passport you hold. But I thought I had more protection because I am Caucasian." Uli Schmetzer, "Chinese Are Taking 'Commercial Hostages,'" *Chicago Tribune*, 27 March 1995, 6; see also "Shanghaied," *FEER*, 6 April 1995, 22.

18. Min Chen, "Technological Transfer to China: Major Rules and Issues," *International Journal of Technology Management* 10, nos. 7/8 (1995): 748. See also Karin Holstius, "Cultural Adjustment in International Technology Transfer," *International Journal of Technology Management* 10, nos. 7/8 (1995): 678.

19. For a discussion of the paradoxes involved in FDI as a source of technology transfer in China, see Roger Hayter and Sun Sheng Han, "Reflections on China's Open Policy Towards Foreign Investment," *Regional Studies* 32, no. 1 (February 1998): 1–16.

20. Holstius, "Cultural Adjustment," 677.

21. Tao Qu and Milford B. Green, *Chinese Foreign Direct Investment: A Subnational Perspective on Location* (Aldershot, England: Ashgate, 1997), 135.

22. See Yun-Wing Sung, *The China-Hong Kong Connection: The Key to China's Open Door Policy* (Cambridge: Cambridge University Press, 1991), 57–58; Michael Selwyn, "SE Asian Chinese Head for Home," *Asian Business*, April 1993, 24–25; and Kathy Chen, "China Drafts Measures to Limit Foreign Investment in State Assets," *Wall Street Journal*, 18 November 1994, A12.

23. Vogel, *One Step Ahead*, 181.

24. Yoshihara Kunio, *The Rise of Ersatz Capitalism in South-East Asia* (Singapore: Oxford University Press, 1988), 106–18. See also Paul Krugman, "The Myth of Asia's Miracle," *Foreign Affairs* 73, no. 6 (November/December 1994): 62–78.

25. Lim Soon Neo, "The China Connection," *Singapore Business*, March 1989, 30.

26. Paul Blustein, "Forging 'Greater China,'" *Washington Post*, 1 December 1992, A30.

27. Ping Lan, *Technology Transfer to China Through Foreign Direct Investment* (Aldershot, England: Avebury, 1996), 166–67.

28. The flying geese model describes the rise and decline of industries in a country as that country's comparative advantage changes, as well as the associated transfer of dominant industries from one state to another. The model assumes that Japan is Asia's technology leader. See C. H. Kwan, "The New Wave of Foreign Direct Investment in Asia," *Nomura Asia Focus*, August/September 1994, 9–13.

29. Richard Pomfret, *Investing in China: Ten Years of the Open Door Policy* (Ames: Iowa State University Press, 1991), 129.

30. Min Chen, "Technological Transfer," 750–51.

31. Eric W. K. Tsang, "The Implementation of Technology Transfer in Sino-Foreign Joint Ventures," *International Journal of Technology Management* 10, nos. 7/8 (1995): 760–63.

32. Lucian W. Pye, *Asian Power and Politics: The Cultural Dimensions of Authority* (Cambridge, Mass.: Harvard University Press, 1985), 25–26.

33. For a discussion of the specifics of ethnic Chinese management style, see Huang Cen, "Haiwai huaren he Zhongguo nanbude huazi kuaguo qiye" ("Ethnic Chinese and Transnational Enterprises with Chinese Capital in Southern China"), *Bagui qiao shi* (*Overseas Chinese History of Bagui*), 1997, no. 4:25–31.

34. Interview by author, 1994.

35. See Redding, *Spirit*, chapter 9.

36. Constance Lever-Tracy, David Ip, and Noel Tracy, *The Chinese Diaspora and Mainland China: An Emerging Economic Synergy* (New York: St. Martin's Press, 1996).

37. See UN, *World Investment Report* 1998, 202–3.

38. "Outlook Grim for Foreign Inflows," *South China Morning Post* (Hong Kong), 15 February 2000, Internet edition; "News Digest—Outward Investment by Asian Groups Plummets," *Financial Times* (London), 3 August 1999, Internet edition; "Asia No Longer Looking to Invest Overseas," *Independent* (London), 2 August 1999, Internet edition; and Colin Galloway, "Fall in FDI Tests Economic Resolve," *South China Morning Post* (Hong Kong), 10 June 1999, Internet edition.

39. Li Yanlong, "Article Views Foreign Investment, Exchange Controls," Beijing *Guoji maoyi wenti* (*International Trade Journal*) (6 March 1995), FBIS *DR/China*, 13 April 1995, 29–33.

40. Shen Hongfang, "Jiushi niandai Dongnan Ya guojia yu woguode waizi touzi huanjing bijiao" ("A Comparison of the Foreign Investment Environments of China and the Southeast Asian States in the 1990s"), *Nanyang wenti yanjiu* (*Southeast Asian Affairs*), 1994, no. 2:54–55.

41. U.S. Department of Commerce, Bureau of Economic Affairs, "U.S. Direct Investment Abroad," http://www.bea.doc.gov/bea/di/dia-ctry.htm.

42. Seymour Martin Lipset, *Political Man: The Social Base of Politics* (New York: Doubleday, 1960), 41; see also Larry Diamond, "Economic Development and Democracy Reconsidered," *American Behavioral Scientist* 35, nos. 4/5 (March/June 1992): 450–99.

43. Samuel Huntington, *The Third Wave: Democratization in the Late Twentieth Century* (Norman: University of Oklahoma Press, 1991), 59–72. For an exposition of how rapid economic growth contributed to democratization in Taiwan, see Tun-ren Cheng, "Democratizing the Quasi-Leninist Regime in Taiwan," *World Politics* 41, no. 4 (July 1989): 471–99.

44. For one analysis of the rise of civil society in China, see Barrett L. McCormick, Shaozhi Su, and Xiaoming Xiao, "The 1989 Democracy Movement: A Review of the Prospects for Civil Society in China," *Pacific Affairs* 65, no. 2 (Summer 1992): 182–202. For perspectives that question the utility of civil society as a concept suitable for China, see Timothy Brook and B. Michael Frolic, eds., *Civil Society in China* (Armonk, N.Y.: M. E. Sharpe, 1997).

45. Lee Kuan Yew, untitled, in *World Chinese Entrepreneurs Convention*, ed. Singapore Chinese Chamber of Commerce and Industry (Singapore, 1991), 187, 190–91.

46. Sheila Tefft, "Repatriates Transform Economy, Yet Endure Persistent Resentment," *Christian Science Monitor*, 30 March 1994, 11.

47. Sheila Tefft, "Overseas Investors Elicit Praise and Protest in Fujian Province," *Christian Science Monitor*, 30 March 1994, 13–14; and interview by author, 1994.

48. Interview by author, 1994.

49. Willem Van Kemenade, *China, Hong Kong, Taiwan, Inc.*, trans. Diane Webb (New York: Vintage Books, 1998), 179–80.

50. Dajiong Zha, "A 'Greater China'? The Political Economy of Chinese National Reunification," *Journal of Contemporary China*, no. 5 (Spring 1994): 52.

51. For an analysis of inequalities in China between provinces as well as between rural and urban areas, see World Bank, *Sharing Rising Incomes: Disparities in China* (Washington, D.C.: World Bank, 1997).

52. Edward Friedman, "Ethnic Identity and the De-Nationalization and Democratization of Leninist States," in *The Rising Tide of Cultural Pluralism*, ed. Crawford Young (Madison: University of Wisconsin Press, 1993), 238.

53. Robert Scalapino, "China in the Late Leninist Era," *China Quarterly*, no. 136 (December 1993): 963–65; and "The Ostrich's View of the World," *Economist*, 19 December 1998–1 January 1999, 67–68.

54. Haishun Sun, *Foreign Investment and Economic Development in China: 1979–1996* (Aldershot, England: Ashgate, 1998), 29; and China Council for the Promotion of International Trade, www.ccpit.org.

55. See Pomfret, *Investing in China*, table 5.7, 93; and David Zweig, " 'Developmental Communities' on China's Coast: The Impact of Trade, Investment, and Transnational Alliances," *Comparative Politics* 27, no. 3 (April 1995): table 2, 261 and 265.

56. See, for example, Li Guoliang, Lin Jinzhi, and Cai Renlong, *Huaqiao huaren yu Zhongguo geming he jinshi* (*Overseas Chinese/Ethnic Chinese and Chinese Revolution and Construction*), ed. Lin Jinzhi (Fuzhou: Fujian renmin chubanshe, 1993), 495–97; and Xiang Dayou, "Lun Zhongguo gaige kaifang yu hua zitou xiang qushi" ("On the Reform and Opening Up of China and the Investment Inclination of Overseas Chinese"), *Bagui qiao shi* (*Overseas Chinese History of Bagui*), 1994, no. 1: 6.

57. Rajeswary Ampalavanar-Brown, "Overseas Chinese Investments in China—Patterns of Growth, Diversification, and Finance," *China Quarterly*, no. 155 (September 1998): 619; and Sun, *Foreign Investment*, 28–34. For an account of the importance of foreign investment to Fujian province, see Yu Yunping, "Qian lun qiao wai shang zhijie touzi zai Fujian jingji fazhan zhongde diwei he zuoyong" ("On the Position and Role of Overseas Chinese and Foreign Businesspersons' Direct Investment in the Economic Development of Fujian"), *Nanyang wenti yanjiu* (*Southeast Asian Affairs*), 1996, no. 2: 35–45.

58. Qu and Green, *Chinese Foreign Direct Investment*, 126.

59. East Asia Analytical Unit, Department of Foreign Affairs and Trade, Commonwealth of Australia, *Overseas Chinese Business Networks in Asia* (Canberra: Commonwealth of Australia, 1995), 203–4. See also Lever Tracy et al., *The Chinese Diaspora.*

60. Tu Wei-ming, "Cultural China: The Periphery as the Center," *Daedalus* 120, no. 2 (Spring 1991): 12.

61. Ibid., 26.

62. Helen F. Siu, "Cultural Identity and the Politics of Difference in South China," *Daedalus* 122, no. 2 (Spring 1993): 36.

63. Graham E. Johnson and Woon Yuen-Fong, "The Response to Rural Reform in an Overseas Chinese Area," *Modern Asian Studies* 31, no. 1 (1997): 52–53.

64. For details, see Henny Sender, "Capital Concern," *FEER*, 29 April 1999, 66–67; and Elisabeth Rosenthal, "Capitalists to Be Granted Official Status in Communist China," *New York Times*, 15 March 1999, Internet edition.

65. See Yuen-Fong Woon, "Family Strategies of Prosperous Peasants in an Emigrant Community in South China," *Canadian Journal of Developmental Studies* 15, no. 1 (1994): 9–33.

66. Matt Forney, "Voice of the People," *FEER*, 7 May 1998, 10–12; and Tony Saich, "The Search for Civil Society and Democracy in China," *Current History* 93, no. 584 (September 1994): 260–64.

67. Margaret M. Pearson, *China's New Business Elite: The Political Consequences of Economic Reform* (Berkeley: University of California Press, 1997).

68. Scalapino, "China," 964–65.

69. Simon Long, "Regionalism in Fujian," in *China Deconstructs: Politics, Trade and Regionalism*, ed. David S. G. Goodman and Gerald Segal (New York: Routledge, 1994), 220. However, Long concludes that there is no strong dissatisfaction with Beijing.

70. Maria Hsia Chang, "Greater China and the Chinese 'Global Tribe,'" *Asian Survey* 35, no. 10 (October 1995): 963.

71. See Yu-Min Chou, "The Role of Foreign Investments in the Formation of an Economic Region—With Reference to China," *RIAD Bulletin*, no. 2 (March 1993): 81–83.

72. Xiangming Chen, "China's Growing Integration with the Asia-Pacific Economy," in *What Is in a Rim? Critical Perspectives on the Pacific Region Idea*, ed. Arif Dirlik (Boulder: Westview Press, 1993), 91.

73. For details on various zones, see Chen, "China's," 95–111; Harry Harding, "The Concept of 'Greater China': Themes, Variations and Reservations," *China Quarterly*, no. 136 (December 1993): 671–72; and Fu Mengzi, "Yatai ciquyu jingji hezuode fazhan yu Zhongguo" ("The Development of Asian Subregional Economic Cooperation and China"), *Xianzai guoji guanxi* (*Contemporary International Relations*), 1993, no. 11: 31–32.

CHAPTER 6

International Implications of China's Policies and Ethnic Chinese Investments in China

This chapter examines the international implications of both China's policies to attract economic contributions from ethnic Chinese and the investments of ethnic Chinese in China, with a primary focus on Southeast Asian Chinese. In terms of the diaspora triangle described in the first chapter, connections will be drawn from the first leg of the triangle (China's relationship with the ethnic Chinese) to the second and third legs (the relationship of ethnic Chinese to the states of Southeast Asia and the relationship of China to Southeast Asia).

More specifically, ethnic Chinese investments in China highlight the long-standing issue of the place of Chinese in Southeast Asia. While ethnic Chinese insist that they belong in Southeast Asia and their transactions with China are primarily economic, others raise questions as to their motivations and loyalties. At the same time, ethnic Chinese investments impact state-to-state relations between China and the countries of Southeast Asia in a complex manner. On the one hand, Southeast Asian states fear that China will siphon off investments from their own economies. They are also concerned about growing Chinese power in the region. On the other hand, Southeast Asia is eager to benefit from China's economic growth and peacefully tie China to the region's economy.

The chapter is divided into four sections. The first examines fears, justified or exaggerated, in Southeast Asia regarding China and the ethnic Chinese. These concerns center around potential Chinese ambitions as a great power, the destabilizing influence of an ethnic minority in whose hands are concentrated large proportions of national wealth, and competition from China in attracting investments. The second part looks at the difficulties ethnic Chinese face in Southeast Asia. The third section analyzes how renewed interest in China among ethnic Chinese affects their prospects for assimilation into Southeast Asian societies. The fourth segment discusses relations between China and Southeast Asia. In each of these areas China's policies toward ethnic Chinese and the ethnic Chinese response have had a significant influence.

SOUTHEAST ASIAN FEARS REGARDING CHINA AND THE ETHNIC CHINESE

With the establishment of the PRC in 1949 and the postwar decolonization of Southeast Asia, many of the new states in the region came to view China as a threat. Although during dynastic times the only Southeast Asian country colonized by China was Vietnam, Southeast Asians are sensitive to China's slow expansion southward over the centuries and the tribute paid to China by the native rulers of Southeast Asia. Regardless of China's policies, its size and power have made the smaller states of the region wary of it. In addition, China's communist ideology, coupled with support for guerrilla movements in mostly capitalist Southeast Asia, was seen as threatening through the 1980s. Regional governments took this danger seriously due to the large ethnic Chinese populations in Southeast Asia that some alleged China could manipulate almost at will.[1] China's evacuation of overseas Chinese from Indonesia in the 1950s and 1960s and confrontation with Vietnam over overseas Chinese in the 1970s fueled these concerns.

Since the advent of China's reform period, fears of China have subsided but have not been eliminated. In the 1980s, China ended party-to-party relations with Southeast Asia's communist insurgents, responding to Southeast Asian demands and improving relations with the region's governments. Economic exchanges also increased in the 1990s, and in general relations between China and Southeast Asia have been good. Nevertheless, Southeast Asian governments still view China with caution, although the level of concern varies by country. An article in the Singapore press in 1993, broadly representative of Southeast Asian views, proclaimed, "The traditional concern with China has been resurrected with it emerging as the single greatest source of security threat to Southeast Asia." The article portrayed the two most serious sources of tension as China's South China Sea claims and its strategic alliance with Myanmar.[2] In 1996, Singapore's senior minister Lee Kuan Yew said that China's growing strength worried countries in Southeast Asia and called on the United States to maintain its stabilizing presence in Asia.[3] In 1999, a year in which Philippine naval vessels rammed and sank Chinese fishing boats, Philippine president Joseph Estrada called China the biggest threat to Asia's security, reflecting tension between China and the Philippines over Mischief Reef and Scarborough Shoals since 1995.[4] China's new weapons systems and a growing military budget that is largely secretive add to the sense of unease.

Within this context, China's stance regarding ethnic Chinese is still a sensitive issue. This was especially so in the late 1970s, when China announced its revived policy toward overseas Chinese.[5] Writing in 1979, Wang Gungwu noted four issues regarding China's policy that raised concern among Southeast Asian governments. First, how does China seek to make amends for the damage done to overseas Chinese during the Cultural Revolution, and how will this affect Southeast Asia? Second, what role does China envision for Southeast Asia's Chinese entrepreneurs in promoting the Four Modernizations? Third, in light of the Sino-Vietnamese conflict and the accompanying exodus of ethnic Chinese, who is considered to be Chinese? Finally, China's warm rhetoric toward "overseas Chinese" served to blur the distinction between Chinese and foreign nationals.[6]

Indeed, China's policy was quite ambiguous. A 1978 *Peking Review* article noted that overseas Chinese love their socialist motherland because the founding of "New China" improved their position, leaving them "overseas orphans" no longer. As a result, Chinese abroad were called to be patriotic and contribute to the Four Modernizations. At the same time, they were also encouraged to choose local nationality. If they maintained their Chinese citizenship, they were exhorted to respect the laws and customs of their host countries and refrain from "big-nation chauvinism," all the while continuing to contribute to China's development and friendly relations between China and their countries of residence.[7] The obvious issue this raises is whether one can serve two masters.

Concern over China's policies has continued through the reform period in varying degrees. In 1987, Chang Pao-Min, a professor of political science in Singapore, warned that "in trying to capitalize on the cultural affinities and linguistic skills of the ethnic Chinese in Southeast Asia, China may well be unwittingly performing a disservice to both the 'overseas Chinese' and the Southeast Asian countries and also getting itself into more trouble than it can imagine."[8] An analyst from the Centre for Strategic and International Studies in Indonesia in 1993 warned that China must be careful regarding the question of the loyalty of Southeast Asia's ethnic Chinese, noting that business relations between China and ethnic Chinese are encouraged as long as "they are not seen to translate into political and cultural affinities."[9] In 1999, Wang Gungwu, director of the East Asian Institute at the National University of Singapore, called for China to strengthen its ties with Asian governments and rely less on ethnic Chinese networks.[10]

The concern over China prevalent in Southeast Asia is closely tied to misgivings over the political and social impact of ethnic Chinese minorities. The most salient issue regarding the ethnic Chinese is their loyalty.[11] However, opinions in Southeast Asia differ on this issue. Many see the ethnic Chinese as loyal citizens who are well integrated into their societies. According to this view, few ethnic Chinese consider China as home. Most ethnic Chinese themselves hold this position. However, a second group, composed largely of staunch nationalists and conservative Muslims, sees the ethnic Chinese as separate from the native inhabitants of Southeast Asia, linked more closely to their Chinese networks than their own indigenous neighbors. Thus ethnic Chinese are susceptible to influence by China. Journalists from outside Asia often hold a similar viewpoint.[12]

From the perspective of Southeast Asian governments, one long-term threat from ethnic Chinese is their economic power. This contributes to social tensions, especially in Indonesia, as demonstrated by the riots directed against Chinese in 1998. Many Southeast Asians are also uncomfortable with the alliances between Chinese businesspersons and pragmatic national elites wherein indigenous officials protect and provide contracts for Chinese business leaders in return for financial considerations. Undoubtedly psychological factors operating in the minds of the indigenous people of Southeast Asia also play a role in their perception of an ethnic Chinese threat. Feelings of legitimacy among indigenous groups based on earlier settlement in the land help maintain stereotypes of the ethnic Chinese as having foreign ties.[13] Political competition further keeps issues regarding ethnic Chinese in the public eye. For example, the president of the Malay opposition party Spirit of '46 in 1993 expressed fears over the increasing investments in China by Malaysian Chinese, questioning the loyalty of those who invested in China.[14] In Indonesia, the government has considered ethnic Chinese a threat through which subversion might occur since the failed coup attempt and Suharto's assumption of power in 1965. The 1990s saw suggestions that ethnic Chinese were involved in China due to ethnic ties, with the implication that such motives were unpatriotic.[15]

Another issue of concern for Southeast Asians is the economic competition that they face from China in trade and in attracting investments from both foreigners and their own citizens.[16] China's need for investments is tremendous, reaching many trillions of dollars. In 1994, Ashwin Kongsiri, president of the Industrial Finance Corporation of Thailand, warned at a meeting of the Asian Development Bank that China could drain funds, expertise, and manpower from other developing countries in Asia over the coming years, while the World Bank forecast that China needed $744 billion to fund public infrastructure development from 1995 to 2004.[17] Singapore's prime minister Goh Chok Tong has called economic competition from China ASEAN's greatest challenge.[18] Not only is China attractive as an export base, it also offers a huge (although for many products illusory) domestic market as well. The problem is compounded by the major reduction in Japanese loans and investments in Southeast Asia.

Others have also expressed anxiety about China's attraction of investments, focusing on investments from ethnic Chinese in Southeast Asia. This attitude is not new. Purcell noted that in the late 1950s the Indonesian government "took the view that profits made by foreign business men in Indonesia should be spent or invested in Indonesia and not sent abroad."[19] As the scope of investment in China has increased significantly, charges of capital flight have again been leveled at Indonesians of Chinese descent who invest in China.[20] In 1998, reports surfaced that thirteen Indonesian-Chinese businessmen were told by the chief of the Indonesian armed forces that they must repatriate funds to Indonesia.[21] Suspicion regarding Chinese investment has also been expressed in Malaysia. For example, one Malaysian politician exclaimed, "I was happy when China didn't get the Olympics. It would have caused a wave of Chinese chauvinism and they would have poured all their money into China. The Chinese are an immigrant race, their loyalty is to where the money is."[22] In the Philippines, ethnic Chinese investments in China have come under fire too. In 1994, President Fidel Ramos told Manila's "six taipans," all wealthy ethnic Chinese Filipinos, that he was concerned that they were investing in China rather than the Philippines. Ramos further threatened a Senate investigation of their overseas investments. As a result, these businessmen were pressured into forming a $21.9 million corporation, "Emerging Dragon," to invest in Philippine infrastructure improvements.[23] Press reports in the Philippines have also described investments in China by Chinese-Filipinos as unpatriotic.[24]

Concern over China absorbing investments that might otherwise have gone to Southeast Asia, from both ethnic Chinese and others, is justified by statistics that demonstrate investments in China greatly surpassing those in Southeast Asia in the 1990s. As table 6.1 demonstrates, FDI in the original ASEAN states (Indonesia, Malaysia, the Philippines, Singapore, and Thailand) exceeded investments in China through 1992. However, in 1993 foreign investments in China nearly doubled those in ASEAN, a pattern that remained consistent through 1997 but has not worsened for Southeast Asia.

In response to dropping investments, Southeast Asian governments have provided new incentives for investors throughout the 1980s and 1990s, both individually and through ASEAN. Malaysia cut taxes and increased spending on infrastructure. Indonesia reduced tariffs, dropped restrictions on foreign investment in strategic sectors, eliminated regional restrictions, ended minimum capital requirements, extended the time that foreign investors can operate in Indone-

Table 6.1
Foreign Direct Investment in China and Southeast Asia[a]
(millions of dollars)

Year	China	Southeast Asia
1985–90 annual avg.	2,654	5,987
1991	4,366	12,925
1992	11,156	11,506
1993	27,515	14,738
1994	33,787	17,732
1995	35,849	20,151
1996	40,800	24,094
1997	45,300	23,957

[a] Indonesia, Malaysia, the Philippines, Singapore, and Thailand.

Source: Calculated from United Nations Conference on Trade and Development, *World Investment Report 1997* (New York: United Nations, 1997), 306, and the 1998 edition, 364.

sia, and simplified customs procedures. Similarly, the Philippines ended some restrictions limiting foreign equity, liberalized foreign exchange transactions, reformed the tax system, and allowed more foreign banks to operate in the country. ASEAN countries have collectively offered tax holidays, duty exemptions on imported capital goods, and access to the domestic market of host countries.

Competition between China and the ASEAN states also manifests itself in trade. A Singapore government report cites "substantial overlap" between low-end exports to the United States between China and Thailand, Indonesia, Malaysia, and the Philippines.[25] This competition will become more serious for Southeast Asia as greater numbers of Western and Japanese firms invest in China, raising the level of competition to include more higher-end products as well.

Mainland scholars and officials have recognized the competition that China poses to Southeast Asia in attracting investments from foreigners and ethnic Chinese. There are two primary responses to this rivalry. One is to recognize that a competitive relationship does indeed exist, using the contest as leverage to call for additional reforms in China in order to remain competitive with Southeast Asia.[26] However, many public analyses are designed to downplay any negative effects of the competition on Southeast Asia and point out the benefits for Southeast Asia of the region's companies investing in China. Thus Chinese analysts state that as a result of Southeast Asian investment in China, tax revenues on investment profits return to the home countries, trade with China increases, and relations with China improve. Furthermore, the competition from China prods Southeast Asian countries to improve their own investment environments, while at the same time the economic complementarity between China and Southeast Asia is increasing.[27] One writer suggests that China be sensitive to tensions in Indonesia regarding ethnic Chinese investments by attracting native Indonesians to invest as partners with Chinese-Indonesians in China, helping avoid charges of capital flight.[28]

Officials in Fuzhou also acknowledged the problem of Southeast Asian suspicions regarding ethnic Chinese investments in China. One noted that, in the case of Indonesian entrepreneurs, most of the capital that is invested in China has been earned from operations outside Indonesia. Nevertheless, the Chinese government has encouraged its own state-run corporations to invest in Indonesia to improve the overall business climate. Officials further respond to the problem of Indonesian sensitivity by refraining from making investments public.[29]

Chinese commentators are correct to assert that Southeast Asian investments are beneficial to home countries as well as China. China provides economic opportunities to Southeast Asia, and the competition that China presents is a natural component of the international political economy. Nevertheless, China's size and political influence make it a formidable economic competitor. The fact that it is at a similar stage of development with Southeast Asia further intensifies economic competition. Moreover, as long as China continues to appeal specifically to ethnic Chinese for aid in furthering its development, concerns in Southeast Asia regarding Chinese intentions will not disappear.

DIFFICULTIES OF ETHNIC CHINESE IN SOUTHEAST ASIA

If Southeast Asian "natives" have been afraid of ethnic Chinese, Chinese have had good reason to fear for their own well being and safety too. Across the centuries there have been periodic purges of Chinese in Southeast Asia, including instances since 1949. For example, in Indonesia thousands of Chinese were killed in 1965 during the slaughter of suspected communist sympathizers following the murder of military generals by Indonesia's Communist Party, the PKI (Partai Komunis Indonesia). During the communist uprising in Malaysia that began in the late 1940s, ethnic Chinese were placed in camps, while thousands of Chinese were forced out of Vietnam in the late 1970s. Governments have also enforced discriminatory policies against the ethnic Chinese. These include restrictions on capital ownership, exclusion from some industries, the forced transfer of equity to indigenous partners, and limitations on licenses and school admissions. Malaysia's New Economic Policy, begun in 1971, is one such example. Thus, Leo Suryadinata notes that although most Chinese in Southeast Asia have local citizenship, many states consider them to be only " 'half' Southeast Asian."[30]

There are several reasons for this discrimination. Questions over the loyalty of ethnic Chinese, the economic disparity between ethnic Chinese and indigenes, fears of China, charges of capital flight, and nationalism have already been discussed. The perception of Chinese as immigrant outsiders, even after many generations, plays a major role as well.[31] In all of this China has never had the power to protect its nationals in Southeast Asia, let alone Chinese who are Southeast Asian citizens. Stephen Douglas summarizes the situation succinctly by noting that the main source of the problem of ethnic Chinese in Southeast Asia is "economic success unmatched by political participation." This is compounded by an incongruent international context where the ethnic Chinese operate in a global business environment while politics is embedded at the level of the nation-state.[32]

It is in this context that China's post-1978 policy and investments by ethnic Chinese are embedded. Overt attempts by China to attract the capital of Southeast Asian Chinese and investments by ethnic Chinese have the potential to raise anxiety levels in Southeast Asia and consequently make life there more difficult for Chinese. This possibility rises as China grows stronger economically and militarily. Not only does China become more of a potential political threat to nations in the region, it also exudes a new cultural pride that is attractive to some ethnic Chinese but uncomfortable for others. Thus in a paradoxical way, China's rise now may bode ill for Southeast Asian ethnic Chinese. However, this trend is moderated to the extent that China can maintain friendly political relations with the states of the region.

One example of Chinese economic might and influence creating discomfort for ethnic Chinese is in Myanmar. Mainland Chinese money is flowing into parts of the country such as Mandalay, where it is used to purchase restaurants, hotels, and shops, sometimes displacing native Burmese. Even Myanmar citizenship can be bought. This creates resentment on the part of the locals. It also makes life more difficult for ethnic Chinese who have lived in Myanmar for generations. Many are unhappy with the mainlanders who flood in and stir up anger against Chinese.[33]

Much more serious displays of rage directed toward ethnic Chinese occurred in Indonesia, where Chinese comprise 4 percent of the population yet control a majority of the economy, in 1994, and especially 1998. In April 1994, a wave of rioting against Chinese broke out in Medan. About 150 shops were looted and one man was killed before the military restored order. In June of that same year another rampage occurred fifty miles south of Jakarta. Anti-Chinese leaflets were also distributed in Jakarta and Bandung, one of which read "My brothers . . . chase the Chinese from our beloved country of ours. What is more clear, let us crush them." As a result of these incidents, many Chinese fled the country in fear.[34] While these attacks were related more to circumstances in Indonesia than to connections between ethnic Chinese and China, they illustrate the tensions that exist in Indonesian society. Even in Malaysia British Broadcasting Corporaton (BBC) coverage of the Medan riots was censored due to fears of a spillover of the violence.

In May 1998, rioting again rocked Indonesia, directed primarily at ethnic Chinese. Thousands of shops, offices, and vehicles were burned, with rioters reportedly chanting, "Let's kill the Chinese . . . let's wipe out the Chinese." Indonesia's National Human Rights Commission reported that 1,188 people were killed during the rioting. In addition, over 150 ethnic Chinese women were raped. The rioting, which brought widespread international condemnation and contributed to the downfall of Suharto, sent shock waves through the Chinese community. Many Chinese fled abroad, and by the time of legislative elections in 1999 it was reported that as much as $80 billion in Chinese money had left Indonesia due to fears of new violence.[35] However, the riots also brought about a resurgence in Chinese activism. Support groups were formed, a mass organization was started to support Chinese rights, and the first political party organized by ethnic Chinese was established.

The indigenous Indonesian response to the riots took two forms. One response was to blame the Chinese themselves for the violence and impose greater restrictions on Chinese. For instance, the mayor of Central Jakarta criticized Indonesian Chinese for not associating with local residents and for acting as if all problems can be solved with money. Others referred to Chinese rudeness and currency manipulation by Chinese speculators.[36] In April 1999, the government imposed a travel ban on numerous ethnic Chinese bankers to keep them from fleeing Indonesia before the upcoming election. The second response was to end, at least officially, state-sanctioned racial discrimination against Chinese. Thus, President Habibie ordered a halt to the requirement that Indonesian-Chinese present certificates of Indonesian nationality when dealing with the government. He also ordered that the teaching of the Chinese language again be allowed. Nevertheless, human rights activists insist that discrimination still occurs.

In light of the difficult domestic circumstances facing ethnic Chinese, it is not surprising that many are sensitive about charges of being tied too closely to China. For example, the president of the Malaysian Chinese Association criticized *Time* and the *Economist* for positing a blood linkage between China and ethnic Chinese. He went on to say that "for the vast majority of us South-East Asian Chinese, home is where we are born. If we invest in China, it is to make profit, not for sentimental tuggings of the heartstrings or because we want to return to the land of our forefathers."[37] Similarly, a scholar in Singapore noted that terms such as "Greater China" are dangerous when used by foreign scholars because they suggest a unity between China and ethnic Chinese that does not exist. Such phrases can make things difficult for ethnic Chinese living in Southeast Asia.[38]

China demonstrates some sensitivity to the "China problem" in Southeast Asia. For example, China's decision to end support for revolutionary parties in the region in the 1980s was an important step toward easing fears regarding ethnic Chinese. In 1993, then foreign minister Qian Qichen publicly denied the existence of an entity labeled "Greater China," emphasizing that Southeast Asia's ethnic Chinese are in a different category from residents of Hong Kong and Taiwan.[39] This is in line with China's efforts to distinguish between its own citizens and foreign nationals of Chinese descent in Southeast Asia. Nevertheless, China's overall policy of attracting the investments of all ethnic Chinese regardless of citizenship can exacerbate local tensions. China's appeals to one specific ethnic group unavoidably highlight the ethnic divisions within Southeast Asia.

ASSIMILATION AND IDENTIFICATION

As the length of time the Chinese have lived in Southeast Asia increases (although there is now further Chinese migration into some Southeast Asian states), there are differences of opinion as to whether ethnic Chinese have been assimilated into Southeast Asian societies. There are also differing interests regarding this issue. Generally speaking, Southeast Asian governments prefer to see an acceleration of assimilation, while China wants to see the maintenance of Chinese culture and identity. Ethnic Chinese themselves also differ as to the level of assimilation they themselves wish to reach. This section focuses on China's approach to this issue and the way in which China's policies toward ethnic Chinese and the ethnic Chinese response affect the process of assimilation.

First, assimilation is a vague concept, and can be perceived as having stringent or loose requirements. At one end, assimilation can be defined as total absorption of a minority into the host country's society and culture. In this case minority language, identification, and culture are effectively lost. Northern European immigrants to the United States usually attained this level of assimilation in a relatively short period of time. At a minimal level, assimilation may be thought of in terms of political loyalty, coupled with an acceding to a core set of beliefs that varies from country to country. For instance, in Thailand a commitment to Thai nationalism, belief in Buddhism, and loyalty to the king are expected of Thai citizens.[40] The level of assimilation that an ethnic majority can legitimately demand of a minority in any society is a controversial question. For instance, in the United States disagreements surround English-only laws, bilingual education, and the search for metaphors for the normative immigrant experience. Nevertheless, it has become increasingly clear in Southeast Asia that ethnic Chinese are not going to blend into the native population over time and lose their ethnic identity.

Looking at the Chinese experience in Southeast Asia, history demonstrates that when assimilation does occur (even at a substantial level) it is not necessarily permanent. During the nineteenth century thousands of Chinese migrated to Southeast Asia. Many became comfortable in their new homes, adopting the local language and giving their loyalty to the lands where they resided. However, the rise of Chinese nationalism in the late nineteenth and early twentieth centuries, along with continued immigration, challenged this local identity throughout Southeast Asia. Slogans such as "once a Chinese always a Chinese" became popular and Chinese identity was reasserted. In the Straits Settlements, as well as elsewhere, this nationalist movement reversed the local loyalties that had been developing.[41] In other words, ethnic Chinese stopped considering themselves as Southeast Asians and began thinking of themselves as Chinese, demonstrating that ethnic and political identities are to at least some extent social constructs rather than fixed attributes.

Many today assert that assimilation of the ethnic Chinese has already occurred to a great extent in Southeast Asia. For example, Leo Suryadinata argues that a Southeast Asianization of ethnic Chinese is occurring and will continue.[42] Individual Chinese often proclaim that their identity lies with Southeast Asia as well. For example, Liew Chen Chuan, editor of a Malaysian Chinese language newspaper, states, "My generation thinks of ourselves as Malaysian first."[43] Others doubt that assimilation has occurred or even can occur, citing a wide variety of obstacles. Lucian Pye points to the difficulties that Chinese have with creating bonds outside nonfamilial relationships and a confusion regarding the distinction between biology and culture. As a result, the underlying sentiment of Southeast Asian Chinese is that "it would be grotesquely abnormal for any Chinese to lose his identification with the roots of Chinese greatness."[44] Others have referred to the lack of common education between Chinese and indigenes, weak intercultural influences, links among Chinese business enterprises, the lack of opportunity for Chinese outside Chinese structures, and insecurity among native Southeast Asians coupled with Islamic resurgence as obstacles to assimilation. Even Malaysian prime minister Mahathir has concluded, "We must accept the fact that the Chinese are not a group that could be assimilated easily."[45]

Ethnic Chinese scholars themselves often point to the sojourner theme when discussing Southeast Asia's ethnic Chinese and assimilation. For example, Harvard's Tu Wei-ming states that "many diaspora Chinese possess a sojourner mentality and lack a sense of permanence in their adopted country."[46] Similarly, Wang Gungwu notes how immigrant Chinese in the past saw their moves to Southeast Asia as being sojourning, not permanent settlement. Modern technology now provides for multigenerational sojourners to maintain links with the home country. Although the Chinese are loyal citizens of Southeast Asia, technological links "may ultimately encourage the globalization of . . . sojourning— being temporarily away from home for generations. The new communications links would enable many migrants or migrant communities to live, behave, think, and feel as if they had never really left home."[47]

Nevertheless, Chinese have become assimilated to varying degrees in the countries of Southeast Asia based on national policies, the percentage of Chinese in the population, and the religion of the indigenous population.[48] Most analysts agree that, outside Singapore, where both ethnic and Singaporean identities are stressed by the government, assimilation is greatest in Thailand and the Philippines, where "nation" is defined more in cultural than racial terms. However, the process has not always been smooth in either country. In Thailand assimilation was aided by the defeat of the KMT (Kuomintang or Guomindang) on the mainland in 1949, after which expressions of Chinese nationalism were discouraged. As the percentage of Chinese born and educated in Thailand rose, Chinese youth assimilated in large numbers. Also contributing was the new Thai policy in 1956 that accepted anyone born in Thailand as a Thai citizen.[49] Even so, in Thailand ethnic Chinese identity is strong, as is evidenced by the widespread use of Chinese language, the importance of Chinese associations, and the practice of Chinese culture.[50] In the Philippines, integration of Chinese into Filipino society accelerated after the conversion of Chinese schools in 1973 and a 1975 presidential decree that allowed for the mass naturalization of Chinese.[51]

Indonesia and Malaysia have seen the least amount of assimilation. In both states there are barriers to intermarriage presented by Islam. In Malaysia assimilation is hindered by the fact that Chinese make up 30 percent of the population. Thus, the government maintains an accommodationist policy, guaranteeing Chinese cultural rights and recognizing that Malaysia is a multiethnic society.[52] In Indonesia, although citizenship has been opened to most ethnic Chinese, state policies have prohibited public expressions of Chinese culture and discriminated against Chinese citizens. Such policies have served to remind the Chinese of their identity.[53] It remains to be seen if recent promises to eliminate official discrimination will be carried out. In Vietnam some discrimination continues to exist as well.

The question of assimilation can also be viewed from the perspective of the individual. One way of redirecting the debate over assimilation is to no longer view Southeast Asia's ethnic Chinese as a group, but to recognize the differences that exist among them. The Chinese are separated by generation, place of origin, educational attainment, language, and citizenship. Thus, individuals in each country of Southeast Asia are assimilated to a varying extent. Indeed, individuals differ in the degree to which they wish to become assimilated. Even more important, people have multiple identities. For instance, Wang Gungwu posits four norms that affect the identities of Southeast Asian Chinese. Physical norms shape an ethnic identity. Political norms refer to the political loyalty given to the state. Economic norms determine class identity, while cultural norms reflect both traditional Chinese and modern values. All four norms work together in every individual.[54] The challenge, then, is whether a nation-state can accept the various identities of minority members in a competitive international environment.

Events in China clearly impact the assimilation of Chinese in Southeast Asia. China's economic growth and rise to greater prominence over the past two decades slows the process of assimilation in Southeast Asia. For instance, there has been a revival of interest in Chinese culture and language throughout the region.[55] Doing business in China also strengthens the ethnic identity of Chinese in Southeast Asia. If we accept the stringent definition of assimilation, ethnic Chinese who deal with China are less likely to become assimilated. Dealings with China mean entering the world of Chinese language, culture, and politics. Old contacts are reestablished and new friendships are made in China, shaping a person's cultural identity.

However, if we take a position closer to the minimal view of assimilation and bear in mind the possibility that one can hold numerous identities, there is no evidence that Southeast Asian Chinese are shifting loyalties to China. Thus, while cultural and economic norms may be changing, political norms are not. In fact, China has little to offer in terms of political norms. This is not to say that the situation could not change. It is possible that certain segments of Southeast Asia's ethnic Chinese population could shift their political loyalties to China. However, the cause of this shift would be widespread discrimination and persecution in Southeast Asia. Thus, the loyalties of the ethnic Chinese lie predominantly in Southeast Asia's hands rather than China's.

China has an interest in the issue of the assimilation of Southeast Asian Chinese as well. Most important is its desire to prevent the forced assimilation of ethnic Chinese. In its 1978 editorial reinstating overseas Chinese policy, the *Renmin ribao* called for foreign governments to "protect the legitimate rights and interests of overseas Chinese and respect their national traditions, customs and habits." Although China has not always acted to protect these "rights and interests" when they have been violated due to conflicting foreign policy objectives, protection is an explicitly stated goal. In 1997, Sun Xingcheng of China's State Council Overseas Chinese Affairs Office asserted that forced assimilation violates the laws of history and is therefore unworkable. He criticized Southeast Asian states that have required ethnic Chinese to become citizens, forced name changes and religious conversion, limited economic freedoms for Chinese, and forbidden Chinese schools, associations, and newspapers.[56]

Moreover, China's policies have seemingly been designed to help preserve a separate identity for ethnic Chinese. By referring to them as kin, providing special privileges, and actively courting their investments and skills, China has reinforced Chinese identity and links with the mainland. Moreover, a 1991 article in the mainland press, which may well reflect official views, criticized Singapore's Lee Kuan Yew for proposing that an East Asian civilization might be developed to replace Chinese civilization as the dominant influence in the region. The article called Lee's remarks a warning to China, commenting that China must take the initiative to preserve the trust and spiritual support of Asia's Chinese.[57]

Mainland Chinese writers focus on several themes when writing on assimilation.[58] First, it is almost universally asserted that political loyalty is a completely separate issue from ethnic identity. Thus, Southeast Asian Chinese can both be loyal citizens of their states and maintain Chinese culture, customs, and habits. Most writers assert that Chinese ethnic identity will be maintained over time, with some defending this view by claiming that Chinese ethnicity and culture is genetically based and thus impossible to change.[59] While attempts at forced assimilation, as has occurred in Indonesia, are condemned and judged ultimately fruitless, there is recognition that some assimilation will occur. However, there are different understandings of what assimilation is. Many think of assimilation as an exchange of cultures between ethnic groups, where the indigenous race both influences and is influenced by the Chinese. Moreover, according to this view assimilation does not mean the extinguishing of any culture. It is difficult for a culture to lose essential characteristics because, as one scholar in Xiamen phrased it, each race has its own mentality (*minzhu xingli*).[60] Thus, even in Thailand, where assimilation has proceeded furthest, those Chinese families that have been in Thailand for generations still maintain elements of their Chinese character. Other Chinese scholars are not eager to see even limited assimilation.[61] Additional debates in China center on the state of Chinese language learning among Southeast Asia's ethnic Chinese, whether specific ethnic Chinese societies exist in various countries, and how relations between China and ethnic Chinese should be conducted.[62]

CHINESE-SOUTHEAST ASIAN RELATIONS

We now examine how China's policies toward ethnic Chinese and ethnic Chinese investments in China affect the country's relations with Southeast Asian governments. Throughout the early and mid-1990s, Chinese analysts viewed the international situation as being one of multipolarity in politics and internationalization in economics, a time of continuing post–cold war change characterized above all by economic competition.[63] One of China's national objectives in such an environment was to build its own economy and technological base as a foundation for national power. By the late 1990s, China was becoming much more concerned with perceived U.S. hegemony, especially after NATO's war to establish an autonomous Kosovo and subsequent bombing of the Chinese embassy in Belgrade, the strengthening of U.S.-Japanese security relations, and Taiwan's insistence on "special state-to-state" relations with the mainland. However, China still placed high priority on economic development as ultimately the only way to match U.S. power. Because regional stability is essential to China's development strategy, China during the reform era has generally adhered to *zhoubian* diplomacy, or a good neighbor strategy, toward Southeast Asia.

However, China also views Southeast Asia as a neighboring area in which it has important economic interests, a region that is open to Chinese influence and where China has clear advantages in economic exchanges. Southeast Asia's natural resources are seen by Beijing as being important to China's future development too. In an international environment of established regional blocs, such as NAFTA and the EU, Beijing believes that Southeast Asia should be closely tied to China.[64] Similarly, China further promotes good ties with Southeast Asia due to its fears of Japanese ambitions in the region.

Still, there are several problems that create tensions between China and Southeast Asia. Most immediate is the territorial dispute over the South China Sea islands, especially the Spratlys. China has alternated between conciliation and belligerence on this issue, leaving the problem's ultimate resolution in some doubt. The Taiwan issue has also proven to be an obstacle, especially with President Lee Teng-hui's step toward independence in 1999. Beijing is suspicious of Taiwan's investments in Southeast Asia and its desire for "substantive relations" with countries of the region. Economic competition with the states of Southeast Asia for investments and markets have created further strains, as do fears that China will manipulate ethnic Chinese for its own purposes.[65]

In regard to the ethnic Chinese, the Chinese government has demonstrated some awareness of the tensions that its policies in the post–World War II era have created and has responded to many of these concerns. Several of the most important sources of tension have been removed. For example, in the 1950s, China rejected dual nationality and began a long process of attempting to clarify citizenship issues for Southeast Asian Chinese. In the 1980s, China ended party-to-party relations with Southeast Asia's communist parties. Furthermore, Beijing has seldom acted to protect the interests of Asia's ethnic Chinese. When China's national interests have clashed with the interests of Southeast Asia's ethnic Chinese, China's government has consistently given national interests precedence.[66]

Another often repeated claim is that ethnic Chinese serve as a bridge between China and the countries of Southeast Asia. As such they help build good will and promote trade and understanding. For example, C.Y. Chang claims that China's Friendship Associations, the promotion of ethnic Chinese tourism in China, open remittance policies, invitations for education in China, and promotion of trade with Chinese communities abroad are measures that will "strengthen the role of the Chinese community as a legitimate channel to win the trust of the nations in which they live."[67] For most of the PRC's history, however, ethnic Chinese have been more of a liability than a bridge. In this regard it has been argued that China suffers from a perception gap, believing that ethnic Chinese are a political asset when in fact they have been a liability for China.[68] Southeast Asian governments feared subversion from their ethnic Chinese populations while indigenes resented their higher living standards. Thus, ethnic Chinese could not serve as a bridge because they were not trusted in Southeast Asia. For a bridge to work, it must be secured on both sides of a gulf.

However, during the late 1980s and 1990s, ethnic Chinese did begin to realize their potential as a bridge as economic relations between China and the ASEAN states made great strides forward. Chapter 4 demonstrated the increase in investments in China by ASEAN. Trade, especially exports from the ASEAN states to China, also increased. From 1990 to 1997, China's total trade with Indonesia, Malaysia, the Philippines, Singapore, and Thailand rose from $6.87 billion to $22.80 billion, a 3.3–fold increase. At the same time, China's trade with the world increased 2.8–fold. As of 1997, China's trade with ASEAN accounted for 7.0 percent of its total world trade, although in 1998, China's exports to ASEAN actually fell as a result of the Asian economic crisis.[69]

This bettering of economic relations with China is partially the result of a conscious decision by Southeast Asian governments.[70] These governments face a dilemma. On the one hand, they are eager to benefit from China's tremendous economic growth. Some governments also share a political interest with China in rebuffing Western demands regarding human rights. On the other hand, regional governments are concerned that an economically dynamic China will one day assert hegemonic influence over the area, a region that China views as within its sphere of influence and an arena of competition with Japan. This concern is compounded by the domestic political costs of policies that disproportionately benefit the Chinese segment of their populations, as well as the fear that ethnic Chinese participation in China's economy will loosen their ties to Southeast Asia. Ross states the dilemma baldly: Southeast Asian governments can either cut themselves off from the benefits of participation in the Chinese economy, or risk the cohesiveness of their domestic societies.[71] In recent years it has become clear that Southeast Asian governments, broadly speaking, have seen engaging China to be the best strategy. Malaysia, Singapore, Thailand, and Myanmar have the best relations with China. Vietnam, the Philippines, and Indonesia see more of a threat.

The country that has made the biggest turnabout in its relations with China is Malaysia. During the early part of China's reform period relations between Malaysia and China were cool. Chinese support for the Malaysian Communist Party and overtures toward ethnic Chinese were major irritants from Malaysia's point of view, while Prime Minister Mahathir was seen as less friendly toward China than his predecessors.[72] In addition, during the New Economic Policy Malaysia attempted to increase the economic holdings of the *bumiputeras* (indigenous Malaysians) in proportion to holdings by Chinese and foreigners. Thus, in 1986, Malaysia complained to China that Beijing was trading with Malaysia through Singaporean agents instead of Malaysian import-export companies. The Malaysian government was also unhappy that direct Sino-Malaysian trade was conducted through Malaysia's ethnic Chinese, which Malaysia saw as interfering with its New Economic Policy.[73]

Although Mahathir led a trade delegation to China in 1985, it was in the early 1990s that Malaysia's policy shifted to embrace economic ties with China, with Mahathir's visit to China in 1993 marking a turning point.[74] Altogether Prime Minister Mahathir has visited China with delegations of businesspersons five times since 1985, the most recent visit occurring in August 1999 to commemorate twenty-five years of diplomatic relations with China. From 1990 to 1997, Malaysia's trade with China increased from $1.2 billion to $4.4 billion. Moreover, in 1996, Malaysia hosted the second Fujianese World Convention, with Mahathir himself delivering the opening address.[75] This had great importance in that it symbolized Mahathir's acceptance of ethnic Chinese business networks. The Malaysian government has thus not only encouraged ethnic Chinese investment in China, but has also urged ethnic Chinese to use their influence to attract Chinese investments to Malaysia. On his 1999 trip to China Mahathir negotiated for a $1.5 billion Chinese investment in a paper and pulp mill in Malaysia's Sabah state. Malaysia is further attempting to increase the number of Chinese tourists by proposing to waive visa requirements as China becomes an important source of tourists for the region.

Malaysia's establishment of closer ties with China has political as well as economic aspects. For example, in 1994, Malaysia's National Front established party-to-party relations with China's CCP, while in 1999, the two countries agreed to boost defense cooperation. The reasons for closer ties, from Malaysia's perspective, are complex. Economic gain certainly plays a role, but animosity toward the West is also crucial. Mahathir has declared that any threat to Asia comes not from China but the West.[76] This attitude was hardened during the Asian economic crisis, which Mahathir blamed on Western speculators and the erroneous response of international economic institutions dominated by the West. Thus, in 1999, the prime minister, while in Beijing, called for the formation of an Asian Monetary Fund that would eliminate Asian reliance on the International Monetary Fund (IMF). Mahathir has also continued to press for an Asian regional grouping consisting of ASEAN, Japan, China, and South Korea to counter the EU and NAFTA. Thus, the Malaysian government has for now subsumed its concerns over China and its own ethnic Chinese population under other interests.

China's relations with Indonesia, while cordial, are still beset by some suspicion, due in part to events dating back thirty-five years. After the 1965 coup attempt, diplomatic relations between China and Indonesia were frozen, with Jakarta worried about China's relations with the PKI and the issue of Indonesia's ethnic Chinese. Although diplomatic relations were reestablished in 1990, the saliency of Indonesia's continued sensitivity was revealed after the Medan riots in 1994. In April the Chinese Ministry of Foreign Affairs issued a statement of concern, calling on Indonesia to curb the demonstrations aimed at ethnic Chinese. Jakarta reacted strongly, with Justice Minister Utoyo Usman responding that "China had better mind its own internal affairs. Events such as took place in Medan happen in many other countries."[77]

Following the 1998 riots in Indonesia, Beijing took a much stronger stand due to pressure from Taiwan and ethnic Chinese around the world. After initially maintaining silence for nearly two months after the May riots, Beijing said it was "concerned and sympathetic" about the plight of Indonesian-Chinese. Over the next few months Beijing's rhetoric intensified. Foreign Ministry officials called on Indonesia to protect ethnic Chinese and the Chinese media heavily publicized the atrocities the Chinese had suffered. In August a front-page *People's Daily* editorial called for the punishment of those responsible for attacks on ethnic Chinese, while later in the month Xinhua stated, "It is an unshirkable responsibility of the Chinese government to do its utmost to show concern for and give assistance to Indonesian Chinese," noting that Chinese embassy personnel aided not only Chinese nationals during the riots but also Indonesian-Chinese. In September the *China Daily* directly criticized Indonesian president B. J. Habibie for his stance on the rapes of ethnic Chinese women.[78]

Beijing's criticisms of Indonesia were surprising. Chinese leaders are usually careful not to comment on the internal affairs of other countries. By criticizing Indonesian authorities, Beijing legitimized international condemnation of human rights violations. Moreover, Beijing responded, albeit weeks after the May riots and Suharto's removal from office, due to pressures from ethnic Chinese around the world who felt that it was Beijing's responsibility to stand for the interests of Chinese regardless of their citizenship. Presumably Beijing could face similar types of pressure in the future, raising the prospect that China will become more active in speaking out on issues important to the well being of ethnic Chinese in other countries.

There are other irritants to the Sino-Indonesian relationship as well. Beijing was unhappy with Taiwan president Lee Teng-hui's visit to Indonesia in 1994, while Jakarta was displeased by Chinese missile firings in the Taiwan Strait in 1996. Indonesia also has been concerned about Chinese maneuvering in the South China Sea, including claims that appear to threaten Indonesia's exclusive economic zone. Jakarta is further uneasy about Indonesian investments in China, especially at a time when Indonesia itself has faced serious economic hardship. Indonesia's domestic politics play an important role in its relations with China. Unlike Malaysia, Indonesia has not had a New Economic Policy to redistribute wealth to its *pribumi* (indigenous Indonesian) population. Thus, ethnic Chinese continue to play the predominant economic role in Indonesia while many *pribumi* remain mired in poverty. Coupled with this is the fact that many wealthy Chinese made their money through monopolies granted by Suharto. High-level corruption and the accumulation of wealth by Suharto's family produced discontent in Indonesia that ultimately led to Suharto's fall and the discrediting of many wealthy Chinese.

Nevertheless, throughout the 1990s there has been progress in Sino-Indonesian relations. Diplomatic ties were restored in 1990, aided by an Indonesian-

Chinese businessman. Since then China and Indonesia have signed agreements covering natural resources, the citizenship of stateless ethnic Chinese in Indonesia, mutual investment promotion, and scientific cooperation. Investments by both sides have increased, as has trade, which rose from $1.25 billion in 1990 to $4.52 billion in 1997. Moreover, in 1999, there were some signs of a closer strategic relationship between Indonesia and China. Indonesian anger over the West's role in East Timor has led to improved relations with China, and newly elected Indonesian president Abdurrahman Wahid traveled to China for his first overseas state visit, accompanied by eighty business leaders.

The Indonesian government has also taken other steps that serve to better relations. For example, Suharto publicly supported Indonesian investments in China before his ouster. In 1994 Indonesia shortened the procedures and processing time for ethnic Chinese in Indonesia to adopt Indonesian citizenship. Indonesia has also lifted restrictions on the public use of Chinese characters and the teaching of Mandarin due to rising tourism and trade with Hong Kong, Taiwan, and China. In 1999, President Habibie declared that Indonesia had abolished all policies that were discriminatory against Chinese, while the election later that year of Abdurrahman Wahid brought new momentum to reconciliation between ethnic groups. China, too, has taken steps to cement ties. When Jiang Zemin visited Indonesia in 1994, he promised that China would never use people of Chinese origin who live in Indonesia for China's own political or economic gain there. He also expressed appreciation to the Indonesian government for steps it had taken in regard to the citizenship issue for ethnic Chinese and noted satisfaction at the way in which problems between China and Indonesia were being resolved.[79] Nevertheless, the position of Chinese in Indonesia continues to be precarious, and the issue will continue to affect Sino-Indonesian relations.

Thailand's overall relations with China are excellent. Thailand and China have enjoyed smooth political ties, and Thailand's ethnic Chinese are well integrated into Thai society. Thai delegations have gone to China to take advantage of business opportunities, and one of China's largest foreign investors, Charoen Pokphand, is a Thai firm. As a result of Thailand's economic problems during the Asian economic crisis, China increased its purchases of Thai agricultural products. In 1999, in a move that alarmed some of Thailand's ASEAN allies, Thailand signed a unique economic and security accord with China that outlines closer cooperation between the two countries for the 21st century. Nevertheless, Thailand also continues to have close ties with the United States, and many Thais have been concerned with China's calls to confront the United States.[80]

Relations between China and the Philippines have worsened throughout the past decade. President Ramos, although wary of the PRC, took businesspersons to China to explore opportunities in 1993. However, the issue of the Spratly Islands, and especially China's building of military structures on Mischief Reef, has soured relations. Thus, in 1999, President Estrada publicly called Beijing the biggest security threat in the region. There is some concern as well that the Philippines' Chinese community has broken into factions that support mainland China or Taiwan, with the main faction coming under mainland Chinese influence.[81]

This chapter has covered the international implications of China's relationship with ethnic Chinese. China's primary goal in this relationship is to promote its economic development. Thus, ethnic Chinese are encouraged to invest in China and establish trade relationships with Chinese firms. China further hopes that ethnic Chinese will serve as a bridge between China and Southeast Asia, strengthening China's economic ties with a region that it views as a natural economic partner. China's policy creates some tensions with Southeast Asian governments and raises questions in Southeast Asia about the loyalties of ethnic Chinese. China tries to mollify such concerns to a certain degree. Nevertheless, its policy aimed at furthering development through the resources of ethnic Chinese remains unchanged.

The ethnic Chinese have responded to China's policies by increasing investments in China. This has been accompanied by a limited resurgence of interest in China and Chinese culture. Nevertheless, there has been no political reorientation toward China. Furthermore, ethnic Chinese are restrained in their relationship with China by domestic pressures in Southeast Asia. Such domestic pressures rise when Southeast Asian nationalists question the loyalties of ethnic Chinese who invest in China.

Southeast Asian governments are caught between domestic pressures and international realities. Encouraging their ethnic Chinese populations to engage in economic cooperation risks exacerbating domestic fissures. Promoting the economic growth of neighboring China carries risks. However, China presents economic opportunities that cannot be ignored. Most governments have thus decided to endorse the economic relationship between China and ethnic Chinese, at least to some degree, hoping that this will benefit Southeast Asia's economic growth and give China a greater stake in a peaceful, stable regional environment. Moreover, if Southeast Asian countries are to be open to the international economy, their governments cannot stop outgoing investments into China. However, political flashpoints such as the Spratly Islands and perhaps even the Taiwan Strait, as well as potential domestic opposition, cast a shadow over economic ties with China.

NOTES

1. For an example of this viewpoint, written in the cold war context, see Robert S. Elegant, *The Dragon's Seed: Peking and the Overseas Chinese* (New York: St. Martin's Press, 1959). Elegant portrays China as bent on domination of Southeast Asia, aided by the overseas Chinese who serve as the irrational but powerful vanguard of China's aggression.

2. Bilveer Singh, "Article Assesses PRC's 'Threat' to Region," *Business Times* (Singapore) in English (9 June 1993), Foreign Broadcast Information Service (hereafter FBIS) *DR/East Asia*, 10 June 1993, 1–3, quote on 2.

3. "Singapore's Lee Warns of Growing Power of China," *Reuters*, 24 February 1996.

4. "Beijing Is Biggest Security Threat in the Region: Estrada," *Straits Times* (Singapore), 19 May 1999, Internet edition.

5. For a much more detailed account of this policy, see chapter 4.

6. Wang Gungwu, "China and the Region in Relation to Chinese Minorities," *Contemporary Southeast Asia* 1, no. 1 (May 1979): 36–50. See also Leo Suryadinata, *China and the ASEAN States: The Ethnic Chinese Dimension* (Singapore: Singapore University Press, 1985), 122–26. Suryadinata describes how in 1984 Malaysia protested Beijing's granting of special passes to visiting ethnic Chinese who were foreign citizens, leading Beijing to end the practice.

7. Lien Kuan, "History of Overseas Chinese and Their Glorious Tradition," *Peking Review*, 26 May 1978, 12–17. The author was the vice director of the Office of Overseas Chinese Affairs under the State Council.

8. Chang Pao-Min, "China and Southeast Asia: The Problem of a Perception Gap," *Contemporary Southeast Asia* 9, no. 3 (December 1987): 191.

9. Jusuf Wanandi, "China's Asia Card," *Far Eastern Economic Review* (hereafter *FEER*), 25 November 1993, 32.

10. Mary Kwang, "China Should 'Boost Ties with Asia Govts,' " *Straits Times* (Singapore), 28 April 1999, Internet edition.

11. For a discussion of this issue, see Leo Suryadinata, "Ethnic Chinese in Southeast Asia: Overseas Chinese, Chinese Overseas, or Southeast Asians?" in *Ethnic Chinese as Southeast Asians*, ed. Leo Suryadinata (New York: St. Martin's Press, 1997), 1–24.

12. For a summary of this debate, see George Hicks and J.A.C. Mackie, "A Question of Identity," *FEER*, 14 July 1994, 46–48. For an example of the sensitivity that some in Southeast Asia feel toward the subject of the ethnic Chinese, see Kernial Singh Sandhu, "Discussion," in Research Institute for Asian Development, International University of Japan, *Proceedings of Research Institute for Asian Development International Symposium 1992*, 120–22.

13. See Donald L. Horowitz, *Ethnic Groups in Conflict* (Berkeley: University of California Press, 1985), 209.

14. See Ismail Kassim, "Rush by Local Chinese to Invest in China Worries '46," *Straits Times Weekly Edition* (hereafter *STWE*) (Singapore), 15 May 1993, 10; and "Investments in China: Razaleigh Slammed," *STWE*, 22 May 1993, 10.

15. See Susan Sim, "The Ties That Do Not Bind," *STWE*, 24 June 1995, 14.

16. See Tan Kong Yam, "China and ASEAN: Competitive Industrialization Through Foreign Direct Investment," in *The China Circle*, ed. Barry Naughton (Washington, D.C.: Brookings, 1997), 111–35.

17. Joseph Kahn, "Beijing Warily Pushes Shanghai to Resume Role in Global Finance," *Wall Street Journal*, 25 November 1994, A1; R. Stormont, "China Seen Becoming 'Black Hole' for Funds," Reuters, 4 May 1994; and "China Seeks to Calm Fears over Foreign Investment," AFP (Agence France Presse), 9 August 1997.

18. Lee Kim Chew, "Goh Says ASEAN Must Respond to Competition from China," *Straits Times* (Singapore), 28 November 1997, Internet edition.

19. Victor Purcell, *The Chinese in Southeast Asia*, 2nd ed. (London: Oxford University Press, 1965), 487.

20. In this regard, see Sheila Tefft, "Chinese Investors Face Scrutiny as Indonesia Vies in Asian Economy," *Christian Science Monitor*, 6 April 1994, 13–14.

21. Michael Backman, "Blame Indonesia's Chinese?" *FEER*, 5 March 1998, 34.

22 "China's Diaspora Turns Homeward," *Economist*, 27 November 1993, 33.

23. "Intelligence—National Service," *FEER*, 7 April 1994, 12.

24. Theresa Chong Cariño, "The Ethnic Chinese, the Philippine Economy and China," in *Southeast Asian Chinese and China*, ed. Leo Suryadinata (Singapore: Times Academic Press, 1995), 223.

25. Economics Department, Monetary Authority of Singapore, "The Impact of the Asian Crisis on China: An Assessment," Occasional Paper no. 8, October 1998, 7–9.

26. See, for example, "Impact of Neighbors' Foreign Investment Policies," Beijing *Guoji Maoyi Wenti* in Chinese (20 September 1997), FBIS, 7 December 1997.

27. See Zhao Heman, "Huaqiao huaren jingji yu Zhongguo dui wai kaifang" ("The Overseas Chinese and Ethnic Chinese Economy and China's Opening to the World"), *Bagui qiao shi* (*Overseas Chinese History of Bagui*), 1994, no. 1: 11; Ma Zongshi, "China Dream in the Global 1990s and Beyond," *Contemporary International Relations* 3, no. 7 (July 1993): 17; and Jin Dexiang, "The Impact of China's Economic Policies," in *China and Southeast Asia: Into the Twenty-First Century*, ed. Richard L. Grant and Amos A. Jordan (Washington, D.C.: Center for Strategic and International Studies, 1993), 12–29.

28. Huang Dinglan, "Zhong-Yin (ni) fu jiao hou jingmao guanxi wenbu fazhan" ("The Steady Development of Economic and Trade Relations Between China and Indonesia After the Resumption of Diplomatic Relations"), *Nanyang wenti yanjiu* (*Southeast Asian Affairs*), 1993, no. 2:85.

29. Interviews by author, 1994. See also Sheila Tefft, "Overseas Investors Elicit Praise and Protests in Fujian Province," *Christian Science Monitor*, 30 March 1994, 13–14.

30. Suryadinata, "Ethnic Chinese," 9. For policies that discriminate against Chinese in Southeast Asia, see also Yuan-li Wu and Chun-hsi Wu, *Economic Development in Southeast Asia: The Chinese Dimension* (Stanford: Hoover Institution Press, 1980), 37–45, 173–79.

31. For a discussion of this phenomenon more generally, see Walker Conner, "The Impact of Homelands upon Diasporas," in *Modern Diasporas in International Politics*, ed. Gabriel Sheffer (London: Croom Helm, 1986), 16–18.

32. Stephen A. Douglas, "Political Dynamics of the Diaspora: The Chinese in Southeast Asia," paper presented at the Annual Meeting of the International Studies Association, Chicago, Ill., February 1995, 15–16, quote on 15.

33. See Philip Shenon, "Burmese Cry Intrusion (They Lack a Great Wall)," *New York Times*, 29 March 1994, A5; Bertil Lintner and Chiang Saen, "River of Dreams," *FEER*, 22 December 1994, 26; and Bertil Lintner, "Reaching Out," *FEER*, 11 September 1997, 57–58.

34. For details of the disturbances see Margot Cohen, "Days of Rage," *FEER*, 28 April 1994, 14–15; "Chinese 'Flee Indonesia over Latest Threats,'" Reuters, 4 June 1994; and "Angry Indonesians Attack Companies," Reuters, 12 June 1994.

35. Susan Sim, "Chinese 'Moved $136b out of Indonesia,'" *Straits Times* (Singapore), 15 April 1999, Internet edition.

36. "Sino-Indonesians Urged to Take 'Lesson' from Riots," *Jakarta Angkatan Bersenjata* (Internet version) in Indonesian (19 May 1998), FBIS, 19 May 1998; and "Indonesian Chinese Blamed for Riots," *Jakarta Post* in English (30 July 1998), FBIS, 30 July 1998.

37. "Don't Question Loyalty of Overseas Chinese: MCA," *Straits Times* (Singapore), 8 August 1994, 21.

38. Interview by author, 1994.

39. Xie Yining, "Qian Qichen jieshou benbao zhuanfang changlun Zhong-Mei guanxi" ("Qian Qichen Receives a Visit from this Paper to Discuss Chinese-American Relations"), *Qiao bao* (New York), 17 November 1993, 2.

40. See Supang Chantavanich, "From Siamese-Chinese to Chinese-Thai: Political Conditions and Identity Shift among the Chinese in Thailand," in *Ethnic Chinese as Southeast Asians*, ed. Leo Suryadinata (New York: St. Martin's Press, 1997), 254–55.

41. See Wang Gungwu, *China and the Chinese Overseas* (Singapore: Times Academic Press, 1991), 176; and Purcell, *Chinese in Southeast Asia*, especially 445.

42. Suryadinata, *China and the ASEAN States*, chapter 1; see also George Hicks and J.A.C. Mackie, "Tensions Persist," *FEER*, 14 July 1994, 50–51.

43. Michael Vatikiotis, "Malaysian First," *FEER*, 14 July 1994, 49.

44. Lucian W. Pye, *The Spirit of Chinese Politics: A Psychocultural Study of the Authority Crisis in Political Development* (Cambridge, Mass.: MIT Press, 1968), 56–57, quote on 57.

45. "Chinese Not an Easy Race to Assimilate: Mahathir," *STWE* (Singapore), 15 March 1997, 8.

46. Tu Wei-ming, "Cultural China: The Periphery as the Center," *Daedalus* 120, no. 2 (Spring 1991): 17.

47. Wang Gungwu, "Migration and Its Enemies," in *Conceptualizing Global History*, ed. Bruce Mazlish and Ralph Buultjens (Boulder: Westview Press, 1993), 145.

48. Suryadinata, "Ethnic Chinese."

49. See Chantavanich, "From Siamese-Chinese to Chinese-Thai," 232–59.

50. Chan Kwok Bun and Tong Chee Kiong, "Rethinking Assimilation and Ethnicity: The Chinese in Thailand," in *The Chinese Diaspora: Selected Essays*, vol. 2, ed. Wang Ling-chi and Wang Gungwu (Singapore: Times Academic Press, 1998), 1–27. Originally published in *International Migration Review* 27, no. 1 (1993).

51. For details on the Chinese in the Philippines, see Teresita Ang See, "The Ethnic Chinese as Filipinos," in *Ethnic Chinese as Southeast Asians*, ed. Leo Suryadinata (New York: St. Martin's Press, 1997), 158–202; and Carino, "The Ethnic Chinese, 216–29.

52. For details on the Chinese in Malaysia, see Lee Kam Hing, "Malaysian Chinese: Seeking Identity in Wawasan 2020," in *Ethnic Chinese as Southeast Asians*, ed. Leo Suryadinata (New York: St. Martin's Press, 1997), 72–107.

53. See Mely G. Tan, "The Ethnic Chinese in Indonesia: Issues of Identity," in *Ethnic Chinese as Southeast Asians*, ed. Leo Suryadinata (New York: St. Martin's Press, 1997), 33–65.

54. Wang Gungwu, *China and the Overseas Chinese*, chapter 11; see also chapter 16.

55. See, for instance, Edward Tang, "Where Using Chinese is Chic," *Straits Times* (Singapore), 2 September 1999, Internet edition.

56. Sun Xingcheng, "Guanyu mingan wenti" ("Regarding Sensitive Issues"), in *Huaren jingji nianjian 1997–1998* (*Yearbook of the Ethnic Chinese Economy 1997–1998*) (Beijing: Shehui kexue wenxian chubanshe, 1997), 229–31.

57. "Sulian zhengbian hou Zhongguode xianshi ying duiyu zhanlüe xuanze" ("China's Realistic Strategic Choice after the Coup in the Soviet Union"), *Zhongguo qingnian bao* (*China Youth Daily*), 9 September 1991. Reprinted in *Chung-kuo chih ch'un* (*China Spring*), 1992, no. 1:39.

58. See, for instance, Le Shui, "Haiwai huarende zhongzu benzhi nanyi gaibian" ("The Racial Nature of Ethnic Chinese Is Difficult to Change"), *Bagui qiao shi* (*Overseas Chinese History of Bagui*), 1997, no. 1:13–16; and Wu Hongqin, "Haiwai huarende minzu rentong yu guojia guannian bianxi" ("An Analysis of the Ethnic Identity and Sense of Nationality of Ethnic Chinese"), *Huaqiao huaren lishi yanjiu* (*Overseas Chinese and Ethnic Chinese Historical Research*), 1996, no. 1:1–6.

59. See, for example, Sun Xingcheng, "Guanyu," 228–29.

60. Interview by author, 1994.

61. Ibid.

62. See Li Guoliang, "Chinese Scholars' Studies on the Changes of Overseas Chinese and Their Descendants after World War II," *RIAD Bulletin*, no. 2 (March 1993): 121–30.

63. See, for example, Shanghai guoji wenti yanjiusuo, ed., *Guoji xingshi nianjian 1995* (*Survey of International Affairs 1995*) (Shanghai: Shanghai jiaoyu chubanshe, 1995), 3–13.

64. See "Sulian zhengbian hou," 38–39.

65. For an analysis of strains in Chinese-Southeast Asian ties from a Chinese perspective, see Zhao Hong, "Jiushi niandai Zhongguo yu Dongmeng guojiade jingmao hezuo guanxi zhanwang" ("Outlook for Economic and Trade Cooperation Between China and ASEAN in the 1990s"), *Nanyang wenti yanjiu* (*Southeast Asian Studies*), 1993, no. 2: 72–73; and Liao Shaolian, "China-ASEAN Economic Relations: Trends and Problems," *Ritsumeikan Journal of International Relations and Area Studies*, no. 2 (March 1992): 38–40.

66. In this regard see C. Y. Chang, "Overseas Chinese in China's Policy," *China Quarterly*, no. 82 (June 1980): 290–303; see also Suryadinata, *China and the ASEAN States*, chapter 2; and Denny Roy, *China's Foreign Relations* (Lanham, Md.: Rowman and Littlefield, 1998), 183–84.

67. C. Y. Chang, "Overseas Chinese," 303.

68. Chang Pao-Min, "China and Southeast Asia," 181–93; see also Robert S. Ross, "China and the Ethnic Chinese: Political Liability/Economic Asset," in *ASEAN and China: An Evolving Relationship*, ed. Joyce K. Kallgren, Noordin Sopiee, and Soedjati Djiwandono (Berkeley: Institute of East Asian Studies, University of California, 1988), 147–73.

69. Statistics calculated from International Monetary Fund, *Direction of Trade Statistics Yearbook 1997* (Washington, D.C.: IMF, 1997); and International Monetary Fund, *Direction of Trade Statistics Quarterly: June 1999* (Washington, D.C.: IMF, 1999).

70. See "Trick or Treat," *Economist*, 10 July 1993, 28–29.

71. Ross, "China and the Ethnic Chinese," 172.

72. John Wong, *The Political Economy of China's Changing Relations with Southeast Asia* (London: Macmillan, 1984), 113–17.

73. Deborah C. Diamond, "Malaysia's Economic Diplomacy," *China Business Review*, May/June 1986, 4.

74. See, for example, Frank Ching, "Malaysia Charts China Course," *FEER*, 23 February 1995, 32.

75. See Hong Liu, "Old Linkages, New Networks: The Globalization of Overseas Chinese Voluntary Associations and Its Implications," *China Quarterly*, no. 155 (September 1998): 597.

76. See, for example, "West Wants to Dominate Asia: Mahathir," *Straits Times* (Singapore), 1 October 1999, Internet edition; and "Chinese Not an Easy Race," 8.

77. In regard to the Chinese-Indonesian exchange, see Rizal Sukma, "Recent Developments in Sino-Indonesian Relations: An Indonesian View," *Contemporary Southeast Asia* 16, no. 1 (June 1994): 35–45; and "Regional Briefing—'Excessive' Reaction," *FEER*, 5 May 1994, 13.

78. See Michael Vatikiotis, Matt Forney, and Ben Dolven, "Compatriot Games," *FEER*, 20 August 1998; Wang Hui, "Irresponsible Words," *China Daily*, 4 September 1998, Internet edition; and "Indonesian Chinese Suffered in May Riots," Beijing Xinhua in Chinese (13 August 1998), FBIS, 20 August 1998.

79. "Jiang on Overseas Chinese," Beijing Xinhua in English (18 November 1994), FBIS *DR/China*, 21 November 1994, 12.

80. See, for example, "China's Policy of Confrontation," *Bangkok Post*, 12 September 1999, Internet edition.

81. See "Pro-China Chinese Filipinos 'A Worry,'" *Straits Times* (Singapore), 17 May 1999, Internet edition.

CHAPTER 7 ————————————————

Economic Cooperation Between China and Singapore

Whereas previous chapters discussed the economic relationship between China and Asia's ethnic Chinese and the ramifications of this relationship, this chapter specifically focuses on China's economic relationship with Singapore. Singapore is singled out for study because it is an independent state in Southeast Asia with a large ethnic Chinese population. In mid-1998, Singapore's total population was estimated at 3.87 million, with citizens and permanent residents numbering 3.16 million. In this multiethnic state, 77.0 percent of Singaporeans are Chinese, 14.0 percent Malays, 7.6 percent Indian, and 1.4 percent other.[1] Although longtime prime minister and now senior minister Lee Kuan Yew and Singapore's government initially strove to create a Singaporean nationalism and insisted that ethnic Chinese in Singapore were Singaporeans rather than overseas Chinese, more recent efforts have been aimed at resinifying ethnic Chinese.[2]

The fact that Singapore is the only Southeast Asian country where ethnic Chinese control the government separates Singapore's Chinese from those of other Southeast Asian states. Singaporeans are much freer to express their Chinese culture and identity and have a government that encourages economic and social exchanges with China. Indeed, many of Singapore's investments in China are state-linked, made in a context of a close working relationship between the Chinese and Singaporean governments. Thus, in the case of Singapore, the diaspora triangle of chapter 1 is shaped differently than with other ethnic Chinese in Southeast Asia. The most high-profile investments are made by Singapore firms with some connection to Singapore's government. Investments by Chinese-Singaporean firms operating independently of the government play a smaller role.

THE SINGAPOREAN PERSPECTIVE

As one of Asia's four dragons, Singapore has enjoyed a successful economic system.[3] However, its developmental path has not been easy or without detours. Singapore's pre–World War II economy was trade-based, inhibiting the development of a strong manufacturing sector. By 1960, manufacturing only accounted for 11.9 percent of Singapore's GNP, while 94 percent of Singapore's exports consisted of reexports.[4] In the immediate postwar period the ability of Singapore to maintain its entrepôt status appeared in doubt, so its leaders began to adopt an import substitution industrial strategy that envisioned Malaysia as the primary market for Singapore's goods. However, Singapore's separation from Malaysia in 1965 and Britain's announcement that it was closing military bases in Singapore jolted the island's economy and led political leaders to adopt a two-pronged export-oriented manufacturing strategy, based on both attracting multinational firms to Singapore and establishing large government-linked companies. Singapore's government directed this new strategy and took aggressive steps to implement it, including the suppression of independent labor unions, the promotion of education, and continual efforts to attract higher value-added manufacturing.

Singapore has been successful in attracting multinational firms. From 1990 to 1997, foreign firms produced 75.5 percent of Singapore's manufacturing output.[5] However, Singapore's favoring of multinational firms and government-linked companies has also stunted development among the local Chinese bourgeoisie. Thus, Singapore's domestic sector is concentrated in its traditional activities in the tertiary sector, especially commerce, finance, and real estate, with little involvement in manufacturing.[6]

Singapore's economic strategy brought consistent high growth up to the mid-1980s. However, a recession in 1985 jolted the economy, and as a result Singapore's government modified its industrial export-oriented strategy. As part of this altered plan Singapore embarked on a path of "internationalization," an effort to increase investments abroad.[7] The need for internationalization is quite clear. Singapore's population is aging due to lowered birth rates and the emigration of young professionals, and there are fears that the population could actually begin to decline at some point in the future. Investments abroad can help cushion this shock by providing long-term sources of income from outside Singapore. Singapore's small size also limits growth based on domestic demand. Furthermore, investing abroad is necessary to maintain a competitive position internationally, especially as Singapore's labor costs increase. In the second half of the 1980s, internationalization through widescale foreign investment became possible as Singapore became a net lender of capital funds.

The initial focus of Singapore's internationalization effort centered on Europe and North America. However, by the early 1990s, the government began to look to Asia, due to losses incurred in the West and greater perceived opportunities in Asia.[8] Singapore's emphasis thus shifted from internationalization to regionalization, most notably in ties with China. By the end of 1997, 53 percent of Singapore's direct investments abroad were located in Asia.[9] Although the severity of the Asian economic crisis led some to question the wisdom of Singapore's commitment to Asia, leading government officials renewed the country's commitment to regionalization while still acknowledging the importance of diversification.[10]

This new strategy has brought a shift in the focus of Singapore's government but has not reduced its economic activism. Singapore's domestic bourgeoisie is relatively weak, limiting its ability to invest in the region. As Singapore's government played a guiding role in developing Singapore's domestic economy, it is has also led the country's regionalization effort. First, Senior Minister Lee Kuan Yew, Prime Minister Goh Chok Tong, and other government officials have given a variety of speeches providing leadership, setting goals, and encouraging Singaporeans to invest abroad. The government has also sponsored conferences on investing in the region and set up the Institute of East Asian Political Economy, headed by former deputy prime minister Goh Keng Swee, to focus on Asia's economy. (In 1997, this became the East Asian Institute, now headed by Wang Gungwu.) Other steps include tax incentives to promote regionalization and attract the regional headquarters of multinational firms, the formation of the Singapore International Foundation to provide support for Singaporeans living overseas, the promotion of entrepreneurship, and the creation of a government-sponsored venture capital fund aimed at helping new entrepreneurs invest in Asia. In addition, the government committed to invest its own reserves in East Asia.[11]

Although Singapore is promoting investments throughout Asia, a primary target has been China because of cultural affinities and long-standing connections, China's economic potential, and China's status as a regional power. This is illustrated in a speech by Minister for Home Affairs Wong Kan Seng, who claimed that Singapore takes advantage of the fact that most Singaporeans are of Chinese origin and therefore understand the language and culture in China. He went on to point to both the geopolitical and economic aspects of investing in China, stating "Singapore's policy towards China is based only on the simple fact that China is a geopolitical reality. We must live with it and it is in our national interest to have good relations with China. It is also where the greatest economic opportunities lie. If we invest in China, it is because there is money to be made there."[12]

The government has encouraged investments in China through numerous high-level contacts with Chinese officials and special cooperative mechanisms. Senior Minister Lee Kuan Yew, Prime Minister Goh Chok Tong, Deputy Prime Minister Lee Hsien Loong, former president Ong Teng Cheong, and others have been active in visiting China with large delegations of potential investors. In October 1993, Beijing and Singapore signed a memorandum of understanding, establishing a high-level joint government committee to facilitate bilateral economic cooperation, the first agreement of its kind signed by the Chinese central government and a Southeast Asian state. In November 1993, Shandong province and the government of Singapore formally launched the Singapore–Shandong Business Council, while in 1995, Singapore and Sichuan province announced plans to set up a working committee of government officials to see how Singapore can contribute to Sichuan's development. Other government-to-government agreements include the signing of an aviation pact in 1997, an agreement on the exchange of land for diplomatic use in 1998, an MOU on legal cooperation in 1998, a reciprocal training program for foreign ministry officers in 1998, an MOU on educational exchanges in 1999, and a cultural cooperation program signed in 1999. Military ties have been established between Singapore and China, and links have also been formed between the Chinese Communist Party and Singapore's People's Action Party (PAP).

Most important, the government is using its network of boards and government-linked companies to lead the way in investing in China. In January 1993, the Trade Development Board (TDB) announced it would begin helping Singaporean companies invest overseas and later began opening a series of specialty shops to sell Singapore-made goods in China. The National Trades Union Congress signed three agreements with the All-China Federation of Labor to invest over S$10 million[13] in business projects in China in 1993, and Singapore's government holding company, Temasek Holdings, has incorporated a vehicle for investments in China. Bodies such as the TDB and Economic Development Board (EDB) lead groups abroad, host visiting delegations, provide information, promote trade, and themselves make overseas investments. The Singapore Tourism Board has been active in China as well. In all this the government actually guides Singaporean companies in individual investments. Thus, a Chinese source notes that "it is widely believed that the bulk of Singaporean investment in China is made through arrangements by the Economic Development Bureau. . . . With that guidance, the investments have been mostly made in packages with few instances of sporadic investment."[14]

Although Singapore's government is the moving force behind many investments in China, Singapore's Chinese Chamber of Commerce and Industry and various clan associations, representatives of domestic entrepreneurs, also promote business in China. For example, the Chamber is active in arranging trade and investment missions to China, offering training on subjects relevant to conducting business in China, providing Mandarin language courses, and hosting Chinese delegations. While in 1989 the Chamber received fifty-nine delegations and visitors from China, by 1992, the number of Chinese delegations had risen to 142.[15]

Perhaps the most important tool of the Chamber in promoting business is its *guanxi* with people in China. As a publication put out by the Singapore International Foundation proudly states, "The chamber's alliances with China have always been close, and never more so than now. Older businessmen in the chamber already have rapport with and contacts in place in China. In a scenario where relationships—including dialect considerations—can make or break a business deal, this old boy's net*work is in*valuable."[16] The Chamber has continued to foster *guanxi* through its organization of the first World Chinese Entrepreneurs Convention in Singapore in August 1991 and its role in subsequent conventions.

SINGAPORE'S INVESTMENTS IN CHINA

Until 1990, the proportion of Singapore's direct investments in China was minimal. This was due partially to political factors. After Singapore's expulsion in 1965 from the Malaysian Federation, Singapore's government was wary of China or any potential Chinese influence in Singapore. This changed somewhat after Prime Minister Lee Kuan Yew's visit to China in 1976, when Lee realized that China was less of a threat than a tremendous opportunity for Singapore's businesses. In December 1979, a trade agreement between Singapore and China was completed, and in 1981, Singapore established a commercial representative office in Beijing to facilitate the efforts of Singaporean businesspersons. However, investments continued to be slow.

In 1985, Lee Kuan Yew made another trip to China, and this spurred Singapore businesspersons to become more active in investing there. Also important were the 1985 Investment Protection Treaty; a 1986 agreement on mutual cooperation in tourism, civil aviation, and exhibitions; the 1986 Avoidance of Double Taxation Treaty; and the 1989 Shipping Agreement. The treaty on taxation is noteworthy because it not only prevented double taxation on investment profits but also reduced the Chinese government's withholding tax on dividends paid out of profits from Singaporean investments in China. Whereas the usual tax rate for foreign investors was 10 percent, Beijing assessed Singaporean investors a rate of only 7 percent.[17]

At the end of 1985, Singapore companies were involved in approximately ninety-one projects in China worth S$414 million.[18] The vast majority of these were in construction and engineering, and many of the early projects were carried out by those who had long-standing contacts in China. By 1988, Singapore businesspersons had signed 239 contracts worth approximately US$539 million, putting Singapore in fourth place among all investors. About 70 percent of this investment was in hotels and real estate, with the rest in manufacturing and services.[19]

As demonstrated in table 7.1, over the 1988–91 period investments rose modestly. However, diplomatic relations were established between Singapore and China on 3 October 1990, and this contributed to an improved investment climate. (Relations between the two countries were warm well before that time, but Singapore refrained from establishing formal relations with China until after Indonesia had done so.) Then, in 1992, Singapore's contracted investments in China skyrocketed, reaching almost US$1 billion, higher than the cumulative total of the entire 1979–91 period. The jump was due largely to Lee Kuan Yew's trip to China in 1992 and further encouragement from Singapore's government, which repeatedly emphasized the importance of getting into the China market before it was too late. Domestic changes within China also played a role, as Deng Xiaoping made his famed southern tour in 1992. However, in spite of this new activity, Singapore's contracted investments in 1992 were still less than 2 percent of the total US$57.5 billion in contracted foreign investment in China for the year.

Singapore's investments in China jumped again in 1993, reaching US$2.95 billion in contracted investments and US$492 million in utilized investments.[20] Thus, between 1979 and the end of 1993, Singapore invested in 3,122 projects in China with a total contracted value of US$4.8 billion, making Singapore China's fifth largest investor. This equaled 1.7 percent of all foreign-funded projects in China and 2.2 percent of the value of all projects signed.[21]

Singapore's contracted investments in China rose again in 1994 and 1995, but dropped significantly from 1996 to 1998. Nevertheless, utilized investment by Singapore companies has risen every year since 1991. Over a ten-year period, actual Singaporean investments in China rose from $84 million in 1989 to $3.4 billion in 1998. Remarkably for a country the size of Singapore, this compares to $3.90 billion invested by the United States in 1998. Thus, in 1998, Singapore was China's fourth largest investor behind Hong Kong/Macao, the United States, and the Virgin Islands (but ahead of Japan), contributing 7.5 percent of direct foreign investment in China. These recent gains have occurred in spite of the Asian economic crisis. By the end of 1998, Singapore's stock of investments in China stood at US$12.2 billion.[22] Nevertheless, Singapore's falling contracted investment indicates that investment increases may soon be over. This conclusion is supported by business losses and survey results showing growing dissatisfaction with investments in China.[23]

Although Singapore's investments in China have increased at rapid rates, they should be kept in the context of Singapore's expanding investments in the entire region. Singapore's total direct equity investments abroad grew from S$13.6 billion in 1990 to S$70.6 billion by the end of 1997. As of the end of 1993, the largest host countries for Singapore's investments were Malaysia (21.9 percent) and Hong Kong (19 percent). Indonesia held 2.4 percent of direct equity investments (8th overall), while China held 2.1 percent (10th overall), up from 1.6 percent in 1992. By the end of 1997, Malaysia and China were the top investment destinations, each holding 13 percent of Singapore's direct investment abroad.[24]

In regard to the economic sectors in which Singaporeans invest, several patterns stand out. In the early 1980s, much of Singapore's business with China centered around oil. However, this quickly faded. On the other hand, property development, especially the construction and management of hotels, has been consistently important. Examples of hotels with partial or complete Singapore ownership include Beijing's Liangmahe Hotel, Shanghai's Hotel Equatorial, Tianjin's Sheraton Hotel, Guangzhou's Cultural Holiday Inn, Xiamen's Harbour View Hotel, Wuhan's Yangtze Hotel, and Haikou's East Lake Hotel. A Chinese report in 1994 stated that 80 percent of Singapore's investments in China were in real estate projects, which tend to have high earnings and short development cycles.[25]

Table 7.1
Singapore's Investments in China (in million U.S. dollars)

Year	Contracted and Percent Increase		Utilized and Percent Increase	
1979–85	190		n.a.	
1986	140		n.a.	
1987	80	(43%)	22	
1988	140	75%	28	27%
1989	150	7%	84	200%
1990	110	(27%)	50	(40%)
1991	160	45%	58	16%
1992	1,000	525%	122	110%
1993	2,950	195%	492	303%
1994	3,780	28%	1,180	140%
1995	8,690	130%	1,861	58%
1996	6,300	(28%)	2,247	21%
1997	4,470	(29%)	2,607	16%
1998	3,000	(33%)	3,404	31%

Sources: Paul J. Bolt, "The New Economic Partnership Between China and Singapore," *Asian Affairs: An American Review* 23, no. 2 (Summer 1996): 88; Lu Ning, "S'pore Investment in China up 30% Despite Asian Crisis," *Business Times* (Singapore), 15 February 1999, Internet edition; and table 4.1.

Another important sector of Singaporean investment has been infrastructure. Singapore has been involved in port and airport development and management, as well as telecommunications. For example, Singapore's Senchang Group Corp. formed a joint venture in 1985 to develop port facilities on Shenzhen's Nantou peninsula. The Port of Singapore Authority has joint venture container terminals in Fuzhou and Dalian. Sembawang Corp. contracted to service overseas flights at China's airports in 1991, while Singapore Telecom participated in laying fiber-optic undersea cable for communications. Further, Singapore-invested firms set up in China are involved in a number of high-tech areas. These include the development of software, computers, optics, and satellite-based communication networks. Singapore Technologies' plan to launch a satellite in a venture with five Chinese companies, however, was blocked by the U.S. government in 1999.

From the mid-1980s continuing to the present, manufacturing has taken a bigger share of Singaporean investments in China. Most industrial investment has been in light industry, such as appliance factories and food processing. However, Singapore companies are involved in heavy industry too. For example, in 1995, NatSteel entered a joint venture with a state-owned steel maker to produce wire rod in Wujin, while in 1999, it announced plans to expand its steel mill operations in Xiamen. Tibs International signed a joint venture agreement with the Beijing Bus Manufacturing Factory in 1993, while Liang Huat Aluminum set up a joint venture in Hangzhou in 1994. In 1999, the Chinese government approved the construction of a power plant in Hubei owned in part by the Government of Singapore Investment Corp. Singaporean companies have also been heavily involved in the development of industrial parks. Thus, by the end of 1997, manufacturing and real estate were the most important sectors for Singaporean investment.

The sectoral pattern of Singapore's investments reflects both China's domestic needs and Singapore's economic strengths. Early investments in the oil industry are no surprise, considering China's efforts to develop its energy sector and Singapore's position as a base for multinational oil companies. Investments in hotels and real estate reflect Beijing's efforts to develop the tourism industry and the traditional strengths of Singapore's domestic bourgeoisie, while industrial parks mirror the expertise of Singapore's government-linked companies. However, Singapore has not set up widespread manufacturing operations like Hong Kong and Taiwan due to its own lack of domestic entrepreneurs engaged in manufacturing. One Singapore editorial explained: "Singapore is going for niche-slotting by offering its expertise in infrastructure building. . . . Competing with the Taiwanese and Hongkongers in goods and consumer services . . . is an unequal contest."[26]

Singapore's reliance on government-linked companies in providing leadership in investing in China affects the character of Singapore's investments. Instead of moving quickly to take advantage of deals that may present themselves suddenly, Singapore tends to go through official channels and move according to standard operating procedures when it comes to investments. This has the advantage of preserving Singapore's reputation for honesty and straightforwardness in business dealings, a reputation that Singapore's leaders are quick to emphasize. Minister for Home Affairs Wong Kan Seng compared Singapore's reputation for integrity with other countries who have "rapacious businessmen only out to make a quick buck."[27] A Chinese official in Fuzhou province commented that Singapore's businesspersons have a good reputation, although they often complain about the dishonest practices of others.[28] Certainly the style of most Singapore companies prevents them from operating in the more freewheeling manner of Hong Kong and Taiwan firms.

In terms of location of investments, up to the end of 1992, approximately 80 percent of Singapore's holdings were located in Guangdong and Fujian provinces,[29] reflecting economic opportunities there and strong ethnic ties between Singaporeans and the inhabitants of those two provinces. However, beginning in 1993, Singapore companies began to look to other areas due to rising costs in the south, Beijing's promotion of areas farther up the coast, a desire to find locations with less competition from Hong Kong and Taiwan companies, and the increasing governmental direction of Singapore investments. In recent years Shandong province, Jiangsu province, and Shanghai have become popular investment destinations for Singapore firms. Singapore's flagship project in Jiangsu's Suzhou helped attract numerous Singapore companies to that area.

Furthermore, the majority of Singapore firms continue to invest in coastal provinces rather than China's interior. Transportation is a major problem for inland areas, as are shortages of water and power and a lack of knowledge among investors about inland areas. Another contributing factor is that the largest Singapore companies have invested in coastal areas. Small and medium-sized enterprises are then drawn nearby to provide secondary materials.[30] Investing in ancestral hometowns also plays some role in the choice of investment locations for Singaporean enterprises. For example, clan organizations are investing in ancestral hometowns, although not exclusively so. However, these types of investments tend to be small. On major projects where large corporations or government-linked companies are involved, economic and political criteria play the primary role in deciding where to invest.

A prominent trend in Singapore's investment practices during the 1990s was to build townships or industrial parks. Singapore consortiums developed plans for Ningbo, Shanghai, and Beihai City in *Guangxi*. The Yuan Hong Industrial Park in Fujian province is a 5,000 hectare area being developed by a consortium of Singapore firms and Indonesia's Salim Group.[31] The Wuxi–Singapore Industrial Park, with a scale of 1,000 hectares, had fifty investors as of June 1998 with an investment commitment of $600 million. However, the biggest and most publicized project has been the development of a township in Suzhou dubbed "Singapore II." This project illustrates both Singapore's optimism over what it could achieve in China through its partnership with the central government and Singapore's disillusionment upon discovering that even central government support does not guarantee success in China.

In May 1993, the overseas investment vehicle of the Singapore Labour Foundation signed an in-principle agreement to develop a 70-square-kilometer industrial township in Suzhou. The initial plans called for three new towns: a commercial hub, a high-tech hub, and a section for industries that required large amounts of space. In August a government-backed consortium led by the government-linked Keppel Group (which had replaced the Singapore Labour Foundation) signed an agreement with Suzhou to construct the township, giving the Singapore side a 65 percent stake in the deal. In October 1993, the governments of Singapore and Jiangsu province signed a memorandum of understanding on cooperation on the Suzhou township. Finally, in late February 1994, Singapore's prime minister Goh Chok Tong and China's prime minister Li Peng witnessed the signing by Singapore's senior minister Lee Kuan Yew and Chinese vice premier Li Lanqing of a national-level agreement on the Suzhou township called the Suzhou Industrial Park (SIP). The final agreement called for a "transfer of public administration software from Singapore to China."[32] Singapore promised to transfer knowledge in economic management and public administration, which China could then utilize for future developments. Both national governments were firmly committed to the park, with the project touted as an example of state-to-state cooperation.

In August 1994, piling work began on the first factory. By September 1995, approximately forty international investors, including companies from Singapore, Europe, the United States, South Korea, Japan, Hong Kong, and New Zealand had committed US$1.5 billion to the township. At that time the township was expected to eventually house six hundred thousand people. Total investment in the project was expected to reach US$30 billion, making it a major competitor for investments with Shandong's Pudong area.

The Singapore–Suzhou project in 1997 was granted the same status as a special economic zone. However, what has made this project unique is the governmental involvement on both the Chinese and Singaporean sides. The project is overseen by the Suzhou Industrial Park Joint Coordinating Council, co-chaired by Chinese vice premier Li Lanqing and Singapore deputy prime minister Lee Hsien Loong (son of Lee Kuan Yew and probable successor to Prime Minister Goh Chok Tong). Both governments once emphasized that much more is involved than economics. Li Lanqing commented, "This is a new mode of cooperation between two governments, which has never been seen before. It is a strategic step, rather than a commercial venture."[33] Similarly, Lee Hsien Loong stated that although Singapore has paid for part of the software transfer, "finance is not an important part of this project." He went on to say that Singapore will gain by developing "a long-term understanding with Chinese officials at many levels who would rise over the years."[34]

This project had great symbolism for Singapore. Singapore was building "Singapore II" inside China, with big plans for further industrial parks and housing complexes. However, by 1997, it had become obvious that the project was not going well. In December of that year Lee Kuan Yew publicly expressed dissatisfaction with the Chinese side, citing "different work habits" and competition from the Suzhou New District, a rival industrial park established by the Suzhou government in 1990. Although Chinese president Jiang Zemin gave his personal support to the Singapore project and called it a "priority of priorities," Lee Kuan Yew was critical of China's central government for not forcing greater cooperation on the part of Suzhou authorities.

By 1999, dissatisfaction on the part of the Singaporeans came to a head. In May it was reported that the China–Singapore Suzhou Industrial Park Development Company was having difficulty repaying its loans. Although by that summer the park had over ninety companies in operation with approved investment of $3.76 billion, in June the company needed new loans. By the end of 2000, the company will have lost an accumulated total of approximately $90 million. Singaporean leaders claimed that problems were due to unfair competition from the rival Suzhou park. Therefore in June an agreement was made whereby the Singapore consortium would reduce its stake in the project from 65 percent to 35 percent and hand over management of the park to the Chinese side on 1 January 2001. By that time 8 square kilometers out of the projected 70 will have been completed.

Taiwan's *United Daily News* described Singapore's frustrations in Suzhou as "Singapore waking up from an unrequited love for the Chinese."[35] Singapore had committed a great deal to this project. In addition to its prestige, Singapore statutory boards and government-linked companies had as of August 1999 invested $147 million in the Suzhou project. In addition, over six hundred Chinese bureaucrats and technocrats had been sent to Singapore for training.[36] Singapore failed because it overestimated the leverage that Beijing had over a local government and underestimated the quality of competition that a domestically run industrial park could provide. The uneasy coexistence of both financial and political goals for the project also caused problems. Singapore's minister for trade and industry George Yeo, giving a broader analysis, claimed that the problems in Suzhou were due to cultural differences, demonstrating how different Chinese and Singaporeans really are. He concluded that China would always be different from Singapore.[37] Thus, a project initially dubbed as "Singapore II" came to symbolize the stark differences between Singapore and China and the difficulty of exporting the "Singapore model" of economic development.

THE CHINESE PERSPECTIVE

China's interest in Singapore is rooted in economic and political objectives. Economically, Beijing has encouraged Singaporean investments and trade with Singapore. Indeed, China's trade with Singapore has expanded rapidly, although the total percentage of each country in the other's trade is still relatively low. In addition, Chinese companies are using Singapore as a base to raise capital and expand into Southeast Asia. Politically, Beijing is appreciative of Singapore's foreign policy, which recognizes that China has an important role in maintaining stability in Asia. Beijing also supports Singapore's role as a mediator in mainland–Taiwan relations and its place as a center of Chinese culture in Southeast Asia.[38] Closer economic ties between China and Singapore promote both Beijing's economic and political objectives.

However, Singapore took a cautious approach toward China throughout the 1980s. In the early days of reform, China was particularly interested in learning from Singapore how to take advantage of Western multinational corporations. In line with this, it was reported that China wanted Singapore to invest heavily in one of the special economic zones and make it successful.[39] That never happened due to Singapore's unwillingness to jump into China until the 1990s, although the initiation of the Suzhou project in 1994 was the equivalent of a special economic zone. Later, in 1993, the Chinese ambassador to Singapore, Yang Wenchang, promised that the Chinese embassy would try to minimize risks for Singapore investors and called on Singapore's businesspersons to invest along the upper and middle Yangtze and in northern China.[40] Subsequently the Chinese press wrote enthusiastically about Singapore's leap in investments, noting in the mid-1990s that Singapore had a "China fever" while Chinese had a "Singapore fever." Chinese sources also referred to an "economic honeymoon" after the establishment of diplomatic relations in 1990.[41]

However, there has been evidence of past Chinese dissatisfaction with the level of Singaporean involvement in China's economy. In 1991, Shanghai offered the Singapore government land for development in Pudong but Singapore declined. In the spring of 1993, then Chinese trade minister Madame Wu Yi complained that Singapore investors "are not daring enough to go for the big projects" in China.[42] However, seven months later Singapore had signed on to several mega-projects. Wu Yi has also suggested that Singapore use Chinese workers in Singapore. Although Singapore was slow to consider this, by 1995, there were over twenty thousand Chinese working on the island. By 1999, it was estimated that the number of Chinese nationals living in Singapore had risen to sixty thousand, including many skilled in technical fields. This is significant in that the use of foreign labor is a delicate political issue in Singapore.[43] Beijing has taken the initiative in other areas as well. For example, it was reported that the impetus for Singapore's major Suzhou investment came from Beijing.[44]

Moreover, China is not simply attempting to import Singapore businesses and export Chinese labor. China is also increasing its presence in Singapore both economically and culturally. As of October 1995, there were an estimated 150 Chinese companies in Singapore, and the numbers have increased. However, Singapore's Department of Statistics does not release data on these companies, perhaps because their presence is politically sensitive due to Singapore's multiethnic makeup.[45] A major share of Chinese companies in Singapore is in the financial sector. Examples include the Bank of Communications, the Industrial Commercial Bank of China, the Agricultural Bank of China, and the People's Construction Bank.

One attraction of Singapore is that Chinese firms have found it possible to raise hard currency there. Chinese firms tend to use Singapore more as a base to raise capital than as a site at which to invest it. As early as 1986, China's Fujian Investment Loan Enterprise Corporation attempted to raise US$50 million in Singapore's international capital market for projects in Fujian. The Bank of China, Bank of Communications, and the Shanghai International Trust and Investment Corporation have also raised hard currency in Singapore. In 1995, Chinese and Singapore officials signed a memorandum of understanding to make it less complicated for Chinese firms to list in Singapore. As a result, Chinese companies are now on the Singapore bourse.

Chinese firms also use Singapore as a base from which to expand into other ASEAN markets. Singapore is valuable because it is Southeast Asia's business center, with excellent transportation facilities and banking services. It is useful for gaining market information and business intelligence on Southeast Asia, as well as for establishing connections with the region's ethnic Chinese companies.

In the first ten months of 1998, seven Chinese firms set up trading units in Singapore to engage in reexport trade, joining several Chinese foreign trade corporations already in Singapore.[46]

In line with closer economic and political relations, the 1990s saw a large increase in the number of Chinese visitors to Singapore. The number of Chinese entrants for 1990 stood at 27,573. The figure for 1991 increased by over 50 percent to 41,709. By 1993, the figure had risen to 230,388, almost two-and-a-half times the previous year's figure and over eight times the 1990 level. By 1998, in spite of the Asian economic crisis, over 293,000 visits to Singapore were made by Chinese.[47]

Some of these visitors are members of the numerous trade and investment missions that go to the city-state. For example, in 1993, China sent a team of fifty senior officials led by Foreign Trade Minister Wu Yi to Singapore offering US$5 billion in joint venture projects to Singapore companies. Various localities in China also compete with each other for Singapore's investments. For example, Shandong and Suzhou were both candidates to host Singapore's township project. Before the final decision was made on where to locate the project, Shandong governor Zhao Zhihao, preceded by an advance party of about fifty and accompanied by six mayors, spent one week in Singapore lobbying for Shandong. Ultimately his attempt failed, but the extent of his effort is noteworthy.[48]

However, although China strives for expanding interactions with Singapore, it does not want these to come at the expense of Hong Kong. In 1990, Xinhua criticized Chinese corporations for holding too many trade fairs in Singapore. Not only were these portrayed as wasteful, they were also viewed as politically harmful to the future of Hong Kong and threatening to Hong Kong's status as an international trade center.[49] Due to Hong Kong returning to full Chinese sovereignty in 1997, Chinese officials did not wish to see any diminution in Hong Kong's status before the handover, while after the handover Hong Kong's economic health is still important for all of China. In this sense, Singapore's efforts to lure regional corporate headquarters, attract Hong Kong-based firms concerned about Hong Kong's future, and compete with Hong Kong as a financial center to service China's growth do not coincide with Beijing's interests. Although often denied, there is a strong rivalry between Hong Kong and Singapore. On the other hand, there are also cooperative elements to the relationship, as indicated by discussion in late 1999 of linking the two cities' stock exchanges.

RAMIFICATIONS

We have seen that Singapore developed deeper economic and political links with China during the 1990s, although Singapore's unhappiness over the Suzhou project has erased any idealism that may once have inflated the hopes of Singaporeans. These linkages carry implications in several areas. First is the extent to which China views Singapore as a model for both economic and political development. Second, Singapore has found it necessary to defend its place in

Southeast Asia as its relations with China have improved. Third, Singapore's domestic society must adjust to a new emphasis on Chinese culture within Singapore.

In spite of its small size and unique circumstances, many developing countries have looked to Singapore as a model of efficiency and modernity.[50] China has been especially interested in the Singapore model due to Singapore's Chinese character, its economic success, its strict social order, its one-party dominant political system, and its government's attacks on Western concepts of human rights. As a result, Chinese praise for Singapore has come from a variety of leaders, including Deng Xiaoping. When Deng visited Singapore in 1978, he was impressed by the city-state and exclaimed that Singapore should be a model for China. In 1992, Deng again complimented Singapore. In discussing socialism with Chinese characteristics, he proclaimed, "We can inspire ourselves using the Singapore social model and then do better."[51] In 1990, Li Peng was impressed with Singapore's economy, cleanliness, and social order, stating, "We should learn from and draw upon the host of invaluable experiences that the Singaporean people have accumulated in their nation-building." He further praised Singapore for maintaining its "oriental cultural heritage."[52]

Other evidence of China viewing Singapore as a model is found in the naming of Singaporeans as advisors in China, such as former first deputy prime minister Goh Keng Swee, MP Fong Sip Chee, former chief planner of Singapore Liu Thai Ker, and MP and trade unionist John Chen. Furthermore, scholarly articles have examined Singapore's success and in so doing subtly hint at recommendations regarding Chinese policies.[53]

Singapore's new township in Suzhou was also clearly meant to be a model of economic efficiency and stability with its transfer of "public administration software." As such it was envisioned to be a demonstration of how to provide an environment that will attract sophisticated multinational manufacturers. A comment by Suzhou's mayor Zhang Xinsheng is illustrative of the importance of ethnic ties as well, indicating how cultural attitudes affect Singapore's role as a model for China. At the signing of the earliest agreement on the building of "Singapore II," Zhang stated that Singapore is right for the job because it has developed its city and industrial estates while maintaining social order. He further noted: "We share the same cultural background . . . we share the same concept of values, native to the East."[54] Nevertheless, the outcome of "Singapore II" has left Singaporeans questioning whether Chinese and Singaporeans really do share the same cultural background and values.

Lee Kuan Yew clearly has considered ethnic Chinese, and particularly Singapore, to be models for China. This was expressed at the first World Chinese Entrepreneurs Convention in Singapore in 1991:

Indeed just by being ourselves, making progress in our lives, Chinese abroad become a powerful pull factor in China's evolution forward. We are living examples of Chinese people, imbued with Chinese culture doing immensely better because we work under a different system, and not because we are better.

In this respect, Singapore has an unusual place. The Chinese media has never held out Taiwan or Hong Kong as models for China. These are too close for comfort, politically too sensitive. On the other hand, Singapore far enough away, has been cited regularly as a model.[55]

Lee specifically points to the People's Action Party's continuous one-party rule and transforming of society as worthy of emulation. However, in 1999, after more experience with China, Lee denied that Singapore had offered itself as a model or that China was using Singapore as a model, blaming the Western press for the misperception.[56]

References on the part of Chinese leaders to Singapore's "social order" or "Asian values" highlight the Communist Party's fear of chaos. Economic reforms have brought many sources of instability, including inflation, deflation, unemployment, housing shortages, fears of foreign exploitation, and an influx of ideas from abroad. Singapore has faced most of these threats while maintaining its one-party dominant system and "social order." Similarly, Beijing can take little comfort from broader political trends in Asia. In the past several years genuine multiparty competition has come to South Korea, Taiwan, Japan, and, most recently Indonesia. Singapore, however, has sustained rapid growth while maintaining a regime that does not tolerate genuine competition.

Thus, a former Chinese Foreign Ministry official commented that Chinese leaders appreciate many aspects of Singapore's style: its authoritarianism, discipline, limited freedoms, one-party rule, absence of corruption, high growth rates, and skillful management of public affairs. However, the former official went on to say that Singapore is too small to be a true model. Although China can learn some strategies from Singapore, Singapore's experiences can not be duplicated by a great power.[57] This is of course true to a certain extent. China cannot take cues from Singapore on, for instance, resolving contradictions between Beijing and the provinces. Nevertheless, there is no other Chinese society that China will openly model as closely as Singapore, and there is evidence that Singapore does indeed serve as an example and inspiration for China.

Second, Singapore's wider international relations are affected by its deepening links with China. Because Singapore is a predominantly Chinese city-state nestled between the predominantly Malay states of Malaysia and Indonesia, Singapore's government must continue to stress publicly that Singapore is a Southeast Asian country in more than just a geographic sense. There has in fact been criticism of Singapore's ties with China. For example, Gerald Segal writes, "While the overseas Chinese as a business community help pull coastal China further out into the world of international interdependence, Lee Kuan Yew is seen to be strengthening Chinese nationalism and in effect souring relations in South-east Asia."[58]

Singapore is quick to defend itself against such charges. Responding to a question about Singapore's relations with China, Prime Minister Goh stated, "We are very clear in our minds that geographically, politically and socially, we belong to South-east Asia and we have to be South-east Asians first. If

Singaporeans don't understand that . . . that will spell trouble for us."[59] As such he has regularly warned against allowing traditional links with Malaysia and Indonesia to be weakened. Singapore officials have further spoken out concerning Southeast Asia's fears regarding the South China Sea. Nevertheless, as Singapore's relations with Indonesia and Malaysia deteriorated in the late 1990s due to various disputes, Singapore's position in Southeast Asia became more of an issue.

Singapore is investing in other countries in Asia too, both as an economic strategy and to prevent perceptions that it has become an appendage of China. Singapore is a major trading partner with Vietnam and also a significant investor, with an industrial park and technical training center in Vietnam. Malaysia is still the number one host of cumulative Singaporean investment. Indonesia comes in at fifth place and is host to at least four major Singaporean industrial parks. Singapore has also attempted to build stronger economic ties with Thailand, the Philippines, India, Myanmar, Kampuchea, and Laos.

A closely related issue is the relationship between Singapore and the ethnic Chinese throughout Southeast Asia. The Singapore government sometimes speaks for Southeast Asia's ethnic Chinese population, defending the loyalty of ethnic Chinese to their home governments. For example, Lee Kuan Yew was called upon to be a spokesman for ethnic Chinese at the Second World Chinese Entrepreneurs Convention, held in November 1993 in Hong Kong. Lee gave the keynote address, in which he encouraged ethnic Chinese businesspersons in their networking and investments, yet tried to reassure worried Southeast Asians about the loyalties of their ethnic Chinese compatriots. Similarly, then minister for information and the arts George Yeo, speaking at the opening of Singapore's Chinese Heritage Center in May 1995, called on ethnic Chinese to keep cultural and family connections with China separate from their political loyalties to their home countries. He went on to say that "long-term peace and stability in the Asia Pacific will partly depend on this clear distinction being made, not just by ethnic Chinese outside China but also by China herself."[60] When Lee Kuan Yew addressed the 1999 World Chinese Entrepreneurs Convention in Melbourne, he implored ethnic Chinese to give political loyalty to their current homelands, separating political and cultural identities.

A third ramification of the deepening Sino-Singaporean relationship is the effect that it is having on Singapore's domestic society. For many years Singapore's government tried to create a Singaporean identity. Now, however, the government has shifted to an emphasis on ethnic and racial roots, encouraging resinification for ethnic Chinese.[61] Through its Speak Mandarin Campaign, emphasis on Confucianism, encouragement of Chinese art, and other programs, the government is actively encouraging Chinese language and identity.

As a result, the overt promotion of Chinese culture is now much more acceptable in Singapore than before. Former Singapore Chinese Chamber of Commerce and Industry chairman K. C. Tan, commenting on this situation, notes: "If we had come out strongly to promote Chinese culture, especially during the

1970s, we would have been branded chauvinists. The conditions have changed because society is more mature."[62] Singapore's expanding links with China encourage this trend, which some have protested. There are still deep divisions in Singapore over race, culture, and religion. The government's efforts to raise Chinese language proficiency and transmit Chinese culture create controversy both within the Chinese community and among the Chinese, Malays, and Indians.

Senior Minister Lee Kuan Yew himself has contributed to Singapore's new emphasis on Chinese culture. Lee is a frequent visitor to China. In 1994, Lee became the honorary chairman of the International Confucian Association, and in late 1994, he donated royalties from the Chinese version of his collection of speeches to a village library project in China. In a story which may be suggestive of Lee's interest in his heritage, a Singapore newspaper reported in October 1994 that Lee, on a two-week official visit to China, visited Taishan in Shandong province, where "Chinese emperors used to ascend the mountains to make offerings to the gods."[63]

CONCLUSIONS

There are four chief conclusions to this chapter. First, the economic relationship between Singapore and China, most notably Singaporean investments in China, cannot be understood merely as the result of market forces. Political and cultural influences have also played major roles as both independent and mediating variables. Throughout the 1980s, when Hong Kong was making numerous investments in China and Taiwan was also jumping into the fray, Singapore largely stayed on the sidelines. This was due to Singapore's reluctance to antagonize its Malaysian and Indonesian neighbors, its economic strategy, the bureaucratized style of government-linked businesses, and the weaknesses of Singapore's domestic entrepreneurs.

When Singapore did begin investing heavily in China in the early 1990s, after suspicions of China in Southeast Asia had subsided and Singapore's own economic policy had shifted focus, investment was encouraged by the government through its statutory boards and government-linked companies. The traditional Chinese bourgeoisie played a much more limited role. In fact, Singapore's leaders are now constantly decrying the lack of entrepreneurs on the island who are willing to invest abroad, promoting programs that they hope will stimulate entrepreneurship and teach creativity. This sets off Singapore's investments from those of other ethnic Chinese, whose investments have been made by family businesses that use their connections in China and can operate more flexibly in China's relatively unstructured environment.

Culture also plays a role in Singapore's investments in China (as well as China's investments in Singapore). This is most obvious in the case of investments by Singapore's domestic bourgeoisie that have long-standing family and linguistic ties with southern China. The Chinese cultural background of most of Singapore's leaders has also made them more eager to become involved in the

Chinese market. This appears to be an interactive process, as the more Singapore becomes involved in China, the more Singapore's leaders feel their own sense of Chineseness.

On the other hand, Singapore's authoritarian, paternalistic, English-educated culture has produced a bureaucratic and cautious style among many of its businesspersons and government-linked companies. This inhibits Singaporean entrepreneurship, as well as investments in a relatively unstructured environment like China. This again differentiates Singaporean companies from those of other ethnic Chinese. It also shapes the type of projects that Singaporean companies tend to be involved in, pushing them toward investments that are supported by the government or negotiated by large companies. By contrast, investments from Taiwan in the mainland tend to involve less capital, are made by small to medium-sized companies that produce consumer goods for export, are more flexible, and are lower in profile. In addition, the failure of the Suzhou project has reminded Singaporeans of the "foreignness" of China and how different Singaporean Chinese are from mainlanders.

Second, Singapore's role in China is a reflection of Asian regionalism. Initially Singapore looked to the West to institute its "internationalization" policy, but this quickly changed when economic and political forces made it appear that "regionalization" was the wave of the future. Although China is Singapore's main focal point, Singapore has also used ethnic and government links to increase investment in and trade with Vietnam, Indonesia, Burma, India, and other Asian states. With the Asian economic crisis, political turmoil in Indonesia, and the bad experience in Suzhou, we can expect some Singaporean investment to shift toward Europe and North America. Indeed, Britain is becoming a popular destination for Singaporean investment and is now in third place on the list of hosts for Singaporean capital.

Third, from the Chinese point of view, Singapore is a good partner in developing China. The two governments share certain ideological presuppositions and rhetorically attack the West in areas such as human rights.[64] Singapore's big projects in China are government-connected, and Singapore is also proving to be a link between China and various multinational firms. Thus, Singapore is everything that Taiwan is not: supportive of Beijing, authoritarian, and pursuing projects that do not threaten the authority of the center. Ironically though, in spite of these positive characteristics, Singapore has only recently begun to make a major impact on China's development, as opposed to Hong Kong and Taiwan firms that have been in China longer.

Fourth, Singapore's new relationship with China presents both opportunities and dangers to Singapore. On the one hand, China is receptive to Singapore's investments and presents major opportunities to Singapore's businesses. This comes at a time when Singapore's own economy has reached a point where currency reserves have been built up, Singapore's small size is a constraining factor on future economic development, and Singapore faces an aging population, making foreign investment an increasingly crucial part of Singapore's economic strategy.

On the other hand, Singapore's involvement in China carries dangers. Internally, Singapore must not let involvement with China and Chinese culture alienate its non-Chinese population. Externally, China's growing economic and military might create security concerns for all the nations of Southeast Asia. At the same time, Singapore's place in the region has been questioned by commentators in Malaysia and Indonesia. For example, in May 1993 Malaysian Spirit of '46 president Tengku Razaleigh Hamzah asked, "What if a commonwealth of Chinese states comprising China, Taiwan, Hongkong and Singapore emerges one day? Will it not pose a threat to other countries in the region?"[65] Similarly, a writer for *Malaysia Business* claimed that Singapore was establishing closer links with China because of geopolitical motives, due in part to the fact that it is surrounded by Islamic Malaysia and Indonesia. He found it suggestive that while Singaporean officials are constantly visiting China, private investors are much more cautious.[66] Singapore must combat such impressions by being restrained in its dealings with China and keeping its neighbors from seriously doubting its commitment to Southeast Asia.

NOTES

1. Singapore Department of Statistics, www.singstat.gov.sg/FACT/SIF/sif3.html.

2. See John Clammer, *Race and State in Independent Singapore, 1965–1990* (Aldershot, England: Ashgate, 1998). For an alternate perspective on Singaporean identity, see Chiew Seen Kong, "From Overseas Chinese to Chinese Singaporeans," in *Ethnic Chinese as Southeast Asians*, ed. Leo Suryadinata (New York: St. Martin's Press, 1997), 211–27.

3. Sources on Singapore's political economy include W. G. Huff, "Turning the Corner in Singapore's Development State?" *Asian Survey* 39, no. 2 (March/April 1999): 214–42; Garry Rodan, ed., *Singapore Changes Guard: Social, Political, and Economic Directions in the 1990s* (New York: St. Martin's Press, 1993); Stephen Haggard, *Pathways from the Periphery: The Politics of Growth in the Newly Industrializing Countries* (Ithaca: Cornell University Press, 1990), chapter 5 and 146–51; Garry Rodan, *The Political Economy of Singapore's Industrialization: National State and International Capital* (New York: St. Martin's Press, 1989); and Kernial Singh Sandhu and Paul Wheatley, eds., *Management of Success: The Moulding of Modern Singapore* (Boulder: Westview Press, 1989).

4. Haggard, *Pathways*, 102.

5. Huff, "Turning the Corner," 222.

6. Gordon Redding notes that Singapore "has marginalized the Chinese family-firm sector" in G. Pierre Goad, "Singapore Takes Steps to Boost Investment and Links in China," *Asian Wall Street Journal*, 17 May 1993, 12. See also Catherine Paix, "The Domestic Bourgeoisie: How Entrepreneurial? How International?" in *Singapore Changes Guard: Social, Political, and Economic Directions in the 1990s*, ed. Garry Rodan (New York: St. Martin's Press, 1993), 184–200.

7. For sources on Singapore's efforts to expand business overseas, see *Singapore: The Next Lap* (Singapore: Government of Singapore, 1991); N. Balakrishnan, "Lion on the Prowl," *Far Eastern Economic Review* (hereafter *FEER*), 23 May 1991, 55–57; and Takao Kanai, "Singapore's New Focus on Regional Business Expansion," *NRI Quarterly* (Autumn 1993): 18–41.

8. In 1996 Singaporean investments in the United States recorded their fifth straight loss. See Chuang Peck Ming, "S'pore Losses from U.S. Investments Soar to US$121m," *Business Times* (Singapore), 21 October 1996, Internet edition. U.S. Bureau of Economic Analysis data also show a 1997 loss.

9. Narendra Aggarwal, "China Closes Gap with Malaysia," *Straits Times* (Singapore), 8 September 1999, Internet edition; see also the government's discussion of regionalization at www.gov.sg/mti.mti5html.

10. See, for instance, Irene Ngoo, "Regionalisation 'Will Continue,'" *Straits Times* (Singapore), 2 July 1999, Internet edition.

11. See Ministry of Finance, Republic of Singapore, *Final Report of the Committee to Promote Enterprise Overseas* (Singapore: SNP Publishers, August 1993).

12. "The Keys to Successful Regionalization," *Petir*, January/February 1994, 51.

13. The rate of exchange for the Singapore dollar to one U.S. dollar ranged from S$1.95 in 1989 to S$1.67 in 1998.

14. Lu Hongyong, "Mainland a Natural for Singapore Investors," *China Daily Business Weekly*, 7 August 1995, 2.

15. Singapore Chinese Chamber of Commerce and Industry, *Annual Report*, various years.

16. Karen Lau, "More Than Business as Usual," *Singapore*, January/February 1994, 13.

17. Wu-Shan Lim, "Pragmatic Partners," *China Business Review*, July/August 1990, 23.

18. Yu Chung-Hsun, "Xin Zhongguo jingji quan yu huan Taipingyang jingji" ("The New Chinese Economic Groupings and Links with the Pacific Economy"), in *Huaqiao huaren wenti lunwenji* (*Essays on the Question of Overseas Chinese and Ethnic Chinese*), ed. Chen Bisheng (Nanchang: Jiangxi renmin chubanshe, 1989), 156.

19. Lim, "Pragmatic Partners," 23.

20. Contracted investments are those agreed to but not yet made. Utilized foreign investment refers to actual investment that has already taken place.

21. Schutz Lee, "S'pore's US$4.8b Investment in China Ranks Fifth," *Business Times* (Singapore), 10 August 1994, 1.

22. "BG Yeo on Visit to China," *Straits Times* (Singapore), 22 August 1999, Internet edition.

23. See, for example, Teh Hooi Ling, "S'pore Firms Less Satisfied with China Ventures," *Business Times* (Singapore), 28 May 1999, Internet edition.

24. Singapore Department of Statistics, *Singapore's Direct Investment Abroad 1993* (Singapore: Department of Statistics, October 1994); Aggarwal, "China Closes Gap"; and "Investments Abroad Surged by End-1997," *Straits Times* (Singapore), 8 September 1999, Internet edition.

25. "Daily Cited on Singapore's Investment in China," Beijing Xinhua in English (14 November 1994), Foreign Broadcast Information Service (hereafter FBIS) *DR/China*, 15 November 1994, 30.

26. "Goh's China Triumph," *Straits Times Weekly Edition* (hereafter *STWE*) (Singapore), 1 May 1993, 12.

27. "Keys," 53.

28. Interview by author, 1994.

29. See Kevin Lim, "S'pore Investors Are Moving Deeper into China," *STWE*, 20 March 1993, 20; and Schutz Lee, "Singapore Firms Give South China a Miss," *Straits Times* (Singapore), 15 February 1994, Life section, 4.

30. See Choo Li Meng, "S'pore SMEs Staying Clear of China's Inner Provinces," *Straits Times* (Singapore), 15 February 1995, 35. Xinhua gives a different perspective, claiming that most Singapore investments, at the direction of Singapore's government, are being made in medium-sized cities, such as Suzhou, Wuxi, Qingdao, Yantai, Xiamen, Dalian, Chengdu, and Chongqing, where competition tends to be less intense. The Singapore government, however, is guiding larger multinationals toward the economic centers of Shanghai and Beijing. See "Daily Cited," 30.

31. For details on the industrial park, see www.pacificrimgroup.com/yuanhong/index.html.

32. For details on the final agreement, see Sunny Goh, "Suzhou Industrial Township Pact Signed," *STWE* (Singapore), 5 March 1994, 3.

33. "Xinhua Praises Suzhou Industrial Park in Jiangsu," Beijing Xinhua in English (25 June 1994), FBIS *DR/China*, 27 June 1994, 69.

34. "Suzhou Project the 'Start of Long-Lasting Ties with China,'" *STWE* (Singapore), 28 May 1994, 2.

35. Quoted in Sunny Goh, "Is the Suzhou Project a Boo-Boo?" *Straits Times* (Singapore), 18 June 1999, Internet edition.

36. Mary Kwang, "Suzhou Park Loss Could Hit $151m," *Straits Times* (Singapore), 15 September 1999, Internet edition; and "Suzhou Industrial Park's Tax Revenue Surges 79%," *Straits Times*, 24 May 1999, Internet edition.

37. "Suzhou Shows how 'Different We Are,'" *Straits Times* (Singapore), 20 June 1999, Internet edition.

38. For an analysis of Beijing's view of Singapore, see Chen Jie, "The 'Taiwan Problem' in Peking's ASEAN Policy," *Issues and Studies* 29, no. 4 (April 1993): 116–22.

39. V. G. Kulkarni, "Hot on a New Trail," *FEER*, 10 October 1985, 107.

40. "China Move to Cut Risks for Singapore Investors," *STWE* (Singapore), 27 March 1993, 4.

41. Ma Chenguang, "Singapore's Investments, PM Welcomed," *China Daily*, 12 May 1995, 1.

42. Sunny Goh, "Why S'pore Choose Not to Go for Big China Projects," *STWE* (Singapore), 24 April 1993, 13; and "S'poreans Overly Cautious about Investing in China: Trade Minister," *STWE*, 24 April 1993, 3.

43. See Phua Kok Kim, "S'pore, China to Form Govt Body to Oversee Cooperation," *STWE* (Singapore), 30 October 1993, 3; Gao Bianhua, "Singapore Trade with China Keeps Thriving," *China Daily*, 11 May 1995, 5; and Ben Dolven, "The China Factor," *FEER*, 18 March 1999, 54–55.

44. Gerald Segal, "Deconstructing Foreign Relations," in *China Deconstructs: Politics, Trade and Regionalism*, ed. David S. G. Goodman and Gerald Segal (New York: Routledge, 1994), 332.

45. Emily Thornton, "Bamboo Brigade," *FEER*, 12 October 1995, 106; and Schutz Lee, "More Than 120 China Firms Have Presence in Singapore," *Business Times* (Singapore), 3 August 1994, 1.

46. Mary Kwang, "Chinese Trading Firms Set Up Base," *Straits Times* (Singapore), 14 December 1998, Internet edition.

47. Singapore Department of Statistics, *Monthly Digest of Statistics* (Singapore: Department of Statistics), various issues.

48. See "Shandong Makes All-Out Bid for Township Deal," *Straits Times* (Singapore), 30 June 1993, 14.

49. "Xinhua Criticizes Singapore Trade Shows," Tokyo Kyodo in English (15 January 1990), FBIS *DR/China*, 23 January 1990, 36.

50. See, for example, Jean-Louise Margolin, "Foreign Models in Singapore's Development and the Idea of a Singaporean Model," in *Singapore Changes Guard: Social, Political, and Economic Directions in the 1990s*, ed. Garry Rodan (New York: St. Martin's Press, 1993), 84–98; and "Selling Success," *Asiaweek*, 13 July 1994, 24–27.

51. "The Success of the New Offensive in Reform Is Tied to Mr. Deng Xiaoping's Health," *Le Monde* (Paris), 22 April 1992, 4.

52. "China and Singapore: Friendly Neighbors," *Beijing Review*," 20–26 August 1990, 10.

53. For example, see Xue Mouhong, "Xinjiabo jingji fazhande ruogan tedian" ("Some Salient Features of Singapore's Economic Development"), *Guoji wenti yanjiu* (*International Studies*) 1990, no. 3:1–10.

54. Han Fook Kwang and Chiang Yin Pheng, "S'pore Firm Signs Accord to Develop Suzhou Township," *STWE* (Singapore), 15 May 1993, 1.

55. Lee Kuan Yew, untitled, in Singapore Chinese Chamber of Commerce and Industry, *World Chinese Entrepreneurs Convention*, 1991, 190–91.

56. "Interview with Singapore's Senior Minister Lee Kuan Yew," *New York Times*, 22 February 1999, Internet edition.

57. Interview by author, 1994.

58. Segal, "Deconstructing," 332.

59. "S'pore's Interests Planted Firmly in S-E Asia: PM," *STWE* (Singapore), 30 January 1993, 3. For details on fears within Southeast Asia concerning Singapore's relationship with China, see Susan Sim, "The Ties That Do Not Bind," *STWE*, 23 June 1995, 14.

60. "Make Distinction in Ties with China, Says BG Yeo," *STWE* (Singapore), 20 May 1995, 24.

61. See David Brown, *The State and Ethnic Politics in Southeast Asia* (New York: Routledge, 1994), chapter 3; and Clammer, *Race and State*.

62. Lau, "More Than Business," 13.

63. Warren Fernandez, "S'pore to Help Shandong Province," *STWE* (Singapore), 8 October 1994, 3.

64. See Denny Roy, "Singapore, China, and the 'Soft Authoritarian' Challenge," *Asian Survey* 34, no. 3 (March 1994): 231–42.

65. Ismail Kassim, "Rush by Local Chinese to Invest in China Worries '46," *STWE* (Singapore), 15 May 1993, 10.

66. Yusman Ahmad, "The China Connection: Private Investors are Approaching China Cautiously," *Malaysian Business*, 16–30 June 1993, 45.

CHAPTER 8 ─────────────────────────────

Conclusion

This study has examined the economic relationship between China and Asia's ethnic Chinese during China's reform period beginning in 1978, as well as the economic and political implications that this relationship has had for China and Southeast Asia. This final chapter reviews important findings and explores their implications for diaspora and state as discussed in chapter 1. The chapter is organized following the three legs of the triangle inherent in a diaspora setting. First, the main focus of the study, China's relationship with Asia's ethnic Chinese, is reviewed. The chapter then moves on to the relationship between ethnic Chinese and Southeast Asian states and, the third leg, ties between China and the countries of Southeast Asia. This is followed by a review of the implications of this study for the concept of Greater China and concluding remarks on states.

THREE LEGS OF THE DIASPORA RELATIONSHIP

The first leg of the diaspora relationship connects China and Asia's ethnic Chinese. Chapter 2 described the long-standing bonds between China and the Chinese diaspora. Many ethnic Chinese in Southeast Asia and China recognize a "Chineseness" that binds them together, although the practical implications resulting from this are shaped by individual preferences, economic forces, and politics. China's diaspora community has been well suited for assisting the country in its development, although it has suffered from the Asian economic crisis. First, the ethnic Chinese business sector has had capital available for investment in China. Second, ethnic Chinese business structures are organized in a manner that provides for flexibility. Third, ethnic Chinese networks are invaluable for providing information and capital, and establishing connections with mainland partners. A familiarity with Chinese language and culture maintained by some Southeast Asian Chinese is also important.

In some respects the connections among various ethnic Chinese can be likened to a "global tribe" due to the worldwide links they share.[1] Nevertheless, the metaphor is incomplete. The tribe is still overshadowed by the Chinese state itself, an entity defined geographically. Thus, although the manner in which the "tribe" interacts outside China is an interesting issue, the ways in which the "tribe" relates to the Chinese state are equally important. Moreover, shared ethnic bonds do not eliminate conflict or ensure cooperation, as the dynamics between the mainland and Taiwan and China's numerous civil wars clearly demonstrate.

Chapters 3 and 4 illustrated China's policy to attract hard currency and investments from Asia's ethnic Chinese. This policy, in various forms, dates back to the last two decades of the Qing Dynasty. Thus, for the past century Chinese governments have, with the exception of the Cultural Revolution era, tried to extract resources from Asia's ethnic Chinese through various government institutions set up for this purpose. Before the current reform period began, the main economic contribution of Southeast Asia's ethnic Chinese to China came in the form of remittances. These remittances were important for balancing China's trade deficits, supporting families, and funding philanthropy. Comparatively little, however, was invested in productive resources due to political uncertainties in China. Those who did invest were often motivated more by filial piety or a search for status than the profit motive. Thus the diaspora Chinese were never able to reach their full potential in helping China modernize.

After the ravages of the Cultural Revolution, China again turned to Asia's ethnic Chinese for assistance in modernization. Post-1978 political statements have referred to Asia's ethnic Chinese as "kin" and called for their support in achieving China's Four Modernizations. To reinforce these appeals, compensation was promised to overseas Chinese and those with overseas connections who had suffered losses during the Cultural Revolution. Special preferences were also given to ethnic Chinese investors (although such preferences later came to be questioned by some in China). Even the location of China's special economic zones was designed to attract ethnic Chinese entrepreneurs. In line with China's policies toward Asia's ethnic Chinese and more general Chinese development goals, government institutions dealing with ethnic Chinese shifted their focus almost completely to attracting capital.

Throughout the reform period the response of ethnic Chinese to China's call for investments has been remarkable. Most foreign investment in China has come from ethnic Chinese. Estimates of the percentage of ethnic Chinese investment out of total investment range from 70 to over 80 percent. Although the level of investment of Southeast Asian Chinese is difficult to determine precisely, estimates here have ranged from 5 percent to 15 percent. Ethnic Chinese have also continued to make charitable contributions and serve as advisors to the mainland government.

The reasons behind the ethnic Chinese response to China's invitation to invest are complex. Profit is central with both entrepreneurs who utilize China as an export platform and those who target China's internal market. However, ethnic bonds and emotional appeals also play some role. This is demonstrated by the frequent placement of investments in ancestral hometowns. Nevertheless, the profit motive and emotional bonds are by no means mutually exclusive. An understanding of how to do business in China and good connections make profits possible. Throughout the reform period as investments have become larger, profit has taken on an even greater role in comparison to sentiment.

The contribution of ethnic Chinese is one major explanatory factor behind China's economic success, especially in comparison with the former Soviet Union. At the outset of the reform period, ethnic Chinese had surplus capital and were equipped for dealing with China's environment. Social and cultural ties with China provided motivation for small-scale investments when profits were uncertain. Once these early investments proved to be successful, the doors were opened for further investments by ethnic Chinese firms and Western and Japanese MNCs. Thus, the ethnic Chinese have played an important role as catalysts for China's economic growth.

Looking at the relationship of China and the ethnic Chinese from the perspective of state-diaspora interactions, it is clear that the strength of the state is important to the kind of resources that it can attract from its diaspora community. During the Qing and KMT periods, the vast majority of resources transferred from the overseas Chinese to China was in the form of remittances to family members rather than investments, due to instability in China and the need of family members of overseas Chinese for money for living expenses. Although overseas Chinese did make limited investments, most turned out as losses as the result of violence and theft. This was a deterrent to further investment. However, during the post-1978 period, in spite of problems with China's investment climate, the Chinese state was able to provide a much more stable environment. Thus, investments could turn a profit, breeding further investment.

However, paradoxically, ethnic Chinese have been more eager to invest in China than other investors due to the weaknesses of the Chinese state. Ethnic Chinese are better equipped to deal with these weaknesses. For example, ethnic Chinese can more easily handle China's undeveloped legal system by establishing connections with local or even national officials. Networks provide information in a society where the free flow of information is limited. In addition, ethnic Chinese firms are well suited for small-scale operations that can turn a profit with the cooperation of local governments.

The response of the ethnic Chinese to China's appeals for investments has clearly met state goals and increased the resources available to the Chinese state. Ethnic Chinese investments have raised China's GNP, increased exports, provided employment, transferred technology and management skills, and developed industries in previously underdeveloped areas. These factors can potentially be tapped by the state to increase state power. Furthermore, ethnic Chinese entrepreneurs serve as partners for MNCs eager to participate in the Chinese market, further contributing to the buildup of China's economy.

On the other hand, some Chinese economists argue that ethnic Chinese provide too high a percentage of China's overall foreign investments. This is a concern for China because technology transfer is a major goal of the Chinese government in attracting foreign investments. Although cultural similarities put the ethnic Chinese in a better position to transfer technology to China, the technology level of ethnic Chinese firms is generally lower than those of Western and Japanese companies. Furthermore, Chinese reliance on Asian investments meant that overall foreign investment in China was significantly affected by the Asian economic crisis. As a result, the Chinese government is attempting to achieve a more balanced mix of foreign investment.

Moreover, ethnic Chinese investments exacerbate other challenges for the current regime. Chapter 5 analyzed the argument that through cooperation with local officials and investing primarily in coastal provinces, ethnic Chinese investments contribute to a dangerous decentralization in Chinese politics and regional economic inequalities. Labor abuses have also been reported, and some accuse ethnic Chinese investors of fostering corruption. Furthermore, theorists of democratization assert that rising incomes, which foreign investment helps bring about, will lead to pressures for democratization.[2] Although the Chinese government supports rationalization, legal reforms, and greater rule by law, at least for business transactions, democratization would be an unacceptable outcome to the current regime, which insists on the continued leadership of the Communist Party.

These threats to the current regime brought about by ethnic Chinese investments are dangerous because of preexisting weaknesses in the Chinese state. Thus, the lack of institutionalized procedures and a tradition of personal rule make the bureaucracy susceptible to corruption. Frequent shifts in recent Chinese history in central-local relations, which still remain unsettled, result in concern over the decentralizing effects of investments. Questions concerning the Beijing regime's legitimacy in the eyes of its population lead to discussion of the democratizing effects of investment. Thus, the entrepreneurial activities of the Chinese diaspora do not create major new problems for the state, but can exacerbate existing contradictions.

In looking at the relationship between the Chinese state and its diaspora community, the Singapore case provides an interesting comparison. Because a large percentage of Singapore investments in China are made by government-linked firms, Singapore investments take on characteristics of a state-to-state relationship. For various reasons Singapore firms were slow to begin investing in China. However, once the government began to push firms to move into China, investments skyrocketed. Various aspects of Singapore's investments in China are affected by the nature of their relationship to the Singapore state, including location and type. Most notable is the Singapore II project in Suzhou, negotiated by the Singapore and Chinese governments and led by the Singapore government-linked Keppel Corporation. The souring of this project has had a detrimental, though not serious, effect on overall Sino-Singaporean relations.

In the second leg of the diaspora triangle, the relationship between Southeast Asia's ethnic Chinese and the nation-states of Southeast Asia, there are three important issues. The first is the loyalty of ethnic Chinese. As ethnic Chinese increase their investments in China, some Southeast Asian observers have raised questions regarding their motivations and whether "capital flight" should be permitted. This is a phenomenon that bears watching, especially in light of the 1998 riots in Indonesia and as transitions occur in the domestic politics of Indonesia and Malaysia. However, this questioning of ethnic Chinese investment is not done overtly by most Southeast Asian governments, several of which are to some degree supportive of investments in China. Furthermore, unlike the early part of this century, there is no resurgence of Chinese nationalism in Southeast Asia. However, renewed interest in China among ethnic Chinese raises questions about the assimilation of Chinese into Southeast Asia. Assimilation can occur at various levels. Thus, although the political assimilation of Chinese into Southeast Asia does not seem to be threatened, increased interactions with China result in greater interest in Chinese culture and language in the region and a government-led process of resinification in Singapore. Indeed, Beijing may make the reinforcement of Chinese culture in Southeast Asia a deliberate policy.

Moving to the state level, some have questioned Singapore's relation to its Southeast Asian neighbors in light of its new economic partnership with China. Singapore's leaders go to great lengths to emphasize that Singapore is part of Southeast Asia and not a third China. Singaporean investments in Southeast Asia continue to be significant as well. Nevertheless, Singapore as a small state is constrained in its relationship with China by regional suspicions regarding its ultimate intentions.

Second, Southeast Asian governments have had to revise their policies regarding investments in their own countries in response to competition from China, to attract both foreign investments and the investments of their own ethnic Chinese. More forceful moves have been taken to keep ethnic Chinese investments in Southeast Asia as well. This illustrates how competition for the investments from multinational actors can drive states to change policies, thus sacrificing some state goals for the advancement of others. Third, the tension between ethnic Chinese and the indigenous societies of Southeast Asia, along with renewed interest in China on the part of Asia's ethnic Chinese, points to the difficulties inherent in a world of state sovereignty and transnational business and cultural interactions. Ethnic Chinese are adopting multiple identities. Such identities require a separation among state, family, business, and cultural loyalties. Such a separation is not always easy for the individuals involved. It can be more difficult for states to accept.

The final leg of the triangle connects China with Southeast Asia. There is competition between China and Southeast Asian states for the investments of ethnic Chinese. Clearly the outcome of this competition is determined to a large extent by market forces. However, each side also has nonmarket claims on the investments of ethnic Chinese. China's claims stem from cultural ties and the fact that it is the ethnic "homeland." Southeast Asian claims stem from the fact that Southeast Asia is the physical and political homeland of ethnic Chinese today. Southeast Asian governments have historically been envious of ethnic Chinese capital flowing to China, even in colonial times, although some governments today have achieved a measure of acceptance of the phenomenon and even encourage it to some degree. This is due in part to an effort to profit from China. It is also due to the belief that a China that is closely tied economically to the region will be a more friendly neighbor.

Southeast Asian suspicion of China is rooted in history and geopolitical realities. During the post–World War II era Southeast Asian governments have feared Chinese hegemony. Any attraction that China held for ethnic Chinese was seen as useful for potential Chinese subversion in Southeast Asia. Although this fear subsided during the 1980s, it has not been completely eliminated. China is aware of this concern and tries to ameliorate it. China desires good relations with its neighbors that will maintain a peaceful environment necessary for its economic growth. However, it also demands respect as a major regional power.

The PRC government has talked of ethnic Chinese as bridges linking China with the countries of Southeast Asia. For a long time this assertion seemed ridiculous because ethnic Chinese were more of a political liability to Beijing than a bridge. Nevertheless, in recent years, as investments in China and trade with China have increased, Asia's ethnic Chinese have finally begun to serve as a bridge. This is demonstrated by increasing trade and investment links between China and Southeast Asia, as well as by Southeast Asian leaders taking large delegations of ethnic Chinese entrepreneurs on state visits to China.

Thus it is evident that transnational economic actors can exacerbate competition between states for resources as well as foster cooperation. Again, the demands of sovereignty and transnational economic activities often clash. However, the contest is not a zero-sum game. The investments of Southeast Asian Chinese in China have benefits for Southeast Asia, as Chinese scholars are quick to point out. At a minimum it lets Southeast Asians participate in China's economic growth and integrates China more closely into the wider Asian economy. Southeast Asian leaders hope that this is good for their economies and security.

GREATER CHINA AND BEYOND

During the past decade the term "Greater China" has become prominent, although as discussed in the first chapter the term has numerous meanings. This study illustrates that economic Greater China has become more of a reality, including not only mainland China, Hong Kong, and Taiwan, but also Southeast

Asia's ethnic Chinese. Strong bonds tie Southeast Asia's ethnic Chinese with the mainland, as well as with Chinese in Hong Kong and Taiwan. As a result, ethnic Chinese business networks crisscross Asia. Furthermore, Southeast Asian Chinese entrepreneurs have contributed to the mainland's development and continue to do so, although the character of their investments differs from those made by Hong Kong and Taiwan Chinese. In addition, a great deal of investment in China combines capital from Hong Kong, Taiwan, and Southeast Asia. In that sense, separating the Southeast Asian Chinese from those who live in Taiwan, Hong Kong, and China is arbitrary.

On the other hand, important reasons can be mustered to exclude Southeast Asia's ethnic Chinese from any conceptualization of Greater China. Chief among them is the fact that Hong Kong has been reunited with China while Beijing claims sovereignty over Taiwan but not the states inhabited by Southeast Asian Chinese. Second, placing Southeast Asian Chinese within Greater China aggravates the suspicions held by Southeast Asian societies regarding their Chinese populations and makes life more difficult for ethnic Chinese. Similarly, Southeast Asian Chinese have been inhibited from participating as fully in the China market as they otherwise might due to the political constraints that they face in their home countries.[3]

In other words, we again see a conflict between the logic of sovereignty and the logic of transnational ethnic connections and business. The implications of an economic Greater China clash with current political realities, creating turbulence.[4] In light of this, using "Greater China" to include Southeast Asian Chinese creates ambiguities and lacks conceptual clarity. "Greater China" has geographic and political implications that do not apply to Southeast Asian Chinese or the countries in which they live.[5] Similarly, it is useful to maintain a distinction between ethnic Chinese who are citizens of Southeast Asian states, *huaqiao*, and residents of Taiwan, Hong Kong, and Macao. Although the economic distinctions are more limited, the political differentiation is important.

Conceptions of Greater China need to be kept in a broader context of developments in China and the world. Ethnic Chinese who invest in China also invest heavily in Southeast Asia and around the globe. At times investments in China are made with Western partners. Furthermore, China itself can be viewed as consisting of numerous economic zones. Thus, even an economic Greater China is by no means an exclusive entity and exists in a context of numerous economic linkages.

This study has also focused on the debate on the current status and future condition of the nation-state. This debate is difficult to definitively answer in the abstract. Instead, the actual role and function of the state must be examined under specific circumstances. This study has demonstrated how the Chinese state, once it had sufficient strength and had shed its inhibiting ideology, was able to utilize ethnic bonds to attract a tremendous amount of investment, propelling its economy into a potential Pacific Century. Asia's ethnic Chinese were a latent comparative advantage that China turned into an active asset. The Chinese state attracted ethnic Chinese investment through a strategy that involved improved treatment of domestic overseas Chinese, emotional appeals to build up the motherland, laws providing special incentives for ethnic Chinese to invest, the utilization of various institutions designed specifically to work with ethnic Chinese abroad, and a broadly improved investment environment. Thus, China used resources available only to a state to attract ethnic Chinese investors.

Moreover, economic networks, to be successful in making money, need strong state institutions. Ethnic Chinese business networks were not able to make long-term profits in China until the reform period, when the state could ensure a minimum amount of order and an appropriate ideological climate that encouraged investment. Even now most investors prefer stronger state legal institutions. State institutions that provide order and allow for investments are grounded in the state's control over a specific geographical territory and thus cannot be replaced by nonstate actors. Moreover, states shape the international environment. Ethnic Chinese are freer to invest in China now that some Southeast Asian governments are mildly supportive. However, renewed opposition on the part of Southeast Asian governments could decrease investment flows. Furthermore, China itself values, at least for now, a peaceful regional environment. If China were to change priorities and undertake military action in regard to Taiwan or the Spratly Islands, the investment environment would immediately change. Economic rationalism can be overridden by other state goals.

However, this study has also demonstrated that the state is one actor among many and the efficacy of state sovereignty is limited. Moreover, the success of state strategies can create unintended challenges to state authority. Thus, China's success in attracting ethnic Chinese investors has led to heightened concerns regarding regionalism, corruption, the conflict between state ideology and the workings of entrepreneurs, and the technology level of investments that are flowing into China. The Chinese state can establish the conditions necessary to attract investors, but once investments are made and investors establish relations with local officials, the economic and political dynamics that are unleashed take on a life of their own.

Whether other countries with diasporas can follow the Chinese model of attracting large-scale diaspora resources is a question that only the future will reveal. Many "home" states, such as India, have large diaspora populations that can contribute to economic development. However, it is doubtful if any diaspora can have the influence of the Chinese. Asia's ethnic Chinese entrepreneurs are noteworthy in terms of their numbers and skills. They will continue to play a major role in China's economy well into the future, a role that will transform China, Asia, and the world economy.

NOTES

1. See Joel Kotkin, *Tribes: How Race, Religion, and Identity Determine Success in the New Global Economy* (New York: Random House, 1993).

2. For a discussion of this issue, see Samuel Huntington, *The Third Wave: Democratization in the Late Twentieth Century* (Norman: University of Oklahoma Press, 1991), 59–72.

3. For a similar view, see Daojiong Zha, "A 'Greater China'? The Political Economy of Chinese National Reunification," *Journal of Contemporary China*, no. 5 (Spring 1994): 42.

4. See James N. Rosenau, *Turbulence in World Politics: A Theory of Continuity and Change* (Princeton, N.J.: Princeton University Press, 1990).

5. The relationship between the mainland and Taiwan is much more complex in terms of sovereignty and even geography than the relationship between Hong Kong and the mainland. Thus including even Taiwan in a conceptualization of Greater China presents ambiguities.

Bibliography

Ampalavanar Brown, Rajeswary. "Introduction: Chinese Business in an Institutional and Historical Perspective." In *Chinese Business Enterprise in Asia*, edited by Rajeswary Ampalavanar Brown, 1–26. London: Routledge, 1995.

———. "Overseas Chinese Investments in China—Patterns of Growth, Diversification, and Finance: The Case of Charoen Pokphand." *China Quarterly*, no. 155 (September 1998): 610–36.

Ash, Robert F., and Y. Y. Kueh. "Economic Integration Within Greater China: Trade and Investment Flows Between China, Hong Kong, and Taiwan." *China Quarterly*, no. 136 (December 1993): 711–45.

Baldinger, Pamela. "The Birth of Greater China." *China Business Review*, May/June 1992, 13–17.

Beetham, David. "The Future of the Nation State." In *The Idea of the Modern State*, edited by Gregor McLennan, David Held, and Stuart Hall, 208–22. Milton Keynes, England: Open University Press, 1984.

Bolt, Paul J. "The New Economic Partnership Between China and Singapore." *Asian Affairs: An American Review* 23, no. 2 (Summer 1996): 83–99.

———. "Looking to the Diaspora: The Overseas Chinese and China's Economic Development." *Diaspora* 5, no. 3 (Winter 1996): 467–96.

———. "Chinese Diaspora Entrepreneurship, Development, and the World Capitalist System." *Diaspora* 6, no. 2 (Fall 1997): 215–35.

Brick, Andrew B. "The Emergence of Greater China: The Diaspora Ascendant." *Heritage Lectures*, no. 411 (1992).

Brook, Timothy, and B. Michael Frolic, eds. *Civil Society in China*. Armonk, N.Y.: M. E. Sharpe, 1997.

Brown, David. "The Corporatist Management of Ethnicity in Contemporary Singapore." In *Singapore Changes Guard: Social, Political, and Economic Directions in the 1990s*, edited by Garry Rodan, 16–33. New York: St. Martin's Press, 1993.

———. *The State and Ethnic Politics in Southeast Asia.* New York: Routledge, 1994.

Cai, Renlong. "'Diyi Taipingyang qiye jituan' chutan" ("Approach to the 'First Pacific Enterprise Group,'"). In *Nanyang yanjiu lunwenji (Essays on Southeast Asian Research)*, edited by Xiamen daxue Nanyang yanjiusuo, 222–33. Xiamen: Xiamen daxue chubanshe, 1992.

Cariño, Theresa Chong. *China and the Overseas Chinese in Southeast Asia.* Quezon City, Philippines: New Day Publishers, 1985.

———. "The Ethnic Chinese, the Philippine Economy and China." In *Southeast Asian Chinese and China*, edited by Leo Suryadinata, 216–29. Singapore: Times Academic Press, 1995.

Chan, Kwok Bun, and Tong Chee Kiong. "Rethinking Assimilation and Ethnicity: The Chinese in Thailand." In *The Chinese Diaspora: Selected Essays*, vol. 2, edited by Wang Ling-chi and Wang Gungwu, 1–27. Singapore: Times Academic Press, 1998. Originally published in *International Migration Review* 27, no. 1 (1993).

Chan, Ngor Chong. "PRC Policy on the Overseas Chinese." In *ASEAN and China: An Evolving Relationship*, edited by Joyce K. Kallgren, Noordin Sopiee, and Soedjati Djiwandono, 125–46. Berkeley: Institute of East Asian Studies, University of California, 1988.

Chang, C. Y. "Overseas Chinese in China's Policy." *China Quarterly*, no. 82 (June 1980): 281–303.

Chang, Maria Hsia. "China's Future: Regionalism, Federation, or Disintegration." *Studies in Comparative Communism* 25, no. 3 (September 1992): 211–27.

———. "Greater China and the Chinese 'Global Tribe.'" *Asian Survey* 35, no. 10 (October 1995): 955–67.

Chang, Pao-Min. "China and Southeast Asia: The Problem of a Perception Gap." *Contemporary Southeast Asia* 9, no. 3 (December 1987): 181–93.

Chantavanich, Supang. "From Siamese-Chinese to Chinese-Thai: Political Conditions and Identity Shifts among the Chinese in Thailand." In *Ethnic Chinese as Southeast Asians*, edited by Leo Suryadinata, 232–59. New York: St. Martin's Press, 1997.

Chen, Jie. "The 'Taiwan Problem' in Peking's ASEAN Policy." *Issues and Studies* 29, no. 4 (April 1993): 95–124.

Chen, Min. "Technological Transfer to China: Major Rules and Issues." *International Journal of Technology Management* 10, nos. 7/8 (1995): 747–56.

Chen, Ta. *Emigrant Communities in South China.* Edited by Bruno Lasker. New York: Institute of Pacific Relations, 1940.

Chen, Xiangming. "China's Growing Integration with the Asia-Pacific Economy." In *What Is in a Rim? Critical Perspectives on the Pacific Region Idea*, edited by Arif Dirlik, 89–119. Boulder: Westview Press, 1993.

Cheng, Tun-ren. "Democratizing the Quasi-Leninist Regime in Taiwan." *World Politics* 41, no. 4 (July 1989): 471–99.

Chiew, Seen Kong. "From Overseas Chinese to Chinese Singaporeans." In *Ethnic Chinese as Southeast Asians*, edited by Leo Suryadinata, 211–27. New York: St. Martin's Press, 1997.

Chou, Yu-Min. "The Role of Foreign Investments in the Formation of an Economic Region—With Reference to China." *RIAD Bulletin*, no. 2 (March 1993): 67–84.

Chung, Stephanie Po-yin. *Chinese Business Groups in Hong Kong and Political Change in South China, 1900–25*. New York: St. Martin's Press, 1998.

Clammer, John. *Race and State in Independent Singapore, 1965–1990*. Aldershot, England: Ashgate, 1998.

Conner, Walker. "The Impact of Homelands upon Diasporas." In *Modern Diasporas in International Politics*, edited by Gabriel Sheffer, 16–46. London: Croom Helm, 1986.

Cui, Geng. "The Emergence of the Chinese Economic Area (CEA)." *Multinational Business Review* 6, no. 1 (Spring 1998): 63–72.

Diamond, Deborah C. "Malaysia's Economic Diplomacy." *China Business Review*, May/June 1986, 4.

Diamond, Larry. "Economic Development and Democracy Reconsidered." *American Behavioral Scientist* 35, nos. 4/5 (March/June 1992): 450–99.

Dikötter, Frank. *The Discourse of Race in Modern China*. Stanford: Stanford University Press, 1992.

———. "Racial Discourse in China: Continuities and Permutations." In *The Construction of Racial Identities in China and Japan*, edited by Frank Dikötter, 12–33. London: Hurst, 1997.

Doremus, Paul E., William W. Keller, Louis W. Pauly, and Simon Reich. *The Myth of the Global Corporation*. Princeton, N.J.: Princeton University Press, 1998.

Dori, John T., and Richard D. Fisher Jr. *U.S. and Asia Statistical Handbook 1998–1999*. Washington, D.C.: Heritage Foundation, 1998.

Douglas, Stephen A. "Political Dynamics of the Diaspora: The Chinese in Southeast Asia." Paper presented at the Annual Meeting of the International Studies Association, Chicago, Ill., February 1995.

East Asia Analytical Unit, Department of Foreign Affairs and Trade, Commonwealth of Australia. *Overseas Chinese Business Networks in Asia*. Canberra: Commonwealth of Australia, 1995.

Economic Research Department, D.B.S. Bank, Singapore. *The Development of Greater China: Prospects and Challenges for ASEAN*. ASEAN Briefing, no. 33, July 1993.

Economics Department, Monetary Authority of Singapore. "The Impact of the Asian Crisis on China: An Assessment." Occasional Paper no. 8, October 1998.

Economist Intelligence Unit. *China/Mongolia*, 1st quarter 1995.

Elegant, Robert S. *The Dragon's Seed: Peking and the Overseas Chinese*. New York: St. Martin's Press, 1959.

Esman, Milton J. "The Chinese Diaspora in Southeast Asia." In *Modern Diasporas in International Politics*, edited by Gabriel Sheffer, 130–63. London: Croom Helm, 1986.

———. "Diasporas and International Relations." In *Modern Diasporas in International Politics*, edited by Gabriel Sheffer, 333–49. London: Croom Helm, 1986.

———. *Ethnic Politics*. Ithaca: Cornell University Press, 1994.

Fang, Chengze Simon. "Why China Has Been Successful in Attracting Foreign Direct Investment: A Transaction Cost Approach." *Journal of Contemporary China* 7, no. 17 (March 1998): 21–32.

Fang, Xiongpu. "Haiwai qiaotuande fazhan yanbian ji qi xiangguan zhengce" ("The Development and Changes in Overseas Chinese Mass Organizations and Related Policies"). *Huaqiao huaren lishi yanjiu (Overseas Chinese and Ethnic Chinese Historical Research)*, 1997, no. 1: 8–11.

Fitzgerald, C. P. *The Third China: The Chinese Communities in Southeast Asia.* Vancouver: University of British Columbia, 1965.

Fitzgerald, Stephen. *China and the Overseas Chinese: A Study of Peking's Changing Policy, 1949–1970.* Cambridge: Cambridge University Press, 1972.

Friedman, Edward. *New Nationalist Identities in Post-Leninist Transformations: The Implications for China.* Hong Kong: Hong Kong Institute of Asia-Pacific Studies, 1992.

———. "Ethnic Identity and the De-Nationalization and Democratization of Leninist States." In *The Rising Tide of Cultural Pluralism*, edited by Crawford Young, 222–41. Madison: University of Wisconsin Press, 1993.

Fu, Mengzi. "Yatai ciquyu jingji hezuode fazhan yu Zhongguo" ("The Development of Asian Subregional Economic Cooperation and China"). *Xianzai guoji guanxi (Contemporary International Relations)*, 1993, no. 11:31–32.

Garver, John W. *Foreign Relations of the People's Republic of China.* Englewood Cliffs, N.J.: Prentice-Hall, 1993.

Gilpin, Robert. "The Politics of Transnational Economic Relations." In *Transnational Relations and World Politics*, edited by Robert O. Keohane and Joseph S. Nye Jr., 48–69. Cambridge, Mass.: Harvard University Press, 1972.

———. *The Political Economy of International Relations.* Princeton, N.J.: Princeton University Press, 1987.

Godley, Michael R. *The Mandarin-Capitalists from Nanyang: Overseas Chinese Enterprises in the Modernization of China 1893–1911.* Cambridge: Cambridge University Press, 1981.

Gold, Thomas B. "Go with Your Feelings: Hong Kong and Taiwan Popular Culture in Greater China." *China Quarterly*, no. 136 (December 1993): 907–25.

Gu, Yuanyang. "China-Singapore Economic Relations: History and Prospects for Development." In *ASEAN-China Economic Relations: Trends and Patterns*, edited by Chia Siow-Yue and Cheng Bifan, 188–209. Singapore: Institute for Southeast Asian Studies, 1987.

Guangzhou shi dui wai jingji maoyi weiyuanhui and Guangzhou shi zhengce yanjiushi (Guangzhou City Foreign Economy and Trade Commission and the Guangzhou City Policy Research Office). *Guangzhou touzi zhinan (Guide to Investment in Guangzhou)*, undated.

Guo, Liang. "Zhan hou Dongnan Ya huaren rentong, tonghua wenti yanjiude jizhong guandian" ("Some Views on the Identification and Assimilation of Ethnic Chinese in Postwar Southeast Asia"). *Nanyang wenti yanjiu (Southeast Asian Affairs)*, 1992, no. 2:12–20.

Haggard, Stephen. *Pathways from the Periphery: The Politics of Growth in the Newly Industrialized Countries.* Ithaca: Cornell University Press, 1990.

Hamrin, Carol Lee. *China and the Challenge of the Future.* Boulder: Westview Press, 1990.

Harding, Harry. *China's Second Revolution.* Washington, D.C.: Brookings, 1987.

———. "The U.S. and Greater China." *China Business Review* (May/June 1992): 18–22.

------. "The Concept of 'Greater China': Themes, Variations, and Reservations." *China Quarterly*, no. 136 (December 1993): 660–86.

Hashida, T. "The Greater China Economic Zone." *Nomura Asia Focus*, June 1992, 16–17.

Hashida, T., and M. Ohkawa. "The Changing Role of Overseas Chinese Businesses." *Nomura Asia Focus*, April 1992, 20–25.

Hayter, Roger, and Sun Sheng Han. "Reflections on China's Open Policy Towards Foreign Investment." *Regional Studies* 32, no. 1 (February 1998): 1–16.

Hicks, George, ed. *Overseas Chinese Remittances from Southeast Asia 1910–1940*. Singapore: Select Books, 1993.

Ho, Samuel P. S., and Ralph W. Huenemann. *China's Open Door Policy: The Quest for Foreign Technology and Capital*. Vancouver: University of British Columbia Press, 1984.

Hodder, Rupert. *Merchant Princes of the East*. Chichester, England: John Wiley, 1996.

Hofheinz, Roy, Jr., and Kent E. Calder. *The Eastasia Edge*. New York: Basic Books, 1982.

Holstius, Karin. "Cultural Adjustment in International Technology Transfer." *International Journal of Technology Management* 10, nos. 7/8 (1995): 676–86.

Horowitz, Donald L. *Ethnic Groups in Conflict*. Berkeley: University of California Press, 1985.

------. "Ethnic and Nationalist Conflict." In *World Security: Challenges for a New Century*, edited by Michael T. Klare and Daniel C. Thomas, 175–87. New York: St. Martin's Press, 1994.

Hou, Chi-ming. *Foreign Investment and Economic Development in China 1840–1937*. Cambridge, Mass.: Harvard University Press, 1965.

Huang, Cen. "Haiwai huaren he Zhongguo nanbude huazi kuaguo qiye" ("Ethnic Chinese and Transnational Enterprises with Chinese Capital in Southern China." *Bagui qiao shi* (*Overseas Chinese History of Bagui*), 1997, no. 4:25–31.

Huang, Dinglan. "Zhong-Yin (ni) fu jiao hou jingmao guanxi wenbu fazhan" ("The Steady Development of Economic and Trade Relations Between China and Indonesia after the Resumption of Diplomatic Relations"). *Nanyang wenti yanjiu (Southeast Asian Affairs)*, 1993, no. 2:81–85.

Huang, Fanzhang. "Yatai jingji geju ji Zhongguode zhanlüe" ("The Asia-Pacific Economic Structure and China's Strategy"). *Xianzai guoji guanxi (Contemporary International Relations)*, 1993, no. 11:27–29.

Huang, Qiwen. "Shantou kai bu yilaide huaqiao touzi yu jinhoude yin zi" ("Overseas Chinese Investment in Shantou after Its Opening and Its Future Attraction of Investment"). *Huqiao yu huaren* (*Chinese Overseas*) 1996, no. 2:40–43.

Huaqiao jingji nianjian 1992 (*Overseas Chinese Economy Yearbook 1992*). Taipei: Republic of China Overseas Chinese Affairs Committee, 1992.

Huff, W. G. "Turning the Corner in Singapore's Development State?" *Asian Survey* 39, no. 2 (March/April 1999): 214–42.

Huntington, Samuel. *The Third Wave: Democratization in the Late Twentieth Century*. Norman: University of Oklahoma Press, 1991.

International Monetary Fund. *Direction of Trade Statistics Yearbook 1997*. Washington, D.C.: IMF, 1997.

------. *Direction of Trade Statistics Quarterly: June 1999*. Washington, D.C.: IMF, 1999.

Jin, Dexiang. "The Impact of China's Economic Policies." In *China and Southeast Asia: Into the Twenty-First Century*, edited by Richard L. Grant and Amos A. Jordan, 12–29. Washington, D.C.: Center for Strategic and International Studies, 1993.

Johnson, Graham E., and Woon Yuen-Fong. "The Response to Rural Reform in an Overseas Chinese Area." *Modern Asian Studies* 31, no. 1 (1997): 31–59.

Kanai, Takao. "Singapore's New Focus on Regional Business Expansion." *NRI Quarterly*, Autumn 1993, 18–41.

Kao, Charng. "A 'Greater China Economic Sphere': Reality and Prospects." *Issues and Studies* 28, no. 11 (November 1992): 49–64.

Kao, John. "The Worldwide Web of Chinese Business." *Harvard Business Review*, March/April 1993, 24–36.

Katzenstein, Peter J., and Takashi Shiraishi, eds. *Network Power: Japan and Asia*. Ithaca: Cornell University Press, 1997.

"The Keys to Successful Regionalization." *Petir*, January/February 1994, 49–53.

Kotkin, Joel. *Tribes: How Race, Religion, and Identity Determine Success in the New Global Economy*. New York: Random House, 1993.

Krasner, Stephen D. "Approaches to the State." *Comparative Politics* 16, no. 2 (January 1984): 223–46.

Krause, Lawrence. "Government as Entrepreneur." In *Management of Success: The Moulding of Modern Singapore*, edited by Kernial Singh Sandhu and Paul Wheatley, 436–51. Boulder: Westview Press, 1989.

Krugman, Paul. "The Myth of Asia's Miracle." *Foreign Affairs* 73, no. 6 (November/December 1994): 62–78.

Ku, Ch'ang-yung. "Cong zhengzhi jingji cengmian lun Zhonggongde Dongnan Ya huaqiao zhengce" ("Economic and Political Perspectives on Peking's Policy Regarding Overseas Chinese in Southeast Asia"). *Zhongguo dalu yanjiu (Mainland China Studies)* 37, no. 9 (September 1994): 15–25.

Kueh, Y. Y. "Foreign Investment and Economic Change in China." *China Quarterly*, no. 131 (September 1992): 637–90.

Kunio, Yoshihara. *The Rise of Ersatz Capitalism in South-East Asia*. Singapore: Oxford University Press, 1988.

Kuo, Alex. "The Engine of Asia." *The World Today* (June 1997): 160–62.

Kwan, C. H. "The New Wave of Foreign Direct Investment in Asia." *Nomura Asia Focus*, August/September 1994, 9–13.

Lampton, David, et al. *The Emergence of 'Greater China': Implications for the United States*. Policy Series, no. 5. New York: National Committee on U.S.-China Relations, October 1992.

Lan, Ping. *Technology Transfer to China Through Foreign Direct Investment*. Aldershot, England: Avebury, 1996.

Landa, Janet T. "The Political Economy of the Ethnically Homogenous Chinese Middleman Group in Southeast Asia: Ethnicity and Entrepreneurship in a Plural Society." In *The Chinese in Southeast Asia*, vol. 1, edited by Linda Y. C. Lim and L. A. Peter Gosling, 86–116. Singapore: Maruzen Asia, 1983.

———. *Trust, Ethnicity, and Identity*. Ann Arbor: University of Michigan Press, 1994.

Lardy, Nicholas R. *China in the World Economy*. Washington, D.C.: Institute for International Economics, 1994.

Lau, Karen. "More Than Business as Usual." *Singapore*, January/February 1994, 10–13.

Lau, Lawson Liat Hoe. "The Technological City: 1984 in Singapore." Ph.D. diss., University of Illinois at Urbana-Champaign, 1992.

Le, Shui. "Haiwai huarende zhongzu benzhi nanyi gaibian" ("The Racial Nature of Ethnic Chinese Is Difficult to Change"). *Bagui qiao shi* (*Overseas Chinese History of Bagui*), 1997, no. 1: 13–16.

Lee, Kam Hing. "Malaysian Chinese: Seeking Identity in Wawasan 2020." In *Ethnic Chinese as Southeast Asians*, edited by Leo Suryadinata, 72–107. New York: St. Martin's Press, 1997.

Lee, Keun. *New East Asian Economic Development: Interacting Capitalism and Socialism.* Armonk, N.Y.: M. E. Sharpe, 1993.

Lee, Kuan Yew. Untitled. In *World Chinese Entrepreneurs Convention*, edited by Singapore Chinese Chamber of Commerce and Industry, 181–92. Singapore, 1991.

Lever-Tracy, Constance, David Ip, and Noel Tracy. *The Chinese Diaspora and Mainland China: An Emerging Economic Synergy.* New York: St. Martin's Press, 1996.

Li, Guoliang. "Chinese Scholars' Studies on the Changes of Overseas Chinese and Their Descendants after World War II." *RIAD Bulletin*, no. 2 (March 1993): 113–30.

———. "Comment to 'Japan's Role in Southeast and East Asia during the Post-Cold War Era: In Relation to the Expanding Economic Power of the Ethnic Chinese.'" In *Proceedings of Research Institute for Asian Development International Symposium 1992*, 115–19. Research Institute for Asian Development, International University of Japan, 1993.

Li, Guoliang, Lin Jinzhi, and Cai Renlong. *Huaqiao huaren yu Zhongguo geming he jinshi* (*Overseas Chinese/Ethnic Chinese and Chinese Revolution and Construction*), edited by Lin Jinzhi. Fuzhou: Fujian renmin chubanshe, 1993.

Li, Hongjie. "Haiwai Anxiren dui jiaxiang jianshede gongxian" ("The Contribution by the Overseas Anxi People for Their Hometown Construction"). *Bagui qiao shi* (*Overseas Chinese History of Bagui*), 1997, no. 3:44–48.

Li, Yanhui. "Zhan hou Zhongguo yu Yinnide guanxi" ("Postwar Sino-Indonesian Relations"). *Nanyang wenti yanjiu (Southeast Asian Affairs)*, 1994, no. 2: 14–22.

Liao, Shaolian. "China-ASEAN Economic Relations: Trends and Problems." *Ritsumeikan Journal of International Relations and Area Studies*, no. 2 (March 1992): 35–43.

Lim, Linda Y. C. "Chinese Business, Multinationals and the State: Manufacturing for Export in Malaysia and Singapore." In *The Chinese in Southeast Asia*, vol. 1, edited by Linda Y. C. Lim and L. A. Peter Gosling, 245–74. Singapore: Maruzen Asia, 1983.

———. "Chinese Economic Activity in Southeast Asia: An Introductory Review." In *The Chinese in Southeast Asia*, vol. 1, edited by Linda Y. C. Lim and L. A. Peter Gosling, 1–29. Singapore: Maruzen Asia, 1983.

———. "The Emergence of a Chinese Economic Zone in Asia?" *Journal of Southeast Asian Business* 8, no. 1 (Winter 1992): 41–46.

Lim, Linda Y. C., and Eng Fong Pang. "The Southeast Asian Economies: Resilient Growth and Expanding Linkages." *Southeast Asian Affairs* (1994): 22–33.

Lim, Soon Neo. "The China Connection." *Singapore Business*, March 1989, 21–32.

Lim, Wu-Shan. "Pragmatic Partners." *China Business Review*, July/August 1990, 22–29.

Limlingan, Victor Simpao. *The Overseas Chinese in ASEAN: Business Strategies and Management Practices*. Manila: Vita Development Corporation, 1986.

Lin, Jinzhi. "Haiwai huaren zai Zhongguo dalude touzi ji qi tedian (1979–1988)" ("The Characteristics of Overseas Ethnic Chinese Investments in Mainland China, 1979–1988"). In *Nanyang yanjiu lunwenji (Essays on Southeast Asian Research)*, edited by Xiamen daxue Nanyang yanjiusuo, 201–21. Xiamen: Xiamen daxue chubanshe, 1992.

———. "Qiaohui dui Zhongguo jingji fazhan yu qiaoxiang jianshede zuoyong" ("The Role of Remittances of Overseas Chinese in the Economic Development of China"). *Nanyang wenti yanjiu (Southeast Asian Affairs)*, 1992, no. 2:21–34.

———. "1979–1992 nian haiwai huaren zai Zhongguo dalu touzide xianzhuang ji qi jinhou fazhan qushi" ("The Current Situation and Future Trends in the Investments of Overseas Ethnic Chinese on the Chinese Mainland, 1979–1992"). *Huaqiao huaren lishi yanjiu (Overseas Chinese and Ethnic Chinese Historical Research)*, 1993, no. 1: 1–14.

———. "Haiwai huaren zai Chao-Shan diqude touzi" ("Overseas Ethnic Chinese Investment in the Chaozhou-Shantou Area"). *Nanyang wenti yanjiu (Southeast Asian Affairs)*, 1994, no. 1:18–27.

Lin, Mei. "Zhong-Tai jingmao guanxi pouxi" ("Economic and Trade Relations Between China and Thailand"). *Nanyang wenti yanjiu (Southeast Asian Affairs)*, 1993, no. 2:76–80.

Lin, Wuguang. "Malaixiya huashang dui Zhongguo dalu touzide xianzhuang yu tedian" ("Investment on the Mainland of China by Overseas Chinese Businessmen in Malaysia and Its Characteristics"). In *Huaren jingji nianjian 1997–1998 (Yearbook of the Huaren Economy 1997–1998)*, 283–89. Beijing: Shehui kexue wenxian chubanshe, 1997.

Lipnack, Jessica, and Jeffrey Stamps. *The Networking Book: People Connecting with People*. New York: Routledge and Kegan Paul, 1986.

Lipset, Seymour Martin. *Political Man: The Social Base of Politics*. New York: Doubleday, 1960.

Liu, Hong. "Old Linkages, New Networks: The Globalization of Overseas Chinese Voluntary Associations and Its Implications." *China Quarterly*, no. 155 (September 1998): 582–609.

Long, Simon. "Regionalism in Fujian." In *China Deconstructs: Politics, Trade and Regionalism*, edited by David S. G. Goodman and Gerald Segal, 202–23. New York: Routledge, 1994.

Lu, Shouwei. "Jiceng qiaowu gongzuo yu yinjin qiao zi" ("Grassroots Overseas Chinese Affairs Work and the Importation of Overseas Chinese Capital"). *Huaqiao yu huaren (The Chinese Overseas)*, 1995, no. 2:26–27, 33.

Ma, Zongshi. "China Dream in the Global 1990s and Beyond." *Contemporary International Relations* 3, no. 7 (July 1993): 1–19.

Mackie, Jamie. "Economic Systems of the Southeast Asian Chinese." In *Southeast Asian Chinese and China*, edited by Leo Suryadinata, 33–65. Singapore: Times Academic Press, 1995.

Manning, Robert A. "The Third World Looks at China." In *China and the Third World: Champion or Challenger*, edited by Lillian Craig Harris and Robert L. Worden, 139–55. Dover, Mass.: Auborn House, 1986.

Margolin, Jean-Louise. "Foreign Models in Singapore's Development and the Idea of a Singaporean Model." In *Singapore Changes Guard: Social, Political, and Economic Directions in the 1990s*, edited by Garry Rodan, 84–98. New York: St. Martin's Press, 1993.

McCormick, Barrett L., Su Shaozhi, and Xiao Xiaoming. "The 1989 Democracy Movement: A Review of the Prospects for Civil Society in China." *Pacific Affairs* 65, no. 2 (Summer 1992): 182–202.

McKeown, Adam. "Conceptualizing Chinese Diasporas, 1842 to 1949." *Journal of Asian Studies* 58, no. 2 (May 1999): 306–37.

Ministry of Finance, Republic of Singapore. *Final Report of the Committee to Promote Enterprise Overseas*. Singapore: SNP Publishers, August 1993.

Moynihan, Daniel Patrick. *Pandaemonium: Ethnicity in International Politics*. Oxford: Oxford University Press, 1993.

Myers, James T., and Donald J. Puchala. " 'Greater China': Some American Reflections." *Asian Affairs: An American Review* 21, no. 1 (Spring 1994): 3–13.

Naisbitt, John. *Megatrends Asia*. New York: Simon and Schuster, 1996.

Naughton, Barry. *Growing Out of the Plan: Chinese Economic Reform, 1978–1993*. New York: Cambridge University Press, 1995.

Nie, Dening. "Jindai Zhongguo yu Xinjiabode jing mao guanxi gaishu" ("Modern Economic Relations Between China and Singapore"). *Nanyang wenti yanjiu (Southeast Asian Affairs)*, 1994, no. 1:58–65.

"1996 nian guonei baokan youguan huaqiao huaren yanjiu wenzhang yao mu" ("Selected Contents of Articles on Overseas Chinese Studies Published in Domestic Newspapers and Periodicals in 1996"). *Huaqiao huaren lishi yanjiu (Overseas Chinese and Ethnic Chinese Historical Research)*, 1997, no. 2:75–80.

Ogden, Suzanne. *China's Unresolved Issues: Politics, Development and Culture*. 2nd ed. Englewood Cliffs, N.J.: Prentice-Hall, 1992.

Ohmae, Kenichi. "The Rise of the Region State." *Foreign Affairs* (Spring 1993): 78–87.

"Overview of Investment Incentives." *China Business Review*, May/June 1986, 20–23.

Paix, Catherine. "The Domestic Bourgeoisie: How Entrepreneurial? How International?" In *Singapore Changes Guard: Social, Political, and Economic Directions in the 1990s*, edited by Garry Rodan, 184–200. New York: St. Martin's Press, 1993.

Pan, Lynn. *Sons of the Yellow Emperor: A History of the Chinese Diaspora*. Boston: Little, Brown, 1990.

Pan, Lynn, ed. *The Encyclopedia of the Chinese Overseas*. Cambridge, Mass.: Harvard University Press, 1999.

Pang, Eng Fong, and Rajah V. Komeran. "Singapore Firms in China." *Singapore Business*, September 1985, 12–15.

Pearson, Margaret. *China's New Business Elite: The Political Consequences of Economic Reform*. Berkeley: University of California Press, 1997.

Pomfret, Richard. *Investing in China: Ten Years of the Open Door Policy*. Ames: Iowa State University Press, 1991.

Poston, Dudley L., Michael Xinxiang Mao, and Mei-Yu Yu. "The Global Distribution of Overseas Chinese Around 1990." *Population and Development Review* 20, no. 3 (September 1994): 631–45.

Purcell, Victor. *The Chinese in Southeast Asia.* 2nd ed. London: Oxford University Press, 1965.

Pye, Lucian W. *The Spirit of Chinese Politics: A Psychocultural Study of the Authority Crisis in Political Development.* Cambridge, Mass.: MIT Press, 1968.

———. *Asian Power and Politics: The Cultural Dimension of Authority.* Cambridge, Mass.: Harvard University Press, 1985.

———. "China: Erratic State, Frustrated Society." *Foreign Affairs* 69, no. 4 (Fall 1990): 56–74.

Qu, Tao, and Milford B. Green. *Chinese Foreign Direct Investment: A Subnational Perspective on Location.* Aldershot, England: Ashgate, 1997.

Ra'anan, Uri. "The Nation-State Fallacy." In *Conflict and Peacemaking in Multiethnic Societies,* edited by Joseph V. Montville, 5–20. Lexington, Mass.: Lexington Books, 1990.

Reardon, Lawrence C. "Learning How to Open the Door: A Reassessment of China's 'Opening' Strategy." *China Quarterly,* no. 155 (September 1998): 479–511.

Redding, S. Gordon. *The Spirit of Chinese Capitalism.* Berlin: Walter de Gruyter, 1993.

Remer, C. F. *Foreign Investments in China.* New York: Macmillan, 1933.

Rodan, Garry. *The Political Economy of Singapore's Industrialization: National State and International Capital.* New York: St. Martin's Press, 1989.

———. "Reconstructing Divisions of Labour: Singapore's New Regional Emphasis." In *Pacific Economic Relations in the 1990s: Cooperation or Conflict?* edited by Richard Higgott, Richard Leaver, and John Ravenhill, 223–49. Boulder: Lynne Rienner Publishers, 1993.

Rodan, Garry, ed. *Singapore Changes Guard: Social, Political, and Economic Directions in the 1990s.* New York: St. Martin's Press, 1993.

Roehrig, Michael Franz. *Foreign Joint Ventures in Contemporary China.* New York: St. Martin's Press, 1994.

Rosenau, James N. *Turbulence in World Politics: A Theory of Continuity and Change.* Princeton, N.J.: Princeton University Press, 1990.

———. *Along the Domestic-Foreign Frontier.* Cambridge: Cambridge University Press, 1997.

Rosenbluth, Eliza. "Preferential Treatment for Taiwan Investors." *China Business Review,* September/October 1990, 36–37.

Ross, Robert S. "China and the Ethnic Chinese: Political Liability/Economic Asset." In *ASEAN and China: An Evolving Relationship,* edited by Joyce K. Kallgren, Noordin Sopiee, and Soedjati Djiwandono, 147–73. Berkeley: Institute of East Asian Studies, University of California, 1988.

———. "China's Strategic View of Southeast Asia: A Region in Transition." *Contemporary Southeast Asia* 12, no. 2 (September 1990): 101–19.

Roy, Denny. "Singapore, China, and the 'Soft Authoritarian' Challenge." *Asian Survey* 34, no. 3 (March 1994): 231–42.

———. *China's Foreign Relations.* Lanham, Md.: Rowman and Littlefield, 1998.

Saich, Tony. "The Search for Civil Society and Democracy in China." *Current History* 93, no. 584 (September 1994): 260–64.

Sandhu, Kernial Singh. "Discussion." In *Proceedings of Research Institute for Asian Development International Symposium 1992,* 120–22. Research Institute for Asian Development, International University of Japan, 1993.

Sandhu, Kernial Singh, and Paul Wheatley, eds. *Management of Success: The Moulding of Modern Singapore.* Boulder: Westview Press, 1989.

Scalapino, Robert A. "The United States and Asia: Future Prospects." *Foreign Affairs* 70, no. 5 (Winter 1991/92): 19–40.

———. "China in the Late Leninist Era." *China Quarterly*, no. 136 (December 1993): 949–71.

Scalapino, Robert A., and George T. Yu. *Modern China and Its Revolutionary Process: Recurrent Challenges to the Traditional Order, 1850–1920.* Berkeley: University of California Press, 1985.

Seagrave, Sterling. *Lords of the Rim: The Invisible Empire of the Overseas Chinese.* New York: G. P. Putnam's Sons, 1995.

See, Teresita Ang. "The Ethnic Chinese as Filipinos." In *Ethnic Chinese as Southeast Asians*, edited by Leo Suryadinata, 158–202. New York: St. Martin's Press, 1997.

Segal, Gerald. "Deconstructing Foreign Relations." In *China Deconstructs: Politics, Trade and Regionalism*, edited by David S. G. Goodman and Gerald Segal, 322–55. New York: Routledge, 1994.

Sender, Henny. "Inside the Overseas Chinese Network." *Institutional Investor*, September 1991, 37–42.

Shambaugh, David. "Introduction: The Emergence of 'Greater China.'" *China Quarterly*, no. 136 (December 1993): 653–59.

Shanghai guoji wenti yanjiusuo, ed. *Guoji xingshi nianjian 1995 (Survey of International Affairs 1995).* Shanghai: Shanghai jiaoyu chubanshe, 1995.

Sheffer, Gabriel. "A New Field of Study: Modern Diasporas in International Politics." In *Modern Diasporas in International Politics*, edited by Gabriel Sheffer, 1–15. London: Croom Helm, 1986.

Shen, Hongfang. "Jiushi niandai Dongnan Ya guojia yu woguode waizi touzi huanjing bijiao" ("A Comparison of the Foreign Investment Environments of China and the Southeast Asian States in the 1990s"). *Nanyang wenti yanjiu (Southeast Asian Affairs)*, 1994, no. 2:49–55.

Shirk, Susan. *The Political Logic of Economic Reform in China.* Berkeley: University of California Press, 1993.

Siddique, Sharon. "Singaporean Identity." In *Management of Success: The Moulding of Modern Singapore*, edited by Kernial Singh Sandhu and Paul Wheatley, 563–77. Boulder: Westview Press, 1989.

Singapore: The Next Lap. Singapore: Government of Singapore, 1991.

Singapore Chinese Chamber of Commerce and Industry. *Annual Report*, various years.

Singapore Department of Statistics. *Singapore's Investments Abroad 1990.* Singapore: Department of Statistics, February 1993.

———. *Singapore's Direct Investment Abroad 1993.* Singapore: Department of Statistics, October 1994.

———. *Monthly Digest of Statistics.* Singapore: Department of Statistics, various issues.

Siu, Helen F. "Cultural Identity and the Politics of Difference in South China." *Daedalus* 122, no. 2 (Spring 1993): 19–41.

Stack, John F., Jr. "Ethnic Groups as Emerging Transnational Actors." In *Ethnic Identities in a Transnational World*, edited by John F. Stack Jr., 17–45. Westport, Conn.: Greenwood Press, 1981.

State Statistical Bureau, People's Republic of China. *Statistical Yearbook of China.* Beijing: China Statistical Publishing House, various years.

Sukma, Rizal. "Recent Developments in Sino-Indonesian Relations: An Indonesian View." *Contemporary Southeast Asia* 16, no. 1 (June 1994): 35–45.

"Sulian zhengbian hou Zhongguode xianshi ying duiyu zhanlüe xuanze" ("China's Realistic Strategic Choice after the Coup in the Soviet Union"). *Zhongguo qingnian bao (China Youth Daily)*, 9 September 1991. Reprinted in *Chung-kuo chih ch'un (China Spring)*, 1992, no. 1:35–39.

Sun, Guoyuan. "Dongmeng tong Zhongguo jingmao guanxide fazhan ji qi qianjing" ("The Development of ASEAN-China Economic Relations and Their Prospects"). In *Zhongguo yu disan shijie (China and the Third World)*, edited by Zhongguo xiandai guoji guanxi yanjiusuo, 144–59. Beijing: Shishi chubanshe, 1990.

Sun, Haishun. *Foreign Investment and Economic Development in China: 1979–1996.* Aldershot, England: Ashgate, 1998.

Sun, Xingcheng. "Guanyu mingan wenti" ("Regarding Sensitive Issues"). In *Huaren jingji nianjian 1997–1998 (Yearbook of the Ethnic Chinese Economy 1997–1998)*, 223–36. Beijing: Shehui kexue wenxian chubanshe, 1997.

Sung, Yun-Wing. *The China-Hong Kong Connection: The Key to China's Open Door Policy.* Cambridge: Cambridge University Press, 1991.

———. "Hong Kong and the Economic Integration of the China Circle." In *The China Circle*, edited by Barry Naughton, 41–80. Washington, D.C.: Brookings, 1997.

Suryadinata, Leo. *China and the ASEAN States: The Ethnic Chinese Dimension.* Singapore: Singapore University Press, 1985.

———. "China's Economic Modernization and the Ethnic Chinese in ASEAN: A Preliminary Study." In *Southeast Asian Chinese and China*, edited by Leo Suryadinata, 193–215. Singapore: Times Academic Press, 1995.

———. "Ethnic Chinese in Southeast Asia: Overseas Chinese, Chinese Overseas, or Southeast Asians?" In *Ethnic Chinese as Southeast Asians*, edited by Leo Suryadinata, 1–24. New York: St. Martin's Press, 1997.

Tan, Kong Yam. "China and ASEAN: Competitive Industrialization Through Foreign Direct Investment." In *The China Circle*, edited by Barry Naughton, 111–35. Washington, D.C.: Brookings, 1997.

Tan, Mely G. "The Ethnic Chinese in Indonesia: Issues of Identity." In *Ethnic Chinese as Southeast Asians*, edited by Leo Suryadinata, 33–65. New York: St. Martin's Press, 1997.

Tang, H. K., and K. T. Yeo. "Technology, Entrepreneurship and National Development: Lessons from Singapore." *International Journal of Technology Management* 10, nos. 7/8 (1995): 797–814.

Taylor, Jay. *China and Southeast Asia: Peking's Relations with Revolutionary Movements.* 2nd ed. New York: Praeger, 1974.

Thomas, Margaret, Peck Ming Chuang, and Soon Neo Lim. "Singapore Inc. Goes Global." *Singapore Business*, September 1989, 28–54.

Ting, Wai. "The Regional and International Implications of the South China Economic Zone." *Issues and Studies* 28, no. 12 (December 1992): 46–72.

Tölölyan, Khachig. "Rethinking Diasporas: Stateless Power in the Transnational Moment." *Diaspora* 5, no. 1 (Spring 1996): 3–36.

Tsang, Eric W. K. "The Implementation of Technology Transfer in Sino-Foreign Joint Ventures." *International Journal of Technology Management* 10, nos. 7/8 (1995): 757–66.

——. "Can Guanxi Be a Source of Sustained Competitive Advantage for Doing Business in China?" *Academy of Management Executive* 12, no. 2 (May 1998): 64–73.

Tu, Wei-ming. "Cultural China: The Periphery as the Center." *Daedalus* 120, no. 2 (Spring 1991): 1–32.

United Nations Conference on Trade and Development. *World Investment Report.* New York: United Nations, various years.

Van Kemenade, Willem. *China, Hong Kong, Taiwan, Inc.* Translated by Diane Webb. New York: Vintage Books, 1998.

Vogel, Ezra. *One Step Ahead in China: Guangdong under Reform.* Cambridge, Mass.: Harvard University Press, 1989.

Wang, Gungwu. "China and the Region in Relation to Chinese Minorities." *Contemporary Southeast Asia* 1, no. 1 (May 1979): 36–50.

——. *Community and Nation: Essays on Southeast Asia and the Chinese.* Singapore: Heinemann Educational Books, 1981.

——. *China and the Chinese Overseas.* Singapore: Times Academic Press, 1991.

——. "Greater China and the Chinese Overseas." *China Quarterly*, no. 136 (December 1993): 926–48.

——. "Migration and Its Enemies." In *Conceptualizing Global History*, edited by Bruce Mazlish and Ralph Buultjens, 131–51. Boulder: Westview Press, 1993.

——. "Upgrading the Migrant: Neither *Huaqiao* nor *Huaren*." In *The Last Half Century of Chinese Overseas*, edited by Elizabeth Sinn, 15–33. Hong Kong: Hong Kong University Press, 1998.

——. "The Status of Overseas Chinese Studies." In *The Chinese Diaspora: Selected Essays*, vol. 1, edited by Wang Ling-chi and Wang Gungwu, 1–13. Singapore: Times Academic Press, 1998).

Wang, Muheng. "Current Situation of Southeast Asian Studies in Mainland China." *RIAD Bulletin*, no. 1 (March 1992): 1–16.

Wang, Qin. "Xinjiabo huaren qiye jituande xingqi ji qi haiwai touzi" ("The Rise and Overseas Investments of Singapore's Chinese Enterprise Groups"). Paper prepared for the International Conference on the World Overseas Chinese and Ethnic Chinese Economy, Xiamen University, Institute of Southeast Asian Studies, undated.

Wei, Shang-Jin, and Jeffrey Frankel. "A 'Greater China' Trade Bloc?" *China Economic Review* 5, no. 2 (1994): 179–90.

Wei, Yanshen, and Yu Kexing. "Role of Hong Kong in China-ASEAN Economic Relations." In *ASEAN-China Economic Relations: In the Context of Pacific Economic Development and Co-operation*, edited by Chia Siow-Yue and Cheng Bifan, 196–215. Singapore: Institute for Southeast Asian Studies, 1992.

Weidenbaum, Murray, and Samuel Hughes. *The Bamboo Network.* New York: The Free Press, 1996.

Weiner, Myron. "People and States in a New Ethnic Order?" *Third World Quarterly* 13, no. 2 (1992): 317–333.

Wilbur, C. Martin. *Sun Yat-sen: Frustrated Patriot.* New York: Columbia University Press, 1976.

Wong, John. *The Political Economy of China's Changing Relations with Southeast Asia.* London: Macmillan, 1984.

Woon, Yuen-Fong. "Family Strategies of Prosperous Peasants in an Emigrant Community in South China." *Canadian Journal of Developmental Studies* 15, no. 1 (1994): 9–33.

World Bank. *Sharing Rising Incomes: Disparities in China.* Washington, D.C.: World Bank, 1997.

Wu, Chun-Hsi. *Dollars, Dependents and Dogma: Overseas Chinese Remittances to Communist China.* Stanford: Hoover Institution, 1967.

Wu, David Yen-ho. "The Construction of Chinese and Non-Chinese Identities." *Daedalus* 120, no. 2 (Spring 1991): 159–79.

Wu, Hongqin. "Haiwai huarende minzu rentong yu guojia guannian bianxi" ("An Analysis of the Ethnic Identity and Sense of Nationality of Ethnic Chinese"). *Huaqiao huaren lishi yanjiu (Overseas Chinese and Ethnic Chinese Historical Research),* 1996, no. 1:1–6.

Wu, Yuan-li, and Chun-hsi Wu. *Economic Development in Southeast Asia: The Chinese Dimension.* Stanford: Hoover Institution Press, 1980.

Xiang, Dayou. "Lun Zhongguo gaige kaifeng yu hua zitou xiang qushi" ("On the Reform and Opening of China and the Investment Inclination of Overseas Chinese"). *Bagui qiao shi (Overseas Chinese History of Bagui),* 1994, no. 1:1–7.

Xu, Jiatun. *Xu Jiatun Xianggang huiyilu (Xu Jiatun's Memoir of His Hong Kong Experience),* vol. 1. Taipei: Lianhe bao, 1993.

Xue, Mouhong. "Xinjiabo jingji fazhande ruogan tedian" ("Some Salient Features of Singapore's Economic Development"). *Guoji wenti yanjiu (International Studies),* 1990, no. 3:1–10.

Yahuda, Michael B. *China's Role in World Affairs.* New York: St. Martin's Press, 1978.

Yamaguchi, Masaaki. "Chinese Money Starts Crossing National Borders." *Nomura Asia Focus,* February 1993, 34–37.

Yen, Ching Hwang. *The Overseas Chinese and the 1911 Revolution: With Special Reference to Singapore and Malaya.* Kuala Lumpur: Oxford University Press, 1976.

———. "Ch'ing China and the Singapore Chinese Chamber of Commerce, 1906–1911." In *Southeast Asian Chinese and China,* edited by Leo Suryadinata, 133–60. Singapore: Times Academic Press, 1995.

Yeo, George. "Asian Civilization in the Pacific Century." In *World Chinese Entrepreneurs Convention,* edited by Singapore Chinese Chamber of Commerce and Industry, 29–42. Singapore, 1991.

Yong, C. F. *Tan Kah-Kee: The Making of an Overseas Chinese Legend.* Singapore: Oxford University Press, 1987.

Yong, Pow Ang. "An Ongoing Romance." *Singapore Business,* February 1992, 44–50.

Yu, Chung-Hsun. "Xin Zhongguo jingji quan yu huan Taipingyang jingji" ("The New Chinese Economic Groupings and Links with the Pacific Economy"). In *Huaqiao huaren wenti lunwenji (Essays on the Question of Overseas Chinese and Ethnic Chinese),* edited by Chen Bisheng, 139–61. Nanchang: Jiangxi renmin chubanshe, 1989.

———. "Japan's Role in Southeast and East Asia During the Post-Cold War Era: In Relation to the Expanding Economic Power of the Ethnic Chinese." In *Proceedings of Research Institute for Asian Development International Symposium*

1992, 99–113. Research Institute for Asian Development, International University of Japan, 1993.

Yu, Elena S. H. "Overseas Remittances in Southeastern China." *China Quarterly*, no. 78 (June 1979): 339–50.

Yu, Yunping. "Qian lun qiao wai shang zhijie touzi zai Fujian jingji fazhan zhongde diwei he zuoyong" ("On the Position and Role of Overseas Chinese and Foreign Businesspersons' Direct Investment in the Economic Development of Fujian"). *Nanyang wenti yanjiu (Southeast Asian Affairs)*, 1996, no. 2: 35–45.

Zha, Daojiong. "A 'Greater China'? The Political Economy of Chinese National Reunification." *Journal of Contemporary China*, no. 5 (Spring 1994):40–63.

Zhang, Xiaowei. "Bawo 'wu ge zhuanwan,' fazhan qiao xiang youshi" (Grasp the 'Five Turns,' Develop the Advantage of Overseas Chinese Hometowns"). *Huaqiao yu huaren (The Chinese Overseas)*, 1995, no. 2:14–16.

Zhao, Heman. "Huaqiao huaren jingji yu Zhongguo dui wai kaifeng" ("The Overseas/Ethnic Chinese Economy and China's Opening to the World"). *Bagui qiao shi (Overseas Chinese History of Bagui)*, 1994, no. 1:8–12.

Zhao, Hong. "Jiushi niandai Zhongguo yu Dongmeng guojiade jingmao hezuo guanxi zhanwang" ("Outlook for Economic and Trade Cooperation Between China and ASEAN in the 1990s"). *Nanyang wenti yanjiu (Southeast Asian Affairs)*, 1993, no. 2: 70–75.

Zhuang, Guotu. "The Policies of the Chinese Government Towards Overseas Chinese (1949–1966)." In *The Chinese Diaspora: Selected Essays*, vol. 1, edited by Wang Ling-chi and Wang Gungwu, 14–28. Singapore: Times Academic Press, 1998.

Zhuhai City International Communication Office. *Zhuhai Special Economic Zone of China*, October 1983.

Zwieg, David. "'Developmental Communities' on China's Coast: The Impact of Trade, Investment, and Transnational Alliances." *Comparative Politics* 27, no. 3 (April 1995): 253–274.

OTHER WORKS CITED

Asian Business
Asian Wall Street Journal
Asiaweek
Bangkok Post (www.bangkokpost.net)
Beijing Review (*Peking Review*)
Business China
Business Times (Singapore) (http://business-times.asial.com.sg)
Chicago Tribune
China Council for the Promotion of International Trade (www.ccpit.org)
China Daily (www.chinadaily.com.cn)
China's Foreign Trade
Embassy of the People's Republic of China, *Newsletter*
Far Eastern Economic Review
Financial Times (London) (www.ft.com)
Foreign Broadcast Information Service reports
Independent (London) (www.independent.co.uk)

Inside China Today (www.insidechina.com)
Le Monde (Paris)
Maclean's
Malaysian Business
Newsweek
New York Times (www.nytimes.com)
Qiao bao (New York)
Renmin ribao (Beijing) (*People's Daily*)
Republic of China on Taiwan Central News Agency (www.taipei.org/teco/cicc/news)
Singapore Department of Statistics (www.singstat.gov.sg)
Sinorama
South China Morning Post (Hong Kong) (www.scmp.com)
Straits Times (Singapore) (www.straitstimes.asia1.com.sg)
Straits Times Weekly Edition (Singapore)
U.S. Department of Commerce, Bureau of Economic Analysis (www.bea.doc.gov)
Washington Post
World Press Review

Index

About the Author

PAUL J. BOLT is Associate Professor of Political Science at the United States Air Force Academy. He has published extensively on Chinese diaspora and economic issues in journals, such as *Diaspora* and *Asian Affairs*.